The Indigenization of Christianity in China II

As the second volume of a three-volume set on the indigenization of Christianity in modern China, this book focuses on Christianity's encounter with the turbulent history of China in the 1920s, the responses of the Chinese Church to criticisms and the backlash against Christianity.

Over the course of its growth in modern China, Christianity has faced many twists and turns in attempting to embed itself in Chinese society and indigenous culture. This three-volume set delineates the genesis and trajectory of Christianity's indigenization in China over the course of the nineteenth and twentieth centuries, highlighting the actions of Chinese Christians and the relationship between the development of Christianity in China and modern Chinese history. This volume re-examines the Condemning Christianity Movement and discusses debates and reflections on the independence and indigenization of the Chinese Church, religious education and the relationship of Christianity with imperialism. The author also demonstrates how historical events and intellectual trends during the period fashioned local believers' national consciousness and their views on foreign missionary societies, imperialism and patriotism, figuring prominently in Chinese Christians' domination of the Church.

The book will appeal to scholars and students interested in the history of Christianity in China and modern Chinese history.

Qi Duan, Professor at the Institute of World Religions of the Chinese Academy of Social Sciences, is a leading scholar specializing in the history of Christianity in modern China and has authored numerous books and articles shedding light on the development of modern Chinese Christianity.

China Perspectives

The *China Perspectives* series focuses on translating and publishing works by leading Chinese scholars, writing about both global topics and China-related themes. It covers Humanities & Social Sciences, Education, Media and Psychology, as well as many interdisciplinary themes.

This is the first time any of these books have been published in English for international readers. The series aims to put forward a Chinese perspective, give insights into cutting-edge academic thinking in China, and inspire researchers globally.

To submit proposals, please contact the Taylor & Francis Publisher for China Publishing Programme, Lian Sun (Lian.Sun@informa.com).

Titles in religion currently include:

The Indigenization of Christianity in China I
1807–1922
Qi Duan

The Indigenization of Christianity in China II
1922–1927
Qi Duan

The Indigenization of Christianity in China III
1927–2000
Qi Duan

For more information, please visit www.routledge.com/China-Perspectives/book-series/CPH

The Indigenization of Christianity in China II
1922–1927

Qi Duan

LONDON AND NEW YORK

First published in English 2023
by Routledge
4 Park Square, Milton Park, Abingdon, Oxon OX14 4RN

and by Routledge
605 Third Avenue, New York, NY 10158

Routledge is an imprint of the Taylor & Francis Group, an informa business

© 2023 Qi Duan

Translated by Luman Wang and Zhen Chi

The right of Qi Duan to be identified as author of this work has been asserted in accordance with sections 77 and 78 of the Copyright, Designs and Patents Act 1988.

All rights reserved. No part of this book may be reprinted or reproduced or utilised in any form or by any electronic, mechanical, or other means, now known or hereafter invented, including photocopying and recording, or in any information storage or retrieval system, without permission in writing from the publishers.

Trademark notice: Product or corporate names may be trademarks or registered trademarks, and are used only for identification and explanation without intent to infringe.

English version by permission of The Commercial Press.

British Library Cataloguing-in-Publication Data
A catalogue record for this book is available from the British Library

Library of Congress Cataloging-in-Publication Data
Names: Duan, Qi, author.
Title: The indigenization of Christianity in China / Qi Duan.
Description: Abingdon, Oxon ; New York, NY : Routledge, [2023] |
Series: China perspectives | Includes bibliographical references and index. |
Identifiers: LCCN 2022031623 (print) | LCCN 2022031624 (ebook) |
ISBN 9781032370224 (v. 1 ; hardback) | ISBN 9781032370316 (v. 1 ; paperback) |
ISBN 9781032384603 (v. 2 ; hardback) | ISBN 9781032384634 (v. 2 ; paperback) |
ISBN 9781032384610 (v. 3 ; hardback) | ISBN 9781032384641 (v. 3 ; paperback) |
ISBN 9781032384627 (hardback) | ISBN 9781032384658 (paperback) |
ISBN 9781003334965 (v. 1 ; ebook) | ISBN 9781003345169 (v. 2 ; ebook) |
ISBN 9781003345176 (v. 3 ; ebook)
Subjects: LCSH: Christianity–China. | Christianity and culture–China.
Classification: LCC BR1285 .D835 2023 (print) |
LCC BR1285 (ebook) | DDC 275.1–dc23/eng/20220907
LC record available at https://lccn.loc.gov/2022031623
LC ebook record available at https://lccn.loc.gov/2022031624

ISBN: 978-1-032-38460-3 (hbk)
ISBN: 978-1-032-38463-4 (pbk)
ISBN: 978-1-003-34516-9 (ebk)

DOI: 10.4324/9781003345169

Typeset in Times New Roman
by Newgen Publishing UK

Contents

1 The Condemning Christianity Movement and
  Christianity in China   1

2 The National Congress of Christianity in 1922   21

3 The Campaign for Taking Back the Right of Education
  and Christianity   95

4 Chinese Christianity in the Shanghai Massacre and the
  Northern Expedition Periods, 1925–1927   153

  Index   215

1 The Condemning Christianity Movement and Christianity in China

The early Condemning Christianity Movement and its intellectual foundation

When the twentieth century dawned, Christianity witnessed a rapid growth in China. It was said that at that time the Christian churches were under construction everywhere and the Christian schools and missionary work were all thriving.[1] In 1913, for instance, 137,579 people from 14 cities listened to the sermons held by two American missionaries, John R. Mott and Sherwood Eddy. Thanks to John Mott's efforts, the missionaries in this year founded the China Continuation Committee (CCC). Headed by Charles L. Boynton and Milton T. Stauffer, the CCC conducted a nationwide survey of Christianity in China. This large-scale, comprehensive survey was completed in 1921. In the next year, the final report, entitled *The Christian Occupation of China*, was published. The bold and aggressive title of this report elicited strong reactions. Many Chinese intellectuals, who were deeply influenced by the May Fourth-New Culture movement and had a very low opinion of Christianity, felt a stronger antipathy towards the *Christian occupation* of China. CCC's report revealed that Christianity had grown very rapidly—the number of Chinese Christian converts, for instance, increased from 80,000 to 360,000 in two decades (1900–1920); and that the missionaries were obsessed with an overweening ambition to have the entire China Christianized. Just at this point, the World Student Christian Federation (WSCF) convened a huge conference in the Beijing-based Qinghua school (the predecessor of Tsinghua University, hereinafter referred to as *Qinghua*) in April 1922. Protesting against WSCF's conference, the Chinese who were critical of Christianity launched China's first Condemning Christianity Movement.

The WSCF, an international association of Christian students, was founded in 1895. John Mott was one of its founders. China's first student YMCA was set up in Fuzhou in 1885. Then, similar student organizations were set up in other Christian schools. When Mott arrived in China in 1896, there had already been five student Christian associations. He and David W. Lyon, the secretary of the YMCA in China, toured several Chinese cities, such as Beijing, Shanghai, Tianjin, Yantai, Hankou and Fuzhou, all of which were renowned for their student Christian groups. Both met students in 40 schools and founded 22 more organizations. In December 1896, 36 delegates from the 27 Chinese student Christian associations gathered together in Shanghai and founded a national YMCA (Chinese name: 中国学塾基督幼徒会), which soon joined the WSCF. In 1897, Chinese delegates, for the first time, attended the WSCF's (second) general assembly held in Williamstown in Massachusetts. By 1907, when the seventh conference was held in Tokyo, the number of Chinese delegates had increased to 70. Then at the tenth (1913) WSCF Conference at Lake Mohonk, China, where Christianity had been very active, was awarded the eleventh conference. Due to the First World War, the Beijing Conference was not convened until 1922.

Some Chinese Christian journals—*The Life Monthly*—were overjoyed, publishing editorials greeting this conference. The WSCF's official journal—*Student World*—at the beginning of 1922 published a series of Chinese Christian-authored articles introducing the foreign readers to China's Christian churches and education system. The YMCA of China's *Progress of the Youth* devoted the entire issue (February 1922) to the WSCF Conference, asserting that the world had started to pay attention to China and that Chinese youth (students) were now in the limelight.[2] It also penned a detailed introduction to the WSCF and its conference.

According to this introduction, the theme of the eleventh conference was Christianity and the change in the world. The conference was comprised of six panels: (1) nation and race; (2) Christianity and social transformation; (3) the dissemination of Christian doctrines and the modern student; (4) the Christianization of school life; (5) the role students could play in the Church; and (6) how to make the WSCF more powerful in the present-day world.[3] Readers heard more details about the WSCF—it was comprised of 2,500 student groups from more than 40 countries and had, in total, 200,000 members.[4] Some pointed out that in the last 25 years the number of YMCA groups in China had increased to 188 and that of the YWCA was 90.[5] These articles gave an expression of expansionistic Christianity. Some felt that the student Christian movement was growing very rapidly in China and the world and the coming Beijing WSCF Conference was no other than a Christian expansion. All these, some concluded, perfectly epitomized the over-ambitious *Christian occupation* of China. Thus, the Chinese critics of Christianity moved against the WSCF Conference.

The young students, who were intellectually open to the communist thinking, took the lead in boycotting the WSCF Conference. In Shanghai, where the Christian churches were very active, in the Spring of 1922, they founded the Condemning Christianity Students Association (CCSA) and published an open statement in a semi-monthly pamphlet entitled *The Pioneer*. The key points of this statement were as follows:[6]

> The CCSA unambiguously is opposed to the WSCF. The reason why we say no to WSCF is that we stand up for the happiness of the people. Now

we explicitly show our attitude [towards Christianity and the Christian Church].

It is well known that Christianity and the Christian Church had been guilty of innumerable sins in history. Now, let us set history aside. How are things now? Christianity and the Christian Church are perpetrating or about to perpetrate crimes. Any person, who has a conscience, uprightness and courage and chooses never to abandon herself or himself to vice, will by no means forgive nor tolerate Christianity and the Christian Church doing evil.

As we know, the modern society is a capitalist society, which is dichotomized into the haves, who are idle and profit by other's toil, and the have-nots, who are kept on short commons in spite of laboring all day long. To put it another way, in this capitalist society, on the one hand, there is the oppressive, exploiting class; and there is the class that is being oppressed and exploited, on the other hand. The modern Christianity and the modern Christian Church are no other than the demon, which helps the oppressive, exploiting class plunder the oppressed and the exploited, meanwhile willingly being the accessary to the oppressive, exploiting class's victimization of the oppressed and the exploited.

We firmly believe that this cruel, oppressive, miserable capitalist society is so irrational and so inhumane that it must be toppled down and reconstructed. Precisely because of this, we take the modern Christianity and the modern Christian Church, the two demons helping the wicked oppressive, exploiting class perpetrate wicked deeds against the oppressed and the exploited, as our arch enemy, to which we decide to fight to the death.

Capitalism has germinated, grown up and started to collapse worldwide. Capitalists in various countries such as Britain, America, Japan and France all panicked and try every way possible to linger on this irrevocably worsening situation. Therefore, they swarm into China by means of the economic invasion. The modern Christianity and the modern Christian Church are, unsurprisingly, daring vanguards of this imperialistic economic aggression.

The reason why capitalists from a variety of countries have set up s Christian Church in China is simply that they are attempting to seduce the Chinese people into accepting capitalism. The goal of the YMCA is to teach the young Chinese to be good-natured but servile stooges of capitalists. In a word, the founding Christian Church is no other than bleeding the Chinese people to the utmost. Thus, we must stand against capitalism and sometimes must be opposed to the modern Christianity and the modern Christian Church supporting capitalism and deceiving the ordinary Chinese.

The WSCF was bred by the modern Christianity and the modern Christian Church. It plans to convene a meeting in Beijing's Tsinghua school, where delegates from all over the world would gather together.

> The topic of this meeting is no more than how to help capitalism have a foothold and grow up in China. For us, the WSCF's meeting is nothing but a conference of banditry, which insults the young Chinese, beguiles the Chinese people and depredates the economic resources of China. We bitterly resent this, deciding to stand up against the WSCF and its conference.
>
> Students, young messieurs, labourers, attention please! None of us are ignorant of the sins committed by capitalism! None of us are unaware of how cruel capitalists are! How can we remain aloof and indifferent when we see [Christian] running dogs of capitalists convening a meeting and discussing how to enslave us? Please, stand up! Stand up, please! We all stand up!
>
> (the Condemning Christianity Student Association, 9 March 1923)

A series of articles echoing this statement came out. They claimed that Christianity and the capitalists were colluding in doing evil;[7] that Christianity was an avatar of capitalism, the Church a tool of exploitation and Christians the lackeys of capitalists;[8] that Jesus was a mean trumpeter of capitalists;[9] and that women in Christianity were merely the appendages to men.[10]

At the same time, the CCSA telegraphed *Qinghua* and other schools nationwide, mobilizing them to say no to the WSCF Conference.[11] This telegraph read:

> To all students of Tsinghua school and its counterparts all over China:
>
> Since the Renaissance, humankind has gradually been enlightened and religion has atrophied increasingly. Consequently, separating government from religion and divorcing education from religion prevails in Europe. Contrary to this, [clergymen and missionaries] who remain too obstinate to be awakened still attempt to help the remaining evil elements of Christianity grow overseas and by doing so they can continue to live a parasitic life; meanwhile, high officials and business tycoons try to use Christianity and the Christian Church as daring vanguards of colonialism. As a result, the Gospel Book, which is escorted by guns and battleships, approaches the Eastern Land, that is, China. [Foreign powers] hope to materially enslave the Chinese by money and spiritually keep the Chinese in bondage by the Gospel. The southeast China, which is renowned for its highly developed culture and civility, is being engulfed by Christians and capitalists. And for no reason at all, the Christian and capitalist influence accumulate constantly in Beijing, the capital of a weak country. The blood and tears of patriotic young people are still wet. How can we force ourselves to praise the alleged supreme deity of Christianity? And besides, since there are many Christian places in Beijing, there is no reason to allow the Christian organization to exclusively use Tsinghua, a

national school, as the meeting place. If we do not refuse it, we will show weakness. We sincerely hope that all young messieurs would like loudly condemn the effrontery and insult of Christianity and keep our education pure and clean forever. We all members of Condemning Christianity Students Association do appreciate your help. (It is penned on day of Hui.)

These powerful words did exert an influence on Chinese society. On 11 March 1922, students from the prestigious Beijing (Peking) University (hereinafter referred to as *Beida*) declared the founding of the Condemning Religion Alliance (CRA) and published an open telegraph and a manifesto.[12] The text of the telegraph and the manifesto were as follows:

The telegraph

(Express telegraph: *Peking Morning*, *Peking Gazette*, and so on [Editor's note: There were 25 newspapers in total and the titles of the remaining 23 newspapers are omitted here to save space].)

To all newspapers, schools, societies, compatriots, overseas Chinese and comrades all over the world:

Christianity is increasingly poisonous. As a consequence, truth easily vanishes, evil doctrines run amuck, and humanity is eclipsed. Originally, China was proudly an atheistic country of free thinkers. It is in modern times that the country is poisoned by Christianity. This situation is worsening in recent decades. We are told the eleventh WSCF Conference will be held in April in Beijing, the capital of China, where Christians attempt to propagate superstitions and help them grow wild. In order to resist this, we start to set up a huge alliance condemning religion. In the light of conscience and enlightenment, we resolve to free all humans from being benighted by religion. At the same time, in the scientific spirit we introduce all humans to the evolutionist thinking. The most basic tenet of our alliance is the condemnation against all religions. The alliance is fully open regardless of race, nationality, sex, age and politics in particular. Welcome is extended to all comrades opposing religions. The independent organizations condemning religion are eligible to join us. For us, there is no room for a middle ground between belief and disbelief in religion. We are of one mind on loving and saving people. We sincerely hope that all comrades make the right decision [to stand against religion] and have no hesitation in joining us immediately. We are really looking forward to your reply! Please send mails to Monsieur Jin Jiafeng, who resides in the First Compound of Peking University. We people, who condemn religion and are from schools of Beijing, do appreciate your help. (The detailed address of the First Compound of Peking University is attached here. It is written on the day of Xian.)

6   *The Condemning Christianity Movement*

The manifesto

We have sworn to wipe out all poisonous religions. We deeply loathe religion, on the grounds it is ten, one hundred, and even ten hundred times more harmful to human society than fierce floods and dreadful monsters. If there is religion, there will be no humanity. If there is humanity, there should be no religion. Humanity and religion are at daggers drawn.

Humanity is an epitome of evolution. Acting against science, religion persists in saying humanity and the myriad things are created [by the alleged God]. Humanity is inherently free and born equal. Running counter to nature, religion is bent on putting shackles on human thought, destroying individual character, performing idolatry and practising monotheism. Humanity intrinsically loves peace. Contrary to this, religion is addicted to sectarianism, innately warmongering and deceitful, meanwhile masquerading as avatar of fraternity. Humanity is, by nature, happy in cherishing life and doing good. Contradicting the human nature, religion tempts people by [the alleged] paradise, intimidates people by [the fictitious] hell, and unduly uses the inhuman authority and morality. Religion is originally created out of nothing. But, in spite of the fact that religion itself is a fabrication, religion is wild about producing superstitions. Religion is meant to be something hypothetical. Nevertheless, it always pretends to be something true. As a result, it harms people to the end. In a word, what on earth is God, which is made of neither physical nor chemical materials? The life of religious patriarchs is beyond people's imagination. Thus, whatever is the life? Following the train of thought of religious believers, there is the Creator. But why did the Creator not invent electric lights and airships earlier? Inasmuch as God has the right to reward and punish, why cannot he transform the entirety of humanity into good persons? The absurd religion is incompatible with science and truth. The evil religion is entirely against humanism.

Globally, China is one piece of pure land, in which free thinkers rather than religious believers predominate. Helplessly, in recent decades, Christianity has been forcibly injected into China, which has no alternative but to expose herself to [the Christian] contamination. Especially in these months, Christianity [and Christian Church] behave with unbearable insolence. For what reason is Christianity much more poisonous and more harmful than other religions? In comparison with other religions' methods of propagation, the one adopted by Christianity can be said to be all-pervasive. The most hateful, most venomous scheme of Christianity is that it stretches resources as far as possible to beguile young students. Young students are originally so intellectually pure that they cannot easily be beguiled. In view of this, Christianity invests the money earned dishonestly in building magnificent houses and has named them the YMCA. Christian missionaries tell young students that the membership of the YMCA is not premised on the belief in Christianity. But in fact, as soon as young students enter the enticing valley [i.e., Christian organizations], they will be, step by step, bewitched by alluring façades [of the Church]. In a nutshell, the YMCA is actually nothing but the preparatory school of Christian converts, or, in other words, an educational institution leading people to convert to Christianity. There are many attractive things, such as a billiard parlor, a sports club, a projector room, celebrity speeches, tea parties, an English corner, an annual conference, (additional) subsidies, jovial receptionists, social butterflies, open secretary and captain positions, and so on, all of which are by nature narcotics and hypnotism. We feel terribly grieved to see this! There are how many poor young people who had been deceived by Christianity? We are really heart-broken! How abominable are these Christians, who try their utmost to distort the personality of young students!

Crimes committed by religion are too numerous to be listed. But in everyday life, many neither observe nor realize how venomous religion is. Witnessing and thinking over this, it is hard for us to avoid feeling grieved. For all persons who are full of sap, they are bound to take immediate actions to defend the truth.

We have reached the end of our forbearance and thus we are founding this huge alliance [condemning religion]. The sole goal of this alliance lies in criticizing religion [and bringing to light the truth about religion]. The alliance, exclusively focusing on the condemnation against religion, is completely immune from political factionalism. It is open to all people regardless of race, nationality, sex and age. It leaves no space for middle ground between the belief and disbelief in religion. All persons, who either enjoy full freedom from religious superstitions or aspire to remove religious poison entirely, are our comrades. We specially prepare this *Manifesto* and publish it nationwide.

In total, 79 people signed this manifesto. Among them, there were some renowned people—Li Dazhao, for instance.

Soon the CRA held a conference in *Beida*. The famous scholars such as Cai Yuanpei, who was *Beida*'s President and had been the Minister of Education, delivered speeches at the conference. Cai asserted that *religion* perpetuated human right violations on the grounds that quite a few religions induced poorly educated people to follow blindly and invaded the spiritual world of humanity. He was strongly against the effort—wherein the young people were tempted to join the church—made by the missionary schools and the student Christian organizations. Cai suggested universities and schools: (1) should abandon theology and have it replaced with the history of religions and the comparative religious studies; (2) should ban all courses advertising religion and all kinds of prayer; and (3) should prohibit professional missionaries from teaching students. Li Shizeng, a prominent educator, in his speech revealed that religion contradicted not only science and scholarship but also morality. He inspiringly pointed out that the good resulting from morality was natural and, by contrast, that from religion was distorted because religion materialistically relied on rewards and punishments.[13]

Beijing's Condemning Christianity Movement was very different from that of Shanghai. First, the membership was much more intellectually diverse. Some were early Marxists, such as Li Dazhao and Chen Duxiu, and some were liberals such as Cai Yuanpei. Second, the Beijing campaigners put not only Christianity but almost all religions under critical scrutiny. Third, the Beijing-style criticism, which underlined the anti-scientific, anti-humanistic and anti-rational nature of religion, was much less radical than its Shanghai counterpart. In view of this, it is safe to say that Beijing's Condemning Christianity Movement was actually an extension of the reasonable criticism of religion in the May Fourth-New Culture movement. Exactly for this reason, it appealed to a large number of intellectuals and young students, exerting a much greater influence on China in comparison with Shanghai. Emulating Beijing, the schools scattering all over the north and south of China set up condemning Christianity organizations and groups and produced publications criticizing Christianity. A nationwide campaign critically reexamining Christianity was thus staged. Take Guangzhou, for example. Wang Jingwei, one of the early leaders of *Kuomintang* (the Nationalist Party), published articles, acrimoniously exposing the inherent fallacies of Christianity and how toxic Christianity was to the people. A repeatedly printed critical article—"What the F*** is Jesus"?—by Zhu Zhixin, a revolutionary theory-builder, interested many students. Due to these efforts, even some industrial workers became critics of Christianity and Guangzhou was thus the South China's condemning Christianity centre. It should be pointed out that the 1920s' campaign was fundamentally different from that led by the Boxers at the dawn of the twentieth century. The Boxers, most of whom were poor peasants, were violently against the Christian churches for extremely complicated socio-historical reasons. Contrary to these armed farmers, the well-educated young Chinese in the 1920s peacefully criticized the Christian dogmata and churches from the perspectives of thought and scholarship.

Nevertheless, paying no heed to the obvious difference, the West indiscriminately denounced the 1920s' intellectual criticism of Christianity as *xenophobic*. Even the Chinese Christian converts found this biased, ungrounded accusation unacceptable. At the same time, the renowned Chinese liberals—Zhou Zuoren, Qian Xuantong, for instance—publicly said people of course fully enjoyed religious freedom and the intellectuals should first of all respect this freedom.[14] Therein lay their discontent with the Condemning Christianity Movement. In the face of the growing criticism, the campaigners rethought their strategy and took measures to prevent the campaign from growing too radical. The CRA published the second open telegram nationwide, defending its endeavour.[15] This telegram read:

> Since the publication of the Telegram of the Day of Xian, we have received an increasing number of replies, all of which unanimously suggest people

abandon religion and choose to be free thinkers. We, encouraged by this, do believe that the force of truth is too powerful to be obstructed by superstitions. But at the same time, many foreigners are unable to grasp the truth. Foreign media misrepresent our endeavour and even throw ungrounded criticism towards us. In these conditions, ordinary Christians naturally foment disunity and dissention and confound right and wrong. Therefore, it is necessary to send another telegram to explain [our motives and sole goal] further.

First, some foreigners suspiciously hold that the Condemning Religion Movement (CRM) might be the same as the Boxer Movement, which resented foreigners very much. They, actually, make a huge mistake. We sincerely tell them that the CRM is aimed exclusively at religion *per se*. Participants and proponents of the CRM, who are all well-educated people, assume a kind, friendly attitude towards foreign countries. How can we be stupidly xenophobic? Furthermore, the Condemning Religion Association (CRA) is open to all foreign nationals. At present, there are indeed some foreigners sympathizing with our endeavour. We do believe that there will be a number of foreign comrades in the CRA in near future. This demonstrates that we do draw a clear line between the belief and disbelief in religion rather than between nationalities. Therefore, the CRM can by no means be xenophobic.

Second, some intentionally foment disunity and dissent, accusing us, who firmly stand against religion, of being radical. This accusation is completely ungrounded. It is absolutely wrong. We again sincerely tell them that the CRM does not have any goals except helping science vanquish religion. Finding solutions to social problems is another matter, being completely irrelevant to the CRA. Thus, no matter who a person is, a noble or a commoner, she or he is eligible to join us, so long as the person is opposed to religion. We never make any distinctions between social ranks of the members.

In brief, in the previous telegram, we have repeatedly stated that the CRA's sole goal is to help people shake off all religious shackles and carry forward science and truth. Inasmuch as the CRA is open to all people regardless of race and nationality, it can by no means be xenophobic. In the same vein, the CRA is absolutely not politically radical, on the grounds that it is completely immune from political factionalism.

After finishing this telegram, we read a declaration, in which a five-man faction led by Zhou Zuoren preaches religious freedom, in the *Morning News*. This faction did not publish its declaration as soon as the WSCF decided to hold a conference in Beijing but printed it out immediately after the founding of the CRA. It unambiguously opposes the setting up of associations against religions and Christianity in particular, meanwhile having no objection to the WSCF Conference. The two points demonstrate that this faction is indeed suspected of supporting religion and abandoning the neutral stance on religion, even though it grandly declares that it does not endorse any religions.

Foregoing discussions focus on the basic attitude of this faction. As far as the true freedom of belief is concerned, we have never done anything against this freedom. Rather, we try our best to protect our own freedom from being infringed [by frenetic religious believers such as Christians]. The WSCF is no more than an alluring propaganda tool of Christianity. When it comes to the true freedom of faith, it is Christian organizations such as the WSCF that shoots first [viz., that provokes free thinkers]. It is not the CRA but the WSCF that infringes [free thinkers'] freedom of belief. Countering the false account of true facts, we make this statement here. (It is candidly penned by the CRA on the Day of Dong.)

After publishing this telegram, some campaigners softened their position when they were criticizing Christianity.

To the disappointment of the campaigners, the eleventh WSCF Conference was held in Beijing as scheduled. Even so, this campaign was a great impetus to the country's rethink of religions and Christianity in particular. Many intellectuals intensively discussed freedom of faith and the validity of the Condemning Christianity Movement. Among those who disagreed with this campaign, Fu Tong and Liang Qichao are worthy of mention. The ideas of Fu and Liang perfectly embodied the scientific and democratic spirit advocated by the New Culture Movement in early twentieth-century China.

Fu, who had been the President of the Xi'an-based Northwest University, in one of his articles academically made a clear distinction between the *scientific* and *religious* Condemning Christianity Movements.[16] Apart from shedding light on the substance and assortment of religion and the correct attitude towards religious studies, Fu emphatically said religion must be *scientifically* reexamined and criticized. It is a pity that, Fu concluded, the Condemning Christianity Movement at that time was neither scientific nor religious and was opposed by both scientists and religionists. Despite this, he held that this campaign attracted a large number of people to join the critical reexamination of religion. As regards the future campaign, Fu suggested the critics should reexamine a specific religion rather than all religions and point their guns at superstition and the corruptive elements of high religions rather than at the ideal, harmless religions. He went further, reminding readers of the best weapons against religion—that is, the *scientific* study in history of religion and the *scientific* comparative religious study.

Liang, one of the leading reformist thinkers in early modern China, adopted a position of reserve towards the CRA. Thoroughly discussing religion in one of his essays, Liang proposed several points.[17] First, religion was purely emotional and thus it could by no means be analysed through reason. Second, the evolution of humankind was dependent on the condensation of strong emotions and this highly condensed emotion was no other than religion. Third, religion was by nature positive and it was not religion itself but the people earning their living by religion that had ruined religion. Fourth, if the Condemning Christianity Movement was driven by a great ideal, it would be respectable; but if not, it would be despicable. Fifth, the Chinese Christian converts should abandon the parochial practice—wherein whether a person was good or bad rested on whether she or he believed in Christianity—and try instead to be more open and more public-spirited. Sixth, the evil cults were much more harmful to society and should be annihilated. Last but not least, China was suffering the loss of faith and the rehabilitation of the lost faith depended on emotion rather than on reason.

The opinions of those who enthusiastically supported the CRA contrasted sharply with above-mentioned ones. But none of them went beyond the New Culture paradigms such as science, democracy, freedom, equality and fraternity. Interestingly, few of them were as radical as the aforementioned CCSA's statement. Take an early Marxist's writing, for example. In March 1922, Chen Duxiu finished *Christianity and the Christian Church*, which was more critical than the one penned two years earlier. He historically reconstructed the Christian Church's evil work oppressing science and freedom of thought, as well as revealing the truth that the Church was exactly the vanguard of colonialism and running dog of capitalists. Chen finally concluded that the corrupt Christian Church was not venerable at all but detestable both in the past and in the present.[18] But at the same time, Chen suggested, a clear distinction between the Christian tenets and the Christian churches must be made. Basically, the Christian tenets—fraternity, sacrifice, for instance—were good. Another leading figure of the early Chinese Marxists—Li Dazhao—shone a critical light on religion from the perspectives of freedom and equality. Li's conclusion was that religion could not bring freedom, equality and universal love to humankind. Both Chen's and Li's writings demonstrated that even the Marxists at that time could not think outside the established *dualistic* New Culture paradigm centred on science and democracy.

The Society for Young China (SYC) played a significant role in the Condemning Christianity Movement. Yu Jiaju, an educator, was the Association's leading critic of Christianity. He set forth his observations on Christianity in an article entitled "Christianity and the Emotional Life".[19] Yu rejected Liang's bold assertion that religion was emotion, as well as strictly pointing out that the problem of religion in China was none other than the problem of Christianity. He paid particular attention to the religious emotional life, contending that the religious emotion was primarily based on adoration, reverence and fear. By having his rethink of Christianity premised on the *reason* independence of emotion, Yu concluded that the religious emotion, which was based on the adoration of supernatural beings, was irreconcilable with reason and thus the Christian emotional life was unreasonable and intolerable. In addition, he suggested that Christianity should be abolished because this religion's expansion grew almost uncontrollable due to its professional and powerful missionary work. Yu denied the Christian faith in light of the religious psychology and the relationship between reason and the religious emotion. This effort still followed the scientific paradigm advocated by the New Culture Movement.

Digging into approximately one hundred papers in support of the Condemning Christianity Movement, all of which were published in 1922, an observer known as Zhang Qinshi (C. S. Chang) drew a conclusion on the reasons why the campaigners were against religion.[20] First, "[r]eligion is out-of-date". Second, "[r]eligion is unfavourable to human progress". Third, "[r]eligion had no connection whatsoever with morality". Fourth, "[r]eligion is not necessary for mankind". As regards the reasons why some attacked Christianity, Zhang said the attackers generally held that the Christian teaching was "unscientific", "contrary to logic" and unable to adapt to modern China.[21] Zhang's analyses indicated that the 1922 Condemning Christianity Movement was totally intellectually based on the New Culture Movement. Nevertheless, it should be pointed out that indeed there were some critics who attempted to go beyond the New Culture paradigms. To be specific, the scholarly reexamination was growing increasingly political and words were being translated into actions. Later, Christianity was denounced as something that was part and parcel of imperialism and should be entirely rejected.

The Chinese Christian Church's response

The 1922 Condemning Christianity Movement was not well organized but spontaneous. It was the brainchild of the intellectuals who were critical of religion in the New Culture Movement. As summer approached, this campaign subsided. It made a great contribution to the indigenization of Christianity in China. In face of the rising tide against Christianity, the Chinese Christian converts, at first, responded with indifference or defense. Some Christian writers published articles in *The Life Monthly*, *Progress of the Youth* and *The True Light*, earnestly defending their faith. But among them, the conservatives and the enlightened were different from each other. Accordingly, the roles the two groups played in the indigenization of Christianity in China differed. When defending the Christian teaching, the enlightened carefully studied the criticisms and started to rethink Christianity. In doing so, they realized that the Chinese Church did need a reform. The articles published in *The Life Monthly* and *Progress of the Youth* reflected this. It was undoubtedly conducive to indigenizing this imported religion. Contrary to the enlightened, the conservatives blindly fought back,[22] paying no attention to the problems attributed to Christianity and the Christian Church themselves. *The True Light* was their mouthpiece.

Zhang Yijing, a Christian apologist, refuted, one by one, more than 20 articles in support of the Condemning Christianity Movement in *The True Light*. Then he published a book entitled *A Critical Review of Criticisms Against Christianity*, which was comprised of 13 chapters and 9 of them were penned by Zhang himself. Acting like an arch-apologist, Zhang, with his sharp tongue, indiscriminately attacked the radical critics of Christianity—the aforementioned Wang Jingwei and Zhu Zhixin, for instance—and the mild, liberal-minded critics, such as Cai Yuanpei and Chen Duxiu. Zhang's writings had a strong smell of gunpowder. He, in one of his essays, vulgarly compared the critics of Christianity to vixens bitching.[23] When arguing against Wang Jingwei's article revealing the three inherent fallacies of Christianity, Zhang frenziedly said Wang's writing was not worth a straw and Wang's critique was insignificant and pointless.[24] Despite his burning anger about the critics of Christianity and his ardent desire to fight back, Zhang and his comrades seldom profoundly rethought their faith and the church. One of the unexpected results of his apologetics was that Zhang himself and *The True Light* were made known to the Chinese. Generally speaking, apart from propagandizing the Christian faith, the conservatives did not make use of the Condemning Christianity Movement to promote the indigenization of Christianity in China.

Being very different from the conservatives, the enlightened, most of whom penned articles for *The Life Monthly* and *Progress of the Youth*, resorted to reason rather than aggressiveness and carefully and deeply reexamined the criticisms against Christianity. They did try their best to defend their faith; but at the same time, they made sincere efforts to create a new Christianity adaptable to Chinese society. Take one piece of writing by Liu Tingfang, who had taught at the Beijing-based Yenching University, for example.[25] Liu wrote:

> This [militant] statement has three features. First, it is stylistically forceful, showcasing the authors' good command of the modern vernacular Chinese. Second, it is intellectually naïve, indicating that the author has fully abandoned himself to emotions. Third, it is entirely propagandistic, uttering ideological paranoia from the beginning to the end.
>
> This statement is a condemnation against Christianity. For this reason, it is unambiguously opposed to the WSCF. But what it criticizes sounds like hullabaloos clamoured by novice Bolsheviks rather than subtle, precise criticisms made by sober, conscientious, and skilled scientists, philosophers or historians.
>
> Where the Christian organization and propagation are concerned, there are indeed many weak points. Even so, the young students' attack on Christianity is still no more than an ineffective attempt. It cannot exert even the slightest influence on Christianity [and the Church]. For the authors [of this statement], attacking Christianity is nothing more than an act of heroism or a show of eloquence, through which she or he pledges loyalty to the radical Bolshevism.
>
> In fact, even though the authors penning this statement do not make any substantial efforts to respect others' freedom of faith, *The Life Monthly* sincerely respects the CCSA's freedom to disseminate its own ideologies. Furthermore, *The Life Monthly* does believe what a saying teaches—straightforward advice from others can help us overcome the shortcomings—and thus reprints this statement. In doing so, we sincerely invite all participants of the WSCF Conference to candidly discuss the following four questions.

First, for what reason are the words and deeds of we Christians and members of the WSCF denounced as the same things done by the running dogs of capitalists?

Second, for what reason do free thinkers hold that our faith, namely, Christianity, helps the wicked oppressive, exploiting class perpetrate crimes against the oppressed and the exploited?

Third, how does the WSCF, which has been set up for 27 years, respond to the worldwide economic injustice and inequality since its very founding? Does it make any suggestions respecting reforming the world economy?

Fourth, how do we, who are members of the WSCF and brethren believing in modern Christianity, perceive the exploiting class and crimes committed by capitalism in the world [and make constructive suggestions for improving the situation]?

Liu's comments and suggestions indicated that, just like their critics, the enlightened Christians followed the New Culture paradigms when defending their beloved faith. Showcasing the Christian democratic spirit, they not only printed the full text of CCSA's statement but also suggested all participants of the WSCF's Conference should rethink Christianity and the Church. Therein lay actually the intellectual foundation of the indigenization of Christianity in China.

In the meantime, *The Life Monthly* published a set of articles penned by leading intellectuals, such as Hu Shi, Zhang Dongsun, Zhou Zuoren, Qian Xuantong and Chen Duxiu. *The Life*'s editors sincerely hoped that this effort could help the one thousand WSCF delegates from all over the world grasp the Chinese intelligentsia's true attitude towards Christianity, on the grounds that in the past the world's understanding of one of the key issues—the relationship between the Chinese and Christianity—unduly relied heavily on the foreign missionaries and Chinese Christian converts' conjectures rather than on the objective observations of the non-Christian, educated Chinese.[26] They promised that the ideas of the intellectuals disagreeing with the Christian teaching would be scientifically studied. This mild stand successfully buried the enmity between the enlightened Chinese Christians and the critics of Christianity.

This rapprochement was perfectly embodied in a statement prepared by the five leaders of the YMCA of China.[27] On the one hand, this statement fairly pointed out that many criticisms of religion were unscientific, ungrounded, arbitrary and parochial; on the other hand, it recognized with magnanimity the contributions these criticisms made to the missions of rethinking and rehabilitating religions and purifying the religious scholarship. It is particularly worth mentioning that this statement, profoundly and critically, rethought traditional Christianity. Most encouragingly, the authors of this statement unambiguously suggested that Christianity in China be Sinicized and (re-)made adaptable to the national spirit of China. To be specific, they pointed out that some critics mistakenly took Christianity as a dead religion and argued instead that the Christianity they believed in was not the ancient or medieval Christianity but the new, vibrant one according with Jesus's ethics and personality and incorporating modern science. This new Christianity, they went on, would be Sinicized and turned into the principal guide and tool in the service of life and society. They freely admitted that indeed there were many bad, inappropriate elements in Christianity, a two-thousand-year-old religion. But this could not overshadow the extraordinariness of Jesus, who created an epoch-making faith. Having their arguments based on the paradigmatic assertion that religion was one of the social systems and would definitely evolve because of the inevitable social evolution, they optimistically and unswervingly believed that Christianity—its tenets, canons, churches, and so on—would surely change and adapt to the spiritual need of the Chinese nation. These elaborations convincingly demonstrated that the enlightened Chinese Christians accepted many reasonable criticisms and were attempting to correct and improve their religion.

The Condemning Christianity Movement did deal a heavy blow to Christianity in China. Compared to this campaign, the critique in the New Culture Movement paled. In some regions—Shanghai, Guangzhou, for instance, even workers joined the critics. The New Culture urged the Chinese Christians to rethink their religion; and the Condemning Christianity Movement forced them to critically reexamine the Christian teaching and the church. In this regard, an observer vividly said the radical critique of Christianity was a head-on blow, whereby the Chinese Christian converts were awakened. The awakened Christians would squarely face the problems confronting the Church.[28] Liu Tingfang, in one editorial, said the Chinese Christians could reap benefits from the Condemning Christianity Movement.[29] First, this campaign helped many people become interested in religion and Christianity in particular. Second, this campaign served as a wake-up call to the Chinese Christians, who were intoxicated by the convening of the WSCF Conference and the National Congress of Christianity and might credit their religion with power it did not possess at all. Third, this campaign forced the Chinese Christians to give up following blindly the herd and picking up what the West said. Fourth, this campaign was a mirror, through which the Christians could discover their mistakes and correct them immediately. As regards the mistakes Christianity had committed, Liu said the worst ones were the undermining of fraternity brought about by the frenetic apologetics and the hindrance of the growth of reason by indulging in emotions.

Echoing Liu's introspection, some suggested the Christian followers and priests should ask themselves several questions: did they truly believe in the Christian teaching or merely live by this religion?; did they put into practice the Christian doctrines such as equality, fraternity, freedom and sacrifice?; did they resolve to abandon all deep-rooted bad habits such as greed, selfishness and hypocrisy?; did they do something for society>; did they aspire to serve humanity?; and did they (the Chinese priests and foreign missionaries in particular) strive hard to improve the social morality and realize Christ's love for the people?[30] Quite a few Chinese Christians shone a critical light on the Church's corrupt practices. Zhao Zichen, a renowned Chinese Christian leader, enumerated the 14 types of malpractice—failing to bring the spiritual and intellectual freedom to humanity, fearing the critical and scientific spirit, remaining indifferent to economic inequality, and so on—of the Church. The reason why the Church became corrupt lay in the ignorance and stupidity of the Christian preachers in China. Zhao explained this in detail, saying inasmuch as the Church in China was not Chinese but Western, the organization, form and mentality of the Church were all inadaptable to the Chinese.[31] Zhao specially said his explanation was inspired by some young Chinese students' discussions.[32] It revealed that the participants of the WSCF Conference had realized the problems of the Church and fiercely rebuked it. Jian Youwen, one of the leaders of the YMCA of China, came to a similar conclusion that the overwhelming majority of Chinese Christian churches were merely vassal organizations of the Western missionary societies.[33] It is evident that Jian was influenced by the critique that Christianity was a running dog of the capitalists. In view of the above discussions, it is safe to say that the enlightened Chinese Christians made a more thorough examination of the Church's problems in comparison with that done by critics in the New Culture Movement. In a word, the Condemning Christianity Movement did exert a positive influence on the Chinese Church.

It was the Condemning Christianity Movement that helped the Chinese Christians realize that the Chinese Church was far gone in a crisis and desperately needed a fundamental reform. In May 1922, the National Congress of Christianity was convened. The Chinese attendees strongly demanded the reform of the Church and the indigenization of Christianity. Many of them concluded that the missionaries should be held responsible for the poor performance of the Chinese Church:

> If the missionaries did not regard the mythologies formulated thousands of years ago as truth, who dares to say that religion is no more than superstition? If the missionaries did not force the followers to believe in the absurd story of pregnant virgin, who dares to say that religion fetters thought; and if the missionaries did not fawn on the capitalists, who dares to say that religion staunchly supports capitalists?[34]

Thus, the enlightened suggested the Chinese Church should place restrictions on the foreign missionaries, try to be independent of the foreign church and transform itself into a national church. The Chinese attendees in the Congress were outspoken in elaborating these ideas.

It was true that the Condemning Christianity Movement was basically an extension of the cultural and academic critique of Christianity in the New Culture Movement; it was also true that Christianity in the 1922 campaign had already been *politically* criticized and related to the oppressive capitalist class. Although this campaign later took measures to prevent the critique from growing too political, this politics-oriented change did stir the Chinese Christianity deeply. Some from the Church started to rethink the relationship involving Christianity, capitalism and socialism. In fact, some in the WSCF's Beijing Conference already discussed the relationships between Christianity and capitalism and between Christianity and war. The pointed out that the Church turned a blind eye to the truth that the growth of capitalism brought about many social problems and did nothing to correct or improve the situation.[35] Then the National Congress of Christianity passed some bills criticizing capitalism. The enlightened faction of the Church demanded a deep study of the relationship of Christianity and capitalism. Some did make an attempt. Liu Tingfang, for instance, held that the Church fairly treated the criticism that the Christian Church belonged to the capitalist class and oppressed the proletariat. To be specific, digging into history, the Church should carefully investigate these issues: did Christianity in the past thousands of years help the proletariat?; did Christianity struggle against the capitalist class with a view to benefiting the proletariat?; and did Christianity collude with the capitalist class in oppressing the proletariat?[36] Zhang Shizhang opined that the Church should not be blindly against socialism but instead thoroughly study it, on the grounds that Jesus himself had a great sympathy for the poor, just as the socialists did. Researching deeply into the relationship of Christianity and socialism, Zhang concluded that the absolute antagonism between Christianity and socialism be abandoned and Christianity and socialism could enjoy an inherent similarity and could peacefully coexist. He asserted that both Christianity and socialism reform themselves. Where the reform of Christianity was concerned, it consisted of the theoretical and practical innovations. In order to theoretically improve itself, Christianity itself should: (1) make the original spirit and teachings of Jesus more conspicuous by abandoning the outdated Western teachings and medieval theological debates; (2) reappraise the value of the Nicene Creed, the Apostles' Creed and the Bible and remake them into the foundation of a more reasonable belief; (3) be more tolerant of the scientists and socialists' criticisms; and (4) be substantially open to the traditional Chinese culture. Besides, the Chinese Christian churches should practically: (1) pay greater attention to active social service rather than to the formalistic personal life; (2) admit more voluntary, free and sincere non-Christians rather than those who enjoyed undeserved fame; (3) train more fair and positive preachers rather than rely on the hypocritical, greedy and arbitrary priests; and (4) give up sectarianism entirely and act in concert with each other. In a nutshell, Zhang earnestly looked forward to the dawning of an indigenized Christianity and a united Church in China.[37] Obviously, the enlightened Chinese Christians' discussion about the interrelation of Christianity, capitalism and socialism was finally channelled to the indigenization of Christianity in China. It shed a revealing light on the truth that the Condemning Christianity Movement and the indigenization of Chinese Christian Church were inextricably interwoven.

Notes

1. Zhang Xiping 张西平 and Zhuo Xinping 卓新平 eds. *The Experiment of Indigenizing Christianity in China* [本色之探] (Beijing: China Radio and Television Press, 1999), 535.
2. Chen Liting 陈立廷, "The WSCF Conference and the Chinese Students" (世界基督教学生同盟大会与中国学生), *Progress of the Youth*, no. 50 (February 1922), 11–13.
3. Bihui 丽诲, "Rethink: The Eleventh WSCF Conference's Theme and Panels" (对于大会总题"基督与世界改造"及分股讨论各问题的感想), ibid., 5–9.
4. Xie Fuya 谢扶雅 (a.k.a. Zia Nai-zing), "WSCF in the Past Quarter Century" (世界基督教学生同盟二十五年小史), ibid., 21.
5. Gu Ziren 顾子仁, "The Declaration of the Eleventh WSCF Conference" (世界基督教学生同盟第十一次大会宣言), ibid., 4.
6. For the full text of this statement, see: vol. 2 of Institute of World Religions of China Academy of Social Sciences, *A Collection of Primary Sources about Religions in the World* [世界宗教资料汇编] (Beijing: Institute of World Religions, CASS, December 1982), 78–79.
7. See: ibid., 92.
8. Ibid., 93.
9. Ibid., 95.
10. Ibid., 92.
11. For the text of this telegram, see: ibid., 79.
12. For the full text of this manifesto, see: ibid., 79–80.
13. For the speeches given by Cai and Li, see: ibid., 199–206.
14. Zhang Qinshi 张钦士, *Trend of Religions in China in Last Decade* [国内近十年来之宗教思潮] (Beijing: Jinghua yinshuju, 1927), 199.
15. For the full text of this telegram, see: vol. 2 of Institute of World Religions of China Academy of Social Sciences, *Shijie zongjiao ziliao huibian*, 81.
16. For the full text of this paper, see: Zhang Qinshi, *Trend of Religions in China in the Last Decade*, 240–260.
17. For this article, see: ibid., 260–271.
18. For Chen's discussion, see: ibid., 193.
19. For this article, see: ibid., 272–304.
20. C. S. Chang (张钦士), "The Anti-Religion Movement", *The Chinese Recorder* (教务杂志), no. 54 (August 1923), 463.
21. Ibid.
22. Zhong Ketuo 钟可讬, "Chinese Christian Churches: A Survey" (中国教会概况), *Annals of Chinese Christian Church* (中华基督教会年鉴), vol. 8 (1925), 9.
23. Zhang Yijing 张亦镜 ed. *A Critical Review of Criticisms Against Christianity* [批评非基督教言论汇编] (Shanghai: Publisher unknown, 1922), 32.
24. For Zhang's refutation of Wang, see: Yang Tianhong 杨天宏, *Christianity and Modern China* [基督教与近代中国] (Chengdu: The People's Press of Sichuan, 1994), 194.
25. Liu Tingfang 刘廷芳, "The CCSA" (非基督教学生同盟), *The Life Monthly* (生命月刊), vol. 2, no. 7 (March 1922), 8–9.
26. See: Anon, "An Editorial" (社论), *The Life Monthly*, ibid., 6.
27. See: Zhang Qinshi, *Trend of Religions in China in the Last Decade*, 207–212.
28. Ibid., 226–227.

29 Liu Tingfang, "On the Condemning Religion Movement" (反对宗教运动), *The Life Monthly*, vol. 2, nos. 9–10 (June 1922), 1–3.
30 See: Zhang Qinshi, *Trend of Religions in China in the Last Decade*, 226.
31 Zhao Zichen 赵紫宸, "A Major Issue Respecting the Future of the Chinese Christian Church" (中国教会前途的一大问题), *The Life Monthly*, vol. 2, no. 8 (1922), 5.
32 Ibid., 6.
33 Jian Youwen 简又文, Part One of "The National Church" (民族的教会), *Progress of the Youth*, no. 52 (April 1922), 33–44.
34 See: Zhang Qinshi, *Trend of Religions in China in the Last Decade*, 228.
35 Lin Ronghong 林荣洪, *The Rise of the Chinese Christian Church in Unrest* [风潮中奋起的中国教会] (Hong Kong: Tien Dao Publishing House, 1980), 132.
36 Liu Tingfang, "The Christian View of Economy and the Church's Responsibility" (基督徒的经济观和基督教教会的责任), *The Life Monthly*, vol. 3, no. 1 (November 1922), 1–3.
37 For a detailed discussion, see Zhang Shizhang 张仕章, "The Chinese Christianity and Socialism" (中国的基督教与社会主义), *Progress of the Youth*, no. 56 (October 1922), 19–20.

Bibliography

Anon. "An Editorial" (社论), *The Life Monthly* (生命月刊). Vol. 2, No. 7 (March 1922).
Bihui 丽诲. "Rethink: The Eleventh WSCF Conference's Theme and Panels" (对于大会总题"基督与世界改造"及分股讨论各问题的感想), *Progress of the Youth* (青年进步). No. 50 (February 1922).
Chang, C. S. 张钦士. "The Anti-Religion Movement", *The Chinese Recorder* (教务杂志). No. 54 (August 1923).
Chen, Liting 陈立廷. "The WSCF Conference and the Chinese Students" (世界基督教学生同盟大会与中国学生), *Progress of the Youth* (青年进步). No. 50 (February 1922).
Gu, Ziren 顾子仁. "The Declaration of the Eleventh WSCF Conference" (世界基督教学生同盟第十一次大会宣言), *Progress of the Youth* (青年进步). No. 50 (February 1922).
Institute of World Religions of China Academy of Social Sciences. *A Collection of Primary Sources about Religions in the World* [世界宗教资料汇编] (Beijing: Institute of World Religions, CASS, 1982).
Jian, Youwen 简又文. "The National Church" (民族的教会), *Progress of the Youth* (青年进步). No. 52 (April 1922), Part One.
Lin, Ronghong 林荣洪. *The Rise of the Chinese Christian Church in Unrest* [风潮中奋起的中国教会] (Hong Kong: Tien Dao Publishing House, 1980).
Liu, Tingfang 刘廷芳. "The CCSA" (非基督学生同盟), *The Life Monthly* (生命月刊). Vol. 2, No. 7 (March 1922).
Liu, Tingfang 刘廷芳. "On the Condemning Religion Movement" (反对宗教运动), *The Life Monthly* (生命月刊). Vol. 2, Nos. 9–10 (June 1922).
Liu, Tingfang 刘廷芳. "The Christian View of Economy and the Church's Responsibility" (基督徒的经济观和基督教教会的责任), *The Life Monthly* (生命月刊). Vol. 3, no. 1 (November 1922).
Xie, Fuya 谢扶雅. "The WSCF in the Past Quarter Century" (世界基督教学生同盟二十五年小史), *Progress of the Youth* (青年进步). No. 50 (February 1922).

Yang, Tianhong 杨天宏. *Christianity and Modern China* [基督教与近代中国] (Chengdu: The People's Press of Sichuan, 1994).

Zhang, Qinshi 张钦士. *Trend of Religions in China in the Last Decade* [国内近十年来之宗教思潮] (Beijing: Jinghua yinshuju, 1927).

Zhang, Shizhang 张仕章. "Chinese Christianity and Socialism" (中国的基督教与社会主义), *Progress of the Youth* (青年进步). No. 56 (October 1922).

Zhang, Xiping 张西平 and Zhuo Xinping 卓新平 eds. *The Experiment of Indigenizing Christianity in China* [本色之探] (Beijing: China Radio and Television Press, 1999).

Zhang, Yijing 张亦镜 ed. *A Critical Review of Criticisms Against Christianity* [批评非基督教言论汇编] (Shanghai: Publisher unknown, 1922).

Zhao, Zichen 赵紫宸. "A Major Issue Respecting the Future of the Chinese Christian Church" (中国教会前途的一大问题), *The Life Monthly* (生命月刊). Vol. 2, No. 8 (1922).

Zhong, Ketuo 钟可讬. "Chinese Christian Churches: A Survey" (中国教会概况), *Annals of the Chinese Christian Church* (中华基督教会年鉴). Vol. 8 (1925).

2 The National Congress of Christianity in 1922

The preparation for and convening of the National Congress of Christianity

On 2 May 1922, the unprecedented National Congress of Christianity (NCC) was convened in the City Hall located on Nanjing Road, Shanghai. It lasted for nine days. According to records, in total, 1,025 (or 1,089) people attended this conference. Among the attendees, there were 568 Chinese delegates, who came from 19 provinces, 6 Christian denominations and 6 organizations.[1] It is particularly worth mentioning that a number of women attended the conference. The NCC's main topic was the Chinese Christian Church. Inasmuch as the NCC was convened merely two months after the outbreak of the Condemning Christianity Movement (CCM), when that social movement was still at its height, it was, in many aspects, deeply influenced by the CCM.

Why was the NCC convened? Some articles published by Christian churches might give some clues. There were three key points in these discussions.

First, the NCC was an extension of the Christian tradition in which converts and churches communicated with each other by means of a conference. Since the arrival of Ma Lixun (Robert Morrison) in China, Christian missionaries had held several national meetings, at which the churches rethought their successes and failures in propagating Christianity and made plans for future work. Moreover, since the 1907 missionary conference celebrating the centenary of the introduction of Protestantism to China, Christianity in China had witnessed a great growth. To be specific, by then, the number of foreign missionaries was over 6,000; the number of Chinese preachers, over 1,000; the number of Chinese Christian converts, 340,000; the number of people working for Christian churches, no less than 25,000; the number of students of missionary schools, approximately 200,000; the number of people attending Sunday school, 220,000; the number of organizations devoted to the propagation of Christianity, over 130; and the number of provincial governments greenlighting the founding of the Christian church among China's 1,713 counties, 1,587. In order for such a huge missionary work in China to be carried out well, it was desperately necessary for missionary organizations and Christian churches to cooperate and coordinate more efficiently. In addition,

DOI: 10.4324/9781003345169-2

American and European missionary societies were sufficiently staffed and more financially prepared after the First World War, so that they attempted to expand the propagation of Christianity in China. Last but not least, Christian churches of all shades in China had their own specific propagation plans and thus they did need to enhance mutual communication.

Second, there had to be a national conference on Christianity, by which missionary societies and churches could adapt to the general situation that was witnessing drastic changes and meet the needs of the Chinese people. In the wake of the 1907 missionary conference, China had experienced a vehement change in politics. Since the commencement of the New Culture Movement (NCM), the Chinese had become increasingly intellectually open, so that they were no longer lukewarm towards politics, society, scholarship and religion, but instead positively sized them up and participated in them. Such a change was a golden opportunity in the eyes of the religionists.[2] Thus, Christianity formulated a scheme, which would cater to the spiritual needs of the Chinese. To be more specific, Christianity in China, which was suddenly enlightened by the CCM driven by the Chinese nationalism unleashed in the NCM, resolved to separate from the Western missionary society and transform itself into a religion that would not only be adaptable to the time and to Chinese society but also be able to convince the Chinese that the Christianity *in* China now was the Christianity *of* China. The Christian Church had to undertake an overall strategy of founding China's own church, through which the propagation of Christianity in China could be more remarkable and the religion itself could be a spiritual guide for the Chinese. On the other hand, due to the influence of the NCM and the CCM, Chinese Christians became increasingly awakened and gradually realized that they had to bear a great deal of responsibility. In the meantime, awakened Chinese Christians eagerly wanted to discuss how to perform the duties of Chinese Christians and how to make the Church a truly Chinese Church.

Third, Christianity in China needed a national associated agency, which had to be set up by means of a national conference. In the past, the Chinese Christian Church had not set up a national coordinating body and the missionary societies all acted according to their own free will. As a result, missionary societies took into account only their own interests and the Chinese Christian Church was actually in a state of lack of integration. The whole of missionary work in China was affected, finally. As Christianity kept growing in China, missionary societies of every hue strongly felt that there should be a united coordinating body. In 1913, due to the influence of ecumenism, the China Continuation Committee (CCC) was set up immediately after the national Protestant meeting. The CCC, acting as an interim national coordinating body, played a leading role in carrying out a national survey of Christian development. But the CCC was not the official agency of the Christian Church. As soon as it had finished its task, it would cease to exist. By then, the development of Christianity in China had grown into an unprecedented mission, which could not be carried out efficiently without a national coordinating body. In a word, in such circumstances, it was imperative to found a coordinating body at the national conference. In fact, convening a national conference on Christianity in 1922 was the right decision, on the grounds that the CCC had finished its national survey in 1921 and published *The Christian Occupation of China* (*Zhonghua guizhu*), a voluminous, highly comprehensive report written in both English and Chinese. This survey helped people gain an insight into the growth of Christianity in China and laid a solid foundation for the national conference on Christianity. In a nutshell, all this led to the convening of the NCC in 1922.

The NCC played quite a significant role in the history of the Chinese Christian Church. The reason was that it made the Chinese core of the Christian Church in China much more conspicuous. This could be corroborated by the NCC's other name—the First National Congress of Chinese Christianity. Before the 1922 NCC, there were indeed three large Protestant meetings held in 1877, 1890 and 1907, respectively. These meetings did attract foreign missionaries nationwide. But none of them were truly *national* (i.e., *Chinese*). Only the 1922 NCC was genuinely *national*, representing the Chinese Christians nationwide. The number of people attending the 1922 NCC was the largest in the history of the Chinese Church. According to the NCC's Constitution, there had to be 1,000 attendees. But in fact, the turnout exceeded 1,000. For this reason, the NCC was praised as an unprecedentedly distinguished gathering of Chinese Christians. Furthermore, some strictly called the NCC the conference of the Chinese Christian Church, because, compared with previous sessions of Protestant meetings, in which no Chinese representatives participated, not only did Chinese delegates account for over 50 per cent of the NCC attendees but also the NCC itself focused on Chinese affairs. To be frank, the NCC demonstrated that Chinese Christians had already cut a splendid figure by the time of this conference.[3] The NCC was also known as the May the Second Conference (MSC), on the grounds that it was convened on 2 May 1922. Some held that the title "MSC" indicated that this conference was just as important as landmark events such as the May Fourth Movement (MFM). In addition, some renamed the NCC "Quanguo dahui" (the National Congress of Women), because they were moved by the number of women representatives attending the conference. Excited observers even replaced the title "quanguo" (全国national) with "quanguo" (全帼all-women). The NCC was open to all applicants, regardless of sex and nationality. It was at the NCC that female Chinese Christians made their national debut. Consequently, not only was the reputation of the women representatives greatly boosted but those who had paid little attention to women's rights were shocked by the female Christians' performance and started to realize that women's rights had been improved greatly within the Church.[4]

The afore-mentioned alternative names for the NCC perfectly reflected the characteristics of this conference. In comparison to previous meetings, the 1922 NCC was more representative (in terms of number of participants and their origins), more democratic (in terms of the Chinese leadership of the

Church), more equal (in terms of female Chinese Christians' presence), and more ecumenical (in terms of the trans-denominational and trans-missionary-societal cooperation and the founding of the National Christian Council of China [NCCC]). Most importantly, the 1922 NCC, for the first time in the history of China, proposed an explicit manifesto voicing the indigenization of the Christian Church in China. All these shed light on how the NCM and the CCM had influenced the Christian Church. For example, the 1922 NCC outdid all previous national meetings of Protestants in attaching importance to female Christians. The NCC's equal treatment of women showed perfectly that the CCM did exert an influence on the Christian Church by strongly condemning the Christian Church's conventional discrimination against women.

The NCC's attempt to carry forward the indigenization of Christianity in China is worthy of further discussion. The NCC's indigenization endeavour was embodied not only in the number of Chinese representatives attending the conference but also in its main topic—*the Chinese Church*. In over one century spanning from 1807, when the Protestant missionary society arrived in China, to the 1920s, there had been several huge meetings of Protestants, among which the 1877, 1890 and 1907 conferences were the most important. Embarrassed but not surprised, none of the Chinese Christians appeared in the three conferences. All attendees were Westerners, without any exceptions. The situation did not change at all until 1913, when 36 Chinese delegates, who accounted for a third of the total number of representatives amounting to 115, participated in the national meeting. The situation did improve. But the meeting itself still focused exclusively on the work of the foreign missionary societies in China. Comparatively, the 1922 NCC made remarkable and substantial progress in terms of form and content of the conference. Not only were over half of attendees Chinese; but the chairman also was a Chinese man, Cheng Jingyi. Moreover, many panel heads were Chinese, too. Most importantly, the main topic of 1922 NCC was the *Chinese Church*. Such a new atmosphere was related to two factors. First, the Chinese Christian Church became increasingly mature and thus the priority of the church's work shifted from the missionary society to the Chinese Church itself and from foreign missionaries to Chinese Christians themselves.[5] In other words, the NCC attempted to transform the old-style practice, in which the missionary society was the centre and had the right to decide all matters, into a new mode, which required that there be a national church independent of the missionary society and it would play a decisive role in routine affairs.[6] Second, the CCM and the NCM in particular directly influenced what took place inside the Christian Church. This is corroborated by the selection of the main topic of the national conference on Christianity. It was in May 1921, when the ninth annual meeting of the CCC's executive office was being held, that attendees intensively discussed the relationship between Christianity and the NCM.

Cheng Jingyi wrote a treatise entitled "The Chinese Christian Church" in preparation for the national meeting, setting forth what the relationship between the national conference on Christianity and the NCM was and how to carry forward the indigenization of Chinese Church. He said:

> The new intellectual trend is very thought-provoking in the eyes of the young Chinese. When young persons are observing the world, they will never take anything for granted, but instead inquire into the root of all things and constantly ask "why." They equally apply such a spirit of questioning and inquiry to Christianity. The young Chinese critically reexamine the history and lessons of the Christian Church. Some hold that Christianity did work in its time (i.e., the past) but by contrast it is wholly lost in the present-day world of science. Some assert that religion can be entirely replaced with the aesthetic education. Some conclude that Christianity does more harm than good to the world. And some contend that Christianity is nothing more than stupidity, conceit and superstition and thus it can by no means find a place in the time of knowledge. In the past two or three years, the number of writings condemning Christianity, such as those opposing Christian beliefs, doctrines, organizations, and followers, has increased significantly compared to the past. All these, however, give us many opportunities to attest our faith in the Lord Christ. But, on the other hand, doubts are indeed sown in our minds. We cannot help asking: "How will the Church respond to such an extraordinary situation?," "Where are the Lord's prophets and the gospels meeting the urgent needs of the time?," "Where is the Christian literature that is the most adaptable to the time and able to meet the needs of ordinary seekers [of true doctrines]?," "Do Christian forces of all shades realize what on earth the current situation really means to us?" And "do they grasp the immediate opportunity to make remarkable progress by thinking and acting in a well-coordinated way?" In answering these questions, we must consider what the success or failure of this effort will bring to the Church and the country.[7]

Cheng's words indicated that the NCM had raised a series of questions, on which the Church had to ruminate. It was in doing so that the indigenization of Christian Church in China was pushed forward.

The preparation work focused on five issues. First, what was the true situation of Christianity in China? Second, how could Christianity in China be successful in the future? Third, what was the mission of the Chinese Christian Church? Fourth, what would be the leadership of the Church? Fifth, how could different churches make a concerted effort and fully cooperate with each other? Simply put, the preparation work was about the present-day church, the future Church, the Church's mission, the Church's leadership and the Church's brotherhood.[8]

The NCC's preparatory committee passed an important resolution, which required: "As far as the third issue respecting the mission of the Church is concerned, we decide that this mission be fully independent of foreign missionaries and completely finished by the Chinese."[9] This resolution was unprecedented in the history of the Christian Church in China. At this point, Liu Tingfang said:

> Passing such a resolution is unprecedentedly remarkable in the history of the Church. The mission of the Church is really important, of great significance to the guiding principles of the Church. In the past, Western missionaries monopolized the discourse on the Church's mission. But on this occasion, the Chinese have full authority to handle this matter and most importantly, it is stipulated that no Westerners are allowed to bother about or intervene in this matter unless all the members of the third section [in charge of this matter] unanimously agree to invite them to be advisors.[10]

Although of the five sections of the preparatory committee only one section was fully operated by the Chinese, it still revealed a lot. Liu Tingfang, explaining this change in detail, summed up why in three reasons.[11] First, unlike Western missionaries, who were so deeply sectarian that they hardly ever attempted to get rid of old thoughts and old customs, the Chinese were almost immune to religious sectarianism and thus were able to avoid being involved in meaningless debates. Second, inasmuch as the mission was the mission of the Chinese Church, which was not set up for Westerners but for the Chinese, it should rightly be carried out by the Chinese. Third, since the Christian Church had developed over one century in China, where it had 6,391 churches, 345,853 Christian converts, and 24,732 Chinese clergy, the Chinese Christians should no longer be dependent on Western missionaries but instead should take on their own responsibilities. In a word, the Chinese Church's consciousness of independence increased constantly after experiencing social movements one after another. The Western missionary societies could not turn a blind eye to this.

Moreover, the preparatory committee specially designated programmes, by which each section would pay greater attention to the indigenization of the Church. For example, the committee required the second section focusing on the future development of the Church to further discuss matters such as the growth of indigenized Chinese Christianity and how the Church could be self-supporting. To put it another way, the second section should answer the following questions: "What is the indigenized Christian Church in China? What is the nature of the existing Christian Church in China? Is it Western? Is it Eastern? Is it neither Western nor Eastern?"[12]

It was in the course of preparing the national conference that many, more profoundly, discussed the main topic. They, having their discussions published in church-run journals, such as *The Life Monthly*, *Progress of the Youth*, *The Christian Occupation of China*, and *Theological Review*, set forth issues such as what the Chinese Church would be, what indigenization meant, what was the relationship between indigenization and the Chinese culture, how the

Church was working at present, what would lie ahead for the Church, and what the leadership of the Chinese Church would be. Discussants did make constructive suggestions, all of which were theoretically conducive to the indigenization of the Christian Church in China.

Cheng Jingyi's "The Chinese Christian Church," which was specially written for the NCC's preparatory work, comprehensively analysed the indigenization of the Christian Church in China. Cheng pointed out that, unlike in the past, when Christianity was strongly European in the incipient stage of its development in China, by then, Christians in the East had already been able to observe Christian gospels from their own perspectives and meanwhile had realized that the goal of Christian occupation of China was not to destroy but to complete the true, the good and the beautiful cherished by the ancient (Chinese) culture. Take ancestral worship, for example. Conventionally, foreign missionaries boorishly rejected all forms of ancestral worship prevailing among the Chinese. This was consequently the biggest obstacle preventing the Chinese from joining the Church. But if Chinese Christian converts could abandon superstitious elements existing in ancestral worship and preserve those in conformity with the Christian doctrine, and at the same time annually hold a Christian-style meeting commemorating deceased ancestors, not only difficulties and misunderstandings besetting the Chinese and Christianity would be eliminated but the simple and sincere ancient custom honouring the ancestors could also be further perfected.[13] Chen went further, analysing the Church's top-heavy phenomenon, in which "[the Chinese Church] can be likened to the small tail of a giant elephant (which symbolizes the missionary society); that is to say, the Church is servilely dependent on the missionary society." The truth was that, in the Church, the Chinese had no right to manage their own affairs and had no alternative but to work as poorly paid assistants of missionaries. Cheng earnestly hoped to change this fundamentally. He had asked: "Who, the Chinese clergy or foreign missionaries, should be the assistants of the Chinese Church?" By definition, in China, it was foreign missionaries who should work as the aids of the Chinese Christian Church.[14] Cheng sharply criticized foreign missionaries' deeply ingrained sectarianism, suggesting the Chinese Church must be united. In the meantime, he analytically pointed out that the rampant illiteracy plaguing the Chinese Christian converts was actually the biggest obstacle to the progress of China. Therefore, Cheng suggested the Chinese Church should make the growth of Christianity in China unobstructed by launching a national campaign eliminating illiteracy. Cheng shed light on the independence of the Church, saying that independence itself should consist of self-support, self-government and self-propagation. He wanted the missionary society to cultivate the independent spirit of Chinese Christians and that the relationship between the missionary society and the Chinese Church should never be financially based. Cheng discussed how the independence of Church could be fulfilled, advising the Church to learn from what other independent churches had done and suggested how to cultivate the Chinese who were able to play a leading role in the Church. In closing,

Cheng discussed how the Church should handle its relationship to China and foreign countries. He held that Chinese Christians should, in association with patriotic students, try their best to protect the country from being bullied by foreign powers. To be specific, they should condemn the unjust treatment of China by imperial Japan, should care for suffering people, should take action to provide disaster relief, and so on. In a word, Chinese Christians should, by means of real actions, help the Chinese people, and Chinese intellectuals in particular, fundamentally change their attitude towards Christianity. Last but not least, Cheng analysed the relationship between indigenization and the NCM, contending that the correlation of indigenization and the NCM, theoretically and practically, showed the orientation of indigenization of Chinese Church.

In one of his treatises, Jian Youwen did an excellent job in explaining what indigenization should be and how the CCM had deeply influenced the definition of the Chinese Christian Church.[15] Jian's definition was that the Chinese Church should be such a church that it could be able to adapt to the true situation of China and meet the needs of the new Chinese culture. In a nutshell, it must be a *national* church. Jian explained this in detail. First, the national church was not the church managed by the state but the church owned by all nationals. Not only was the national church fully independent of the government but it was also able to lead the political life by means of lofty Christian moral teachings. It benefited the nation and the people. Second, the national church did not depend on the foreign church but was a religious institution that belonged to the country. In other words, the national church was neither founded nor ruled by any foreign states and their religious agencies, but instead it disseminated the gospel dedicated to the Chinese nation and devoted itself to cultivating the Chinese Christians. Third, the national church was not abstract but practical. To put it another way, the national church threw itself into Christian national salvation, meanwhile trying its best to adapt itself to Chinese ethics and the spirit of the new culture. Fourth, the national church was neither sectarian nor divisive but united. In other words, it was strongly opposed to the sectarianism brought about by foreign missionary societies. Fifth, the national church was not an exiled or isolated institution but a bridge interconnecting the past and the present. That is, the national church of China, being itself based on ethics, morality, spirit and faith taught by Christ, not only was the true extension of Christianity but also resolved to carry forward good traditions handed down from past churches.

Tianxie (a pen name) shed light on the Sinicized Christianity from a different perspective. According to his definition, the Sinicized Christianity referred to such a Christian religion that was based on the Chinese spirit and concretized in the light of the needs of the Chinese Christians. The Sinicization of Christianity could not be superficially accomplished by simplistically separating the Church from foreigners and having the Church led by the Chinese. One of the characteristics of Christianity was that this religion was able to adapt itself to thought and morality of any nation. The key to Christianity's success lay exclusively in this religion's handling of spiritual matters. Tianxie contended that, where the Christianity brought to China by Westerners was concerned, it was conducive to the Chinese only in terms of the cultivation of the spirit of service. The West's economic aid, he argued, could not help the Chinese Church obtain an independent spirit but instead might be devastating to this spirit. Tianxie held that, only when the power of foreign missionary societies was weakened to some extent and foreign missionaries really worked together with the Chinese Church, would Christianity be truly indigenized in China. At this point, he emphatically stated:

> The birth and growth of indigenized Christianity in China are dependent on how foreign missionaries and Chinese Christians mutually treat each other. For foreign missionaries, they should act more flexibly in Chinese society and abandon the idea of leading the Chinese to live as foreigners do, meanwhile doing their best to teach the Chinese the Christian spirit and have the Christian spirit represented in a Chinese form. [For Chinese Christians, they should assimilate appropriate elements taken from foreign missionaries' experience and advantages.]

In closing, Tianxie discussed how to make the indigenized Christian Church more powerful and should place restrictions on the excessive power of foreign missionary societies, suggesting that all the issues concerning missionary societies and the Chinese Church must be discussed in a joint meeting attended by Chinese and foreign clergy, that the employment of foreign missionaries and their salaries must be approved by the joint meeting; and that Chinese representatives must be part and parcel of the management of the missionary church, its hospitals and other undertakings.[16]

Xingwu (Jia Yuming) insightfully explained the relationship between Christianity and the Chinese national character. He said, although the religious system could change itself in order to adapt itself to society, the religious faith should never change according to societies. For this reason, it would be better for the Chinese Christian Church to make use of the innate Chinese national character to propagate Christianity. Specifically, he said:

> The Christian truth is forever new and fresh. It is always appealing to all nations and all peoples through all ages. But, on the other hand, the time in which people live, ethnic groups, the political culture, human dispositions, general psychologies, common sense, and the social environment are different from one another in different historical periods. As a consequence, how the Christian truth will affect people exposing themselves to this truth will differ accordingly.

Xingwu contended that the Chinese national character was closely related to religion. First, the Chinese national character was conservative. Confucius said: "[I prefer to be a] transmitter and not a maker, believing in and loving the ancients."[17] The Master's words indicated that, although the Chinese people were psychologically tranquil and lukewarm towards Christianity that recently had arrived in the country, they would not easily be deluded by heathen doctrines, provided that they chose to believe in this religion. Second, the Chinese people were good at accommodation. The Chinese always treated religions from the perspective of adjusting to all controversial things. Take Confucian, Daoist and Buddhist teachings, for example. Although the three teachings were very different from one another, they were finally well syncretized together. Such a Chinese-style accommodation or adjustment did matter to the future of the Chinese Christian Church. In the future, the fulfilment of the Lord's ambition to shepherd entire humanity might begin with the Chinese Church, which heralded the advent of grand unity [of all Christians]. Third, mystic thoughts were not uncommon in China. The Chinese believed that they could be enlightened in dreams, their dreams would turn out to be true, and spirits were visible. Although these could be regarded as superstition, they properly indicated that the Chinese strongly believed there was a spiritual world. By appropriate means, these beliefs could be turned into the spiritual interaction of man and the Holy Ghost and of man and the highest Lord. Fourth, the faith of the Chinese was almost unshakable. As far as the Chinese faith was concerned, it was actually stronger than that of any other people. This could be explicitly corroborated by the Chinese people's enthusiasm devoted to images of the deity. Even for Chinese intellectuals, who were usually sceptical about religion, they would adhere to Christian doctrines, so long as they were inspired to believe in Christianity. "The Chinese are born with sincerity and purity of faith." Xingwu finally concluded that, as long as the Chinese Church grasped the intrinsic attributes and specialties of the Chinese and carried them forward, there would be a bright future ahead.[18]

Some others prepared feasible programmes of indigenizing the Christian Church in China. For example, Shen Sizhuang penned an article entitled "Three Manifestos," which was the first programme of the Sinicization of Christianity in history. According to Shen's programme, the reason why Christianity was widely regarded as a *foreign* religion in China was that there were many misunderstandings brought about by foreign missionaries' ignorance and misperception of Chinese social customs. What's worse, some Chinese preachers of Christianity awkwardly imitated foreign missionaries and copied their mistakes mechanically. In view of these, Shen wrote a manifesto advocating the Sinicization of Christianity. His main points were as follows:

1   The Holy Bible should be Sinicized to adapt to the Chinese social psychology. The Sinicization of the Bible consisted of multiple efforts. First, the composed typeface of the Bible should be modernized and all content should be punctuated. Second, all the hymns in the Bible should be rendered into traditional Chinese five- or seven-character verses that were easy to remember. Third, among Sinicized biblical hymns, the

melodies that were unsuitable for reading and singing should be deleted and replaced with popular tunes, such as Baixiang and Changchun, both of which the Chinese knew very well. Western melodies should be indigenized and used by those who had a good knowledge of them. In remote rural areas, Western hymns should be abandoned. Third, the lecture notes should be Sinicized. Fourth, the musical instruments should be Sinicized. For example, huqin (a two-stringed traditional Chinese instrument) and the bamboo flute could replace the piano and the organ, both of which were too expensive and hardly repaired.

2 The Sinicization of Christianity should be reasonable. This endeavour consisted of several aspects. Frist, the Bible should be reasonably interpreted. In other words, the explanation of the Bible should not be based on text only but on history. Second, there should not be any unreasonable theologies but a reasonable theology. Third, there should be reasonable Christian doctrines and unreasonable doctrines should be rectified. Fourth, Christianity and the Church should treat free thinkers reasonably. This religion should be open to those who do not believe in it and those who followed other religions. Christians should read their books or canons. Christianity should be tolerant and refrain from declaring war on other religions.

3 The Sinicization of Christianity should be centred on life. First, the spiritual practice should revolve around life. Prayer and the rest day were all good for the spirit and the body. Christians should never forget life, which should not be dismal but vivid. Second, figuratively, the Sinicization of Christianity was an endeavour of life. To put it another way, the greatest undertaking of Chinese Christianity and its Church was to care for the social life, that is, the society itself, and do work benefitting society. Christianity and the Church should not be indifferent to social affairs nor should both focus exclusively on their own business.[19]

Zhenru made specific suggestions regarding the indigenization of the Christian Church in China. First, the leadership of the Chinese Church should not be exclusively open to elites but also to commoners. Zhenru held that, in his time, the Church was still controlled by a small number of people. It was nothing more than a top-down, elitist politics. He suggested that the Church must be indigenized, break all established Western models and remould itself to be in line with the principles of democracy. In a word, the Chinese Church should abandon vertical leadership and adopt horizontal administration. The remoulded Church should advocate the spirit of self-government among its followers. When it came to the treatment of its followers, the new Church would not be high-handed, but like a parent, in the hope that their autonomous spirit could be aroused. For followers of the new Church, they should actively initiate discussions and in doing so they could gradually realize that they were the true owners of the Church and take responsibility for it. Therefore, Zhenru suggested all members of the Chinese Christian Church should convene a national meeting. Second, the Church should promote economic endeavours to improve the life of the people. In other words, if the Church wanted to be truly independent, it should not be passively dependent on donations but instead take the initiative in developing economic cooperation. There were three types of economic cooperation advocated by the Church, namely, consumptive cooperation, productive cooperation and credit cooperation. Through such cooperation, the Church could be financially independent and its followers could live in abundance and fulfil their obligations. Most importantly, Zhenru suggested the Church should set up a national Christian cooperative bank. Third, the Church should help ordinary Christians improve their academic and intellectual life. In the New Cultural Movement, some free-thinking intellectuals, such as Chen Duxiu, had deeply studied religions including Christianity. In addition, Buddhist scholarship was very active and its profound teachings were particularly attractive to the intelligentsia. In view of this, Zhenru suggested the Chinese Church should learn from the Buddhists. He even proposed founding a Buddhist study programme in Christian theological seminaries. Zhenru laid particular stress on the creation of a Christian library, which might play a pivotal role in the Christian education. Fourth, the form of the Christian Church should be reformed to adapt to Sinicized rituals. That is to say, the Christian Church, learning from Buddhism, should abandon Western rites and institutions that were psychologically discordant to the Chinese and should reshape its form and organization to meet the psychological needs of the Chinese people. The final goal of these efforts was to formulate a Sinicized Christian constitution.[20]

Some expressed their attitude, expectations and advice concerning the NCC in their articles. Take Gu Ziren, for example.[21] He, first of all, recognized that the NCC's exclusive focus on the Chinese Church really met the need of Chinese Christians. Gu pointed out that the five sections of the NCC were all directly related to Chinese Christians. For the first section of the NCC, which focused on the status quo of Christianity in China, it dealt with two questions most appealing to Chinese Christians, that is, the facts concerning the progress and development of the Chinese Church, the true situation in which the Church grew, and the relationship involving the CCM, the NCM and the Church. For the second section, which explored what would lie ahead of the Chinese Church, it shed light on how to cultivate its followers' religious life so that it was uppermost in their minds. The cultivation of religious life had three aspects. First, regarding how to set up an indigenized Chinese Church and help it grow. Chinese Christians had two tendencies regarding this: (1) the Church should be fully independent of Western missionary societies; and (2) the Church should be self-supporting, self-supporting and self-governing and geared to growing into a national church. In order to achieve these, the Chinese Church needed to work with Western missionary societies, because the Church itself was still not a fully-fledged entity. Second, how to make the religious education and Christian texts adaptable to the situation really mattered. Third, the Church should cultivate its followers' self-awareness of the propagation of Christianity. This was very important. Gu set this forth, saying:

> The Church has set up many schools in China. But it is a pity that only a small number of students educated by church-run schools choose to join the mission propagating Christianity in the Chinese land. Among members of the Church, there are quite a few rich people, none of whom think they have the duty to financially support the Church. If we want to lead the Church to grow sound and strong, we must try our best to enlighten Chinese Christians to take the responsibility of propagating the gospel and serving the Church with life and money. The best way to enlighten them was to have Chinese Christians shoulder accumulated responsibility.

For the third section, which concerned itself with the mission of the Chinese Church, it paid particular attention to the social reality of China. For the fourth section, which discussed the leadership of the Chinese Church, it planned to thoroughly investigate and analyse the training and remuneration of people who play a leading role in the Church. Moreover, some Christians, who devoted themselves to writing, would exert an influence on the NCM. For the fifth section, which was responsible for convening a national Christian meeting that interested Chinese Christians most, suggested that there should be a national institution representing churches all over the country and uniting them.

Some fervently discussed the leadership of the Chinese Christian Church. The leading Christians were divided into two groups. One consisted of people who were paid by the Church; the other including those who completely gave up salaries. The unpaid ones were volunteers serving the Church. The paid ones were professional preachers, medical workers, heads of schools, teaching fellows and leading administrators of churches. Christians analysed the advantages and disadvantages of the two groups and what their positions were in the Church. They pointed out that the status of those paid was fully dependent on the favour or disfavour of Western missionaries and on the Church's true needs as well. In other words, they were not appointed according to their talent but in the light of the Church's need. Whenever the Church needed them, they would be sent to do relevant work. Only a very small number of Western missionaries wanted to treat the paid Chinese equally, meanwhile the vast majority of them used those paid as slaves or servants. In most cases, the Western missionaries adopted an obscurantist policy and methods to seduce the Chinese, by which the Chinese would be fooled into serving them for life and allow Western missionaries to do as they pleased. For this reason, the Chinese Church seldom produced talented, qualified people who could lead the followers. As far as the talented, qualified people were concerned, they should have a noble personality, exquisite thinking, a brave spirit and an inclusive attitude and at the same time they should have completed a profound study of the essence of Christian teaching and adapted themselves to the trends of the times.[22] Not only were new leaders of the Chinese Church morally distinguished, well-educated, abundantly intelligent and of a docile disposition, but they were also thoroughly enlightened to shoulder the new mission of building a heaven on earth.[23] Some even dreamt that there would emerge such Christian leaders, who had status and integrity, never fawned upon those in power, possessed a great deal of global experience, and acquired solid knowledge about the Christian theology.[24] Echoing this, some said:

> For those who truly exposed themselves to the higher learning, what they have is more than a diploma. That is to say, the spiritual practice is not an appealing verbal truth but should be embodied in actual efforts; the courage and will power of doing things should not be used to push themselves forward but to benefit the community of Christians. Only those who accomplish doing these are truly qualified candidates for leading positions in the Church.

Regarding the method of recruiting talented people for the Church, it was generally held that Western missionaries' monopoly on personnel administration must be remoulded. Some suggested that there must be a new, powerful organ in charge of screening and selecting talented people recommended by Western missionaries and local churches. Candidates who passed the strict examination constituted the Church's talent pool, which was open to all branches of the Church whenever they had the need.[25] Additionally, some proposed a regular educational programme. According to this programme, the Church would set up seminaries, normal schools, colleges and medical schools, from which it selected students aspiring to be Christian professionals and offered them special training. As soon as these selected students finished their study, they would be appointed to appropriate posts in accordance with their competence.[26] Last but not least, participants analysed why the salaries of the paid leading Chinese Christians were too low.

In fact, not only Chinese Christians but also foreign missionaries joined the discussion. For example, Situ Leideng (John Leighton Stuart), a missionary-turned-politician, wrote an article discussing the independence of the Chinese Christian Church.[27] This Chinese-born American missionary held that the independence of the Chinese Church was extremely slow. This independence could not be accomplished by simply granting economic autonomy. Foreign missionaries were responsible for such slow progress. If foreign missionaries, he said, did not regard Chinese clergy merely as hirelings but treated them as colleagues on an equal footing, Chinese clergy would do a more excellent job and consequently Chinese society would notice the Church's management of talented people. In this sense, the management of Chinese clergy really mattered to the true independence of Chinese Church. Situ even suggested that Chinese Christians should have the right of management of the Church.

Foreign missionaries must make up their mind to transfer the authority for administration to Chinese Christians. Only by doing so would the enthusiasm of Chinese Christians be rekindled and a greater endeavour be launched. Financially, the invigorated community of Chinese Christian converts would donate more money to the Church. For Situ, foreign missionaries must have confidence in Chinese Christians and give them a free hand in propagating Christianity. Only in this way would the independence of the Chinese Christian Church be substantially advanced.

The above-mentioned articles and discussions all appeared in the preparation period. As we can see, the NCC was really well planned and well prepared. These articles and discussions made a great contribution to the indigenization of the Chinese Christian Church.

After careful study and discussions involving many parties, the NCC was formally convened. Many delegates articulated their opinion about Chinese Christian Church and comprehensively explored various aspects of the indigenized Chinese Church. Some gave a speech at the conference. Wu Deshi, the head of the first section of the NCC, delivered a report entitled "The Chinese Church Today," which discussed the status quo of the Church at that time, the progress Christianity had made in China in the 1920s, the social environment in which the Church was developing, and the influence of Christianity in China. Mude (John R. Mott) lectured on the advantages of Christian religion in the present-day world. Zhao Zichen, a renowned Chinese Christian, made a speech: "Advantages and Disadvantages of the Chinese Christian Church." Jia Yuming voiced his ideas in "The Personal Life of Christians." Bi Jiale (C. E. Patton), who headed the second section of the NCC, prepared "The Future Church," in which he outlined the Church's work in the near future, such as the cultivation of the religious life of the Christian community, the improvement of all existing branches and founding branches in new areas. He particularly stressed that the key to the Church's work would lie in indigenization. Cheng Jingyi, who played the leading role in the third section of the NCC, wrote the manifesto of the Church. In addition, Liu Tingfang and Yi Wensi (Robert K. Evans) gave a report: "The Chinese Christian Church" and "What Is the Proper Attitude of Western Missionaries towards the Chinese Church?," respectively. Yu Rizhang, the head of the NCC's fourth section discussing the leadership of Chinese Church, made a distinction between paid and unpaid leading Chinese Christians, analysed the past and the present of the Church's leadership, and set forth how to train the Church's leaders by methods such as preaching work, social service, education, medical work and writing, and explained what had been achieved by these efforts in his report. Shi Hengbai, who was in charge of the fifth section on planning regulation and cooperation of different churches, wrote the report entitled "The Cooperation of the Churches." This report, focusing on the creation of a central council regulating the Church's work nationwide, was comprised of three parts. The first part consisted of the organic law respecting the regulation and cooperation of the Chinese churches and the progress of relevant work; the second part, a motion bill respecting the administration of the Church and interdenominational cooperation; and the third part, a proposal respecting the function, nature and organization of the National Council of Christianity. During the meeting, there were many special study and discussion sessions revolving around these reports. Delegates intensively discussed the indigenization of Christianity in China, the training of leaders of the Church, the religious education in church-run schools and followers' families, the administration and training pertaining to urban and rural churches, and so on. Overall, Chinese delegates had a greater right to speak in this conference. The present author briefly summarizes these reports, by which readers might grasp the relationship between the NCC and the indigenization of the Christian Church in China.

1 "Advantages and disadvantages of the Chinese Christian Church" by Zhao Zichen[28]

This was a powerful speech critically reexamining the Chinese Church. Zhao shed light on the advantages of the Chinese Church. (1) The education of common Christian followers improved significantly. For example, the general knowledge of Chinese Christians was higher than that of Chinese who did not believe in Christianity. Specifically, the literacy of male Christians was 60 per cent; and that of female Christians, 40 per cent. (2) The Chinese Church was renowned for its education. In two decades, the number of young Chinese studying in church-run schools increased by 333 per cent, accounting for one-nineteenth of the total number of students nationwide. (3) The intellectual landscape of the Church had changed fundamentally. In the past, Westerners dictated the intellectual world of the Church. But by now, among Chinese Christians, there were an increasing number of insightful people, who were not inferior but even, sometimes, superior to Western Christian preachers in terms of talents, knowledge, experience, scholarship, morality and thoughts. (4) In the promotion of religious life, the Chinese Church did not rely on the mysterious experience on the grounds that it would prevent the significance of Christ's abandonment of his own life from being carried forward, but instead it laid particular stress on morality.

As far as the disadvantages of the Chinese Church were concerned, there were four points. (1) Except for a few members, the moral awareness of the Chinese Church was overall still insufficient. Zhao made a special analysis of the phenomenon known as *chijiao*, in which some bad persons belonged to the church under the aegis of foreign missionaries, pointing out that, among Western preachers good and bad mixed together just as wheat and weeds were intermingled. In the circumstances, there were, sadly but inevitably, a mixture of loyalists and traitors and good and evil among Chinese Christians. (2) The weakness of the Chinese Church was caused by the Western organization and thought and the widely prevalent sectarianism. Originally, Christianity itself was adaptable to the disposition of the Chinese. Unfortunately, in the face of the rampant sectarianism intrinsic to Christianity and a kaleidoscopic array of Christian organizations, the Chinese people were at a loss as to what to do. As a result, the Chinese felt it was very difficult to make a choice and had their reservations about this religion. Zhao stressed that it was the inappropriateness of Western Christian doctrines and rituals that resulted in the Chinese people's misunderstanding of Christianity. In this regard, he said:

> If we analyse the Chinese people's misunderstandings of Christianity one by one, we will find the reason why they cannot properly apprehend this religion exactly lies in *yangjiao*, viz., that it is generally held that Christianity is nothing more than a *foreign* religion. The foreignness of this religion, plus a dazzling variety of Christian sects and wild Christian sectarianism, make Christianity unbearably Western. [Because sectarianism helps] individualism and belief in the Other World continue to grow and, consequently, the Christian social movement and cosmopolitan idea cannot prevail within the Church, the Church not only becomes increasingly weak but also probably has jeopardized itself.

(3) Christianity, which had to face external criticism against itself and internal confused disagreements, was seemingly unable to cope with the unstable social environment in which China changed constantly. At that time,

> The Chinese academia aspires to learn science and gain scientific experience. Chinese intellectuals and science accord with and complement each other. But at this moment, the Church, far from realizing what the Chinese intelligentsia really needs, regards intellectuals as a grave threat to religion. As a consequence, it treats friends as enemies and reliable partners as worthless grasses. Worst of all, the Church becomes increasingly intellectually stagnant and arbitrary.

Precisely because of the Church's inability to adapt itself to the socio-intellectual environment, it had more disadvantages.

Zhao's entire speech and his reexamination of the Church's weak points in particular were actually the responses to the NCM's and the early CCM's criticisms of Christianity. Zhao's effort indicated that the Chinese Church had fully realized that Christianity and the Church must adapt themselves to China's socio-intellectual environment, abandon its established image of foreign religion, improve the quality of Christian converts, and fulfil indigenization. Only by doing so would there be a future for the Chinese Christian Church. Zhao defined what an indigenized Chinese Church was, saying:

> When the Chinese people finally choose to believe in Christ and blend Christ into their spirit, mind and intelligence in the light of their own national characters, they will set up a church. This church is no other than an indigenized Christian church.[29]

Zhao's profound introspection depicted the truly indigenized Chinese Christian Church that he dreamt of building.

2 "The Chinese Christian Church" by Liu Tingfang[30]

This report, of interest to a huge number of participants of the NCC, reflected that Liu himself was deeply influenced by the NCM. For example, Liu carried forward the NCM's critical spirit, requiring the Chinese Church to fearlessly fight against all evils. For him, the Church should never repeat history, in which the Christian agencies turned a blind eye to socio-personal sins and even pretended to attack evils while giving them a hand; but instead, it should do all it could to combat all evils existing within and outside the Church and plaguing the country, society and the people. Taking into consideration the fact that many NCM activists denounced Christianity as superstitious and anti-scientific, Liu especially pointed out that the Chinese Church must meet God's requirement that the belief in the Bible was sacrosanct and at the same time it should accept the academic consensus that the truth of the Bible must be studied with scientific methods. In other words, not only the Bible but also doctrines, tenets, rites and ceremonies of the Church should all be subject to scientific examination. Liu criticized those Christian clergy who obstinately adhered to old laws and prevented others from applying scientific methods to the study of the Bible, strongly suggesting that Christianity must adopt scientific principles and all Christianity's superstitious elements which clashed with the scientific spirit must be eliminated. Obviously, he was deeply influenced by the scientific spirit advocated by the NCM. In responding to the NCM activists' criticism that Christianity was nothing more than a foreign religion, Liu suggested:

> The Chinese Church should conscientiously serve the Chinese people. It should be a truly independent Chinese church owned and managed by the Chinese. It cannot be an organ oppressing the Chinese citizens but be a servant of the Chinese people.

In order to serve the Chinese people, the Church must preserve all the Chinese spiritual heritage, do a solid study of the existing national essence of China, and lead the Chinese nation to adapt itself to the tide of progress of the world and move forward with the vision of being a teacher and in the spirit of a leader. Liu went further, advising that, when the Church had set up its organizations and made programmes, it should not only assimilate new cultures of different countries but also select the best Chinese spiritual elements representing the noblest Chinese ideals. Moreover, he told the Church that it should never borrow indiscriminately the Western experience but instead should conduct a truly independent study and interpret the Christian truth from the Eastern/Chinese perspective. In doing so, the Chinese Church would make a greater contribution to the world. It is evident that Liu had adopted the nationalism disseminated by the NCM. In the end, Liu required that the Chinese Christianity must be united, must abandon the wild sectarianism that had been established in American and European churches, and must prevent new sects and factions from emerging within the Chinese Church.

In Liu's mind, the indigenized Chinese Church was like this:

> The Chinese Christian Church is the church owned by the Chinese people. The most important task of the Church is to serve the Chinese and rehabilitate the Chinese society. Organizations and programmes of the Church are entirely based on the spirit of the Chinese nation and psychologically according to the Chinese nation. On the one hand, the Church takes inspiration from the brilliant national essence; on the other hand, it assimilates good elements of all civilizations on this planet.[31]

3 "What is the proper attitude of Western missionaries towards the Chinese Church?" by Yi Wensi[32]

Yi's speech pointed out that the Chinese Church had not been the "church in the mission field" mentioned in the 1910 World Missionary Conference held in Edinburgh but the de facto National Church of China. As a consequence, there was an issue concerning Western missionary societies' political status and Western missionaries' personal status in China. Yi held that, now that the Chinese Church already existed, Western missionary societies should not have politico-religious privileges unless the Church wanted to give them some special rights. As regards the personal status of Western missionaries, Yi said this could be divided into two types. For those who came from American and European missionary societies, their job was just to serve the Chinese work of propagating Christianity. For those who regarded themselves as Christians of the Chinese Church, they were same as the Chinese followers in terms of (personal) intelligence and church administration, on the grounds that both were equally members of the Chinese Church. Yi, profoundly and critically, reflected on the Western missionary societies' old practice, in which Westerners monopolized the administration and choked the vitality of the Chinese Christian converts to death. He was deeply ashamed of this mistake. When it came to the assets of missionary societies, Yi suggested that these could either be donated towards the Chinese Church or jointly administered by missionary societies and the Chinese Church. As regards sectarianism, Yi proposed that Chinese Christians should abandon or change all existing Western sects and at the same time Western sects could choose to separate themselves from the Chinese Church. Generally, Yi agreed with the idea that all missionary societies in China should give up their sectarian practice to defend the interests of the Chinese Church. It is evident that Yi's speech was very conducive to the realization of independence of the Chinese Church that was still young.

On the basis of these discussions, the NCC finally passed *The Manifesto of the Chinese Christian Church* (hereinafter referred to as *Chinese Manifesto*) and *The Constitution of the National Christian Council of China*, both of which articulated the spirit of indigenization. Furthermore, the NCC set about founding a national council consisting of all the major Christian sects existing in China.

It must be pointed out that the *Chinese Manifesto* was the brainchild of the Church's Chinese members working for the third section of the NCC, who based this manifesto on an independent study. Digging into the *Chinese Manifesto*, readers will find that not only is one section devoted to the indigenized Chinese Church but also a large number of sections voice the spirit of indigenization. The *Chinese Manifesto* defined what an indigenized church should be, saying:

> An indigenized Christian church should, on the one hand, preserve the historical connection with other denominations worldwide and prevent this connection form breaking; and, on the other hand, truly assimilate the indigenous cultural and spiritual experience of the Chinese nation.

The *Chinese Manifesto* was comprised of two parts. The first part, which was entitled "Warm Notice to Christian Fellows," discussed seven issues, namely, the united church, the indigenous Chinese Church, the profound sanctification of the church, more intensive exposure to the Bible, social rehabilitation, international cooperation and the work of preaching. The second part, which was known as the "Warm Notice to Our Chinese Compatriots," set forth issues such as the glory of Chinese history, the dangers China was facing, the means of saving the nation, and why Christianity mattered to the country. The following paragraphs intensively discussing the indigenization of the Christian Church in China are all taken from the "Second Section of the First Chapter" of the *Chinese Manifesto*.[33]

The Indigenized Chinese Christian Church

(1) We Chinese Christians do believe that the Church is the spiritual home in which Christians are spiritually cultivated. This Christian spiritual cultivation does not run counter to the heritage and spirit of the Chinese nation.
(2) We Chinese Christians extend thanks to the Western missionaries, who, regardless of personal sacrifice, do their utmost to set up churches in China. We also express our sincere thanks to the Western churches, which try their best to donate and earnestly pray for us in the hope that the Chinese Church will be a success. Western missionaries and churches do their bit for what we have achieved.
(3) If we Chinese Christians blindly follow and poorly imitate Western, ancient Christian texts, rites and organizations without critically

examining them, we will be unable to make durable, significant contributions to Chinese Christianity. The entirety of the members of the Chinese Church has reached a consensus on this.

(4) The Chinese Christian Church has consciously realized what its mission and duty are. For this reason, we, formally and solemnly, make this declaration.

(5) Chinese history, the Chinese national character, the nature of Christian work, the enlightenment of experience, the rapid changes taking place in China, all of which require that there must be an indigenized Chinese Christian Church, through which the indigenized Chinese Christianity will be propagated nationwide. We define the indigenized Chinese Christian Church as such a church that it not only keeps the historical connection with Christian denominations worldwide intact but also, truly and practically, adapts itself to the indigenous cultural and spiritual experience of the Chinese nation.

(6) We thus demand that all Chinese followers of Jesus Christ act with united strength to make the Church self-supporting by means of systematic donations, self-governing by means of resolute study, brave experiments and fearless spirit, and self-propagating by means of fully-fledged religious education, cultivation of leadership and cordial and ardent personal sermons.

(7) We declare that the time belonging to us has dawned. We Chinese Christians should carefully study Christian doctrines, boldly make experiments, and independently select and revise the Church's rites, ceremonies, organizations, systems and methods of propagation. In doing so, we benefit the Chinese Christian Church and finally make it a truly indigenized Christian Church.

(8) We sincerely invite leading Western missionaries working for the Chinese Church to give us practical advice, by which Chinese Christians can learn something and make themselves more competent. We also sincerely hope that Western missionaries would allow Chinese Christians to have full freedom in making their experiments.

(9) The Chinese Christian Church was deeply indebted to the help and cultivation of Western churches. We do expect that, after being truly indigenized, the Chinese Church will make remarkable achievements in the growth of Christian thought, religious life and propagation work. All these achievements will, in turn, contribute to the Western churches, from which the Chinese Church stems. We do believe that all these indigenized contributions will make the global Christian life more diverse and more thriving.

Apart from above-cited "Second Section," there was a great amount of content related to the indigenization of the Christian Church in China. For example, the section entitled "The United Church" stressed that sectarianism should be ascribed to the history of Western churches and it had nothing to do with Chinese Christians. It was Western missionaries who had brought sectarianism to China. As a consequence,

> Sectarianism, which fails to be appealing to the Chinese, becomes the main reason of disorder, confusion and inefficiency of the Church ... Present-day China desperately needs a Christian national salvation. It is firmly believed that only a united Christian Church is able to implement the programme of national salvation. The reason is that, without strong solidarity, the Church will be unable to gain enough power to launch grand social projects, such as national salvation.[34]

This section showed the Church what it should do in reshuffling its organization to meet the requirements of indigenization. Moreover, the section entitled "The More Intensive Exposure to the Bible" mentioned the biblical indigenization, pointing out:

> We deeply desire that Chinese Christians eagerly have the Chinese edition of the Bible translated by Chinese translators, just as the English Bible was translated by English scholars and the German Bible was rendered by German scholars. Therefore, the Chinese Bible must be translated by Chinese scholars who piously believe in Christianity. Judging from our experience of propagating Christianity, the surging trend of Chinese scholarship, and the future of the Church, we conclude that there is a desperate need for both an indigenized Church and an indigenized Bible among Chinese Christians.[35]

The Church, driven by the spirit embodied in the above citations, paid greater attention to the Christian textual work. Even the section "International Cooperation" indigenously showcased the patriotic feeling by connecting the invasion of China by the Western powers with Christianity. This might be attributed to the influence exerted by the CCM. For example, it said:

> God created all peoples equally in the light of his own image. [Therefore, he extends the same treatment to all. Even so, the *Chinese Manifesto* admits that Christians really realize that] in the last century, the history of Christian occupation of China is unfortunately inseparable from the grieved experience taking place in the national history of China, viz., that the country is repeatedly invaded, bullied and humiliated by Western powers. In over one hundred years, there have been several rounds of national disgrace, all of which are related to Christianity. As a result, there are a huge number of misunderstandings of Christianity and the propagation of Christianity in China is seriously impeded. In the past, the Chinese Church itself was too weak to prevent the self-declared Western Christian governments from perpetrating anti-Christian sins such as invading and plundering China. [In view of this], we suggest

the Church does its utmost to frequently ask foreign powers to recognize China's inviolable sovereignty, China's interests and China's right to develop and progress, and to refrain from containing China. In the meantime, the Church requires all Chinese clergy to carefully nourish the patriotic feeling of the Chinese nationals and reform the increasingly strong parochial perception of the nation by means of the Christian fraternity. The reason why the Church makes such endeavours is that the love for peace is part of the special, inherent nature of the Chinese nation.

The above citations epitomized the patriotic feeling of Chinese Christians. Again, the *Chinese Manifesto*'s second part, known as the "Warm Notice to Our Chinese Compatriots," expounded the idea of Christian national salvation, clearly stating that Christians were willing to be servants of the people and the Church would like to care about society and set an example of serving China. Overall, the *Chinese Manifesto* could be regarded as the Chinese Church's earliest proclamation of indigenization, which laid the foundation for the Church's theory and practice of indigenization.

Another remarkable achievement made by the NCC was *The Constitution of the National Christian Council of China*, precisely on which the National Christian Council of China (NCCC), an incarnation of the spirit of unity and indigenization, was formally set up. The creation of the NCCC was the embodiment of the Chinese Church's organizational indigenization. This could be corroborated by the aims and responsibilities of the NCCC.

According to Fan Yurong, who was one of the secretaries of the NCCC's department of young female Christians, the NCCC's aims and responsibilities were as follows:[36]

[The aim of the NCCC is twofold]

First, by means of the NCCC, the Chinese Church and its internal departments and organizations achieve unity, cooperation and mutual aid. As we know, Christianity is imported from the West, where countries have very different customs. Therefore, in different mission fields, the work propagating Christianity is not very different from one another. Even so, this work inevitably bears different names. As a consequence, there are misunderstanding due to the difference in form and the Christian Church cannot completely and rapidly be successful. In recent years, the Church has realized this problem and thus resolves to have unity truly fulfilled. The NCCC is thus created.

Second, the Chinese Christian Church should accomplish indigenization. In the past, the Christian Church in China was imported from the West. It was set up by Westerners and leading positions in the church were all occupied by Westerners. As a result, the work of the church was entirely an imitation of the Western Church. There were unavoidably many things incompatible with the Chinese view of religion. For this reason, many Chinese people treat the Christian Church as something purely foreign. In view of this, the NCCC aspires to transform the existing Christian Church in China into a fully independent, self-supporting, self-propagating and self-governing Chinese Church.

[The organization of the NCCC]

The NCCC is comprised of 100 members. The NCCC members are recommended by Christian churches and institutions nationwide. They are representatives of their recommenders. Among the NCCC members, there are 21 women Christians. From the existing 100 members, 21 persons are elected to be executive commissioners, who are responsible for the regular work and programmes.

[The nature of the NCCC]

Although the NCCC represents the Chinese Church, it cannot exercise power independently on the grounds that it is not an independent organ. The existence and operation of the NCCC depend on Christian churches and institutions nationwide. The goal of the NCCC is to grow into a united, cooperative organization. Therefore, whenever the NCCC takes any action, it must first be approved by the member churches and institutions. This reveals that the NCCC is actually an advisory body.

[Responsibilities of the NCCC]

First, the NCCC cultivates and commends the team spirit of Chinese Church.

Second, the NCCC concerns itself with how to make the Chinese Church more self-supporting, self-governing and self-propagating, tries its best to help the Church adapt to the Chinese character and conditions, and promotes all movements accelerating the full independence of the Church.

Third, the NCCC investigates various needs of the Church from a national perspective, plans to have the gospels disseminated nationwide, improves the Church's spiritual cultivation, organizes national prayers, holds national mobilization meetings for propagation work, convenes national Christian conferences, and nourishes the Church's spiritual life and spirit of sermon whenever and wherever.

Fourth, the NCCC suggests leading Chinese Christians completely abandon their sectarian ideas and mutually trust one another instead. It proposes that there should be special training for leading Christians who are competent to handle national and international issues, meanwhile encouraging the Chinese Church to strengthen their communication with foreign churches.

In addition to the above-mentioned responsibilities, the NCCC has other jobs that focus on how to unite all churches' efforts to greet the advent of the Heavenly Kingdom.

The above-mentioned NCCC's aims and responsibilities were all based on *The Constitution of National Christian Council of China* passed at the 1922 NCC. As far as the *Constitution* was concerned, it was comprised of the explanation of reasons why the NCCC was set up, 13 items regarding the NCCC's responsibilities, organizational methods, election of members, and regulations concerning the selection of members, meetings, staff, executive commissioners, offices, funds, and the national conference. Among these, many were related to the indigenization of the Chinese Church. For example, the 13 items regarding the NCCC's responsibilities, directly or indirectly, discussed the indigenization of the Christian Church in China. These items were as follows:[37]

(1) The NCCC should cultivate and carry forward the Chinese Church's spirit of communication and unity, progress to spiritual unity with Christian churches worldwide, and finally lead churches worldwide to pray with one heart and reach an intellectual consensus.
(2) In China, the Christian movement should help ordinary people widely recognize the pivotal role the Chinese Church can play. In the meantime, it should carefully think how to promote being self-supporting, advance the self-government and self-propagation of the Chinese Church and advocate all movements and methods that are conducive to the rapid fulfilment of these goals. Moreover, it should encourage proper campaigns within the Church and in doing so the self-government can be fully realized and do its best to lead the Church to adapt to the Chinese environment and finally grow into a truly Chinese Church.
(3) The NCCC should appraise the Chinese Church's various needs from the national perspective and carefully think how to save the nation by disseminating the gospels nationwide.
(4) The NCCC should attempt to have leaders of the churches, regardless of their nationalities, denominations and residences, know, respect and trust one another and willingly cooperate with each other in finishing plans and proposals well, quickly and naturally.
(5) The NCCC should select the right candidates from churches and missionary societies and train them to be leading Christians, having a national and a global vision in handling religious affairs.
(6) The NCCC should do the preparatory work, by which churches nationwide, branches of missionary societies, their departments and other Christian institutions could strengthen their interactions through discussing various Christian endeavours carried out in the whole of China.
(7) The NCCC should organize special prayers, arrange preaching sessions, make preparations for national Christian conferences, and cultivate the Church's spiritual life and spirit of sermon whenever and wherever.

(8) The NCCC should set up a survey centre, which will be responsible for investigating everything related to the Church and editing various reports. These investigations and reports can be used as guidebooks by churches, missionary societies and their directorates.
(9) The NCCC should collaboratively work with special Christian national associations for general education, medicine and health education.
(10) The NCCC should strengthen communication ties with its counterparts worldwide on behalf of the Chinese Church.
(11) If necessary, the NCCC should arrange a national gathering, in which all churches could make a speech and discuss things item by item.
(12) The NCCC can be commissioned to do the work, if churches in China have special missions.
(13) The NCCC is responsible for arranging and convening the next national Christian conference.

The present author holds that, among the 13 items, the first five could be regarded as the principles illuminating what would lie ahead of the indigenization of the Chinese Church and the last eight ones should be the aims of the Chinese Church's progressive attempts. Just as the last paragraph of the first chapter of *Chinese Manifesto* stated:

> We do believe that Chinese Christians ultimately aspire for a true unity. We boldly hope that the unity of the Chinese Church will encourage Western Christians to put an end to the split of their churches and realize their unification.

This indicated that unity was exactly one of the characteristics of the Chinese indigenization of the Christian Church. The Chinese Church set an example to churches worldwide in terms of unity. It thus can be said that the unity of Chinese churches was directly related to the world's Christian mission.

It is especially worth mentioning that, due to the CCM's influence, the NCC paid particular attention to the question of the workers. This was embodied in the three criteria applied to proposals concerning economy and industry among the proposals discussed in this conference. The three criteria were as follows:

> First, all children under 12 are not permitted to work in any factories. Second, there must be a day for rest in a working week. Third, workers' health must be protected by the limitation for overtime work, hygiene barriers in factory, and safety measures at the work site.[38]

Later, the NCCC especially selected the three criteria as the basic principles guiding the Church's work of realizing fraternity in industries.[39] This was actually a brave, righteous effort made by the Christian Church to challenge capitalist exploitation.[40]

Most people's response to the NCC was positive. Wang Zhixin discussed this in one of his articles.[41] Wang himself was very pleased with the NCC, saying:

> [The reports of five sections and statistics of *The Christian Occupation of China* are all completed after countless rounds of investigation and consideration. Even the follow-up five reports] are all compiled on the basis of the thorough, painstaking investigation, extensive consultation and intensive panel discussions. All programmes and perceptions of this conference are good enough to break a new path for Chinese Christianity and lead the 400,000 male and female Chinese Christians to strive for the fulfilment of building a truly Chinese Church.

Among the more than 1,000 delegates taking part in the NCC, both Westerners and Chinese discussed all aspects of the Christian endeavour in China, regardless of nationalities and races. It is commendable that the majority of the NCC's senior members were Chinese, among whom Cheng Jingyi and Yu Rizhang were elected the President and Executive Chairperson respectively. The NCC did two most admirable things. The first was that the NCC had a great impetus on the unity of the Chinese Church. Originally, the Chinese Church was immune to Western sectarianism. Unfortunately, due to the influence exerted by various Western Christian sects, there were sectarian disputes within the Chinese Church. The NCC, which assembled over 130 sects, pushed Christian unity in China forward to a great extent and made a public joint declaration, which heralded the fulfilment of grand unity of all Chinese churches. The second was that NCC unequivocally indicated the Chinese Church was none other than the indigenized—or Sinicized—Christian Church. As regards the reason why the Christian Church should be indigenized, Wang explained:

> [When the Church is] propagating Christianity in China, it must change its original Western rituals and organizations to be adaptable to the Chinese character. In other words, the Christian Church should not be imported goods but an indigenous product. Now that the Church calls itself the Chinese Church, the Chinese should play a leading role in the Church, take the initiative in shouldering the responsibility and try their best not to fall behind Westerners. In a word, figuratively speaking, the Chinese should turn from guest into host. For Westerners, they have realized that, sooner or later, the Church will be returned to the hands of the Chinese. To put it another way, they know well that they are guests after all, so that they should no longer keep the Chinese Church under their control.

But, on the other hand, Wang criticized the NCC. His greatest dissatisfaction was that there were too many limitations imposed on speech, viz., that only seven hours were left for discussions in ten days. Wang's complaint was that:

[Due to the time limit,] except for a few standard-bearer-like Christians, most of the participants are nothing more than yes-men or voting machines. It can thus be said that the conference could be likened to a puppet play, in which participants are nothing more than dummies.

Zhang Junjun fairly appraised the NCC.[42] He affirmed and also criticized this conference. He pointed out that, although the NCC had itself focused on indigenization, the conference itself was actually very poorly indigenized. For example, the church called itself a Chinese Church; but at the same time, all the speeches were delivered in English. This language policy seriously impeded Chinese delegates from listening to and delivering speeches. In reality, of the 540 participants of the conference, only two-fifths of them barely understood English and for the rest English was way over their head. Ridiculously, this turned the Chinese, who constituted the main body of the conference, into *foreigners*. Moreover, the NCC applied very strict regulations to speeches. All speakers must fill in a form of discussion, which would be strictly reviewed. Consequently, some discussion sessions turned out to be silent except for a few speakers. And, the NCCC was actually compartmentalized according to Christian sects, even though all the Chinese delegates were against sectarianism. Naturally, the number of representatives from huge sects was larger. This created new problems for the unity and indigenization of Christianity in China. Some even denounced the NCC as undemocratic, rebuking, "The preparatory committee prepares a name list beforehand. Then the list is announced in an authoritative manner before the entirety of participants, who are not allowed to discuss it. How arbitrary is this!"[43]

Some totally disavowed the NCC. For example, Zhang Zhimou, who was from Hunan, contended that the conference was fundamentally wrong, questioning: "What is the basis on which the Church can be named after China? And, what is the point of Sinicizing the Church?" He went further, critically pointing out that the Chinese Church and the Sinicized Church were all not orders from God but embodiments of parochial perceptions of nation and state.[44] Evidently, there were different understandings of Sinicization. This revealed that some indeed resisted the indigenization of the Christian Church in China.

Overall, the NCC, which was deeply influenced by the NCM and the CCM, did make great efforts to push forward the indigenization of the Chinese Christian Church. But it must be pointed out that indigenization could by no means be simply achieved by a conference. Rather, the completion of indigenization depended on the steady growth of the Chinese Church itself. Even so, the Chinese Church's indigenization advocated by the NCC exerted a substantial influence on a number of open-minded Chinese Christians. This was corroborated by the fact that, during the years following the conference, some church-run magazines still keenly discussed the issue of indigenization.

The continuation of debates on the indigenization of the Chinese Church

The NCCC, driven by the spirit of the NCC, set up the Committee of the Indigenized Chinese Church (CICC) in 1923. The CICC prepared a five-item compendium, which was as follows:

> First, the relationship between the Chinese Church and missionary societies. Second, the independence of the Chinese Church. Third, the organization and management of the Chinese Church. Fourth, the unity of the Chinese Church. Fifth, the implementation of indigenization of the Chinese Church.

As regards the reason why the Chinese Church should be indigenized, the CICC explained:

> How does the Christian Church take root in China and naturally adapt itself to Chinese conditions? Christianity has been introduced to China for almost one hundred years. By now, it is like a huge tree with luxuriant foliage and looks magnificent. Even so, Christianity still has a bad reputation as *yangjiao* (foreign religion). The name goes too far. But it is not totally ungrounded. For the Church itself, it should learn lessons from the past, avoid make similar mistakes in future, cultivate itself deeply and thoroughly, and make itself more competent, more diverse and more decent. Such an indigenized Chinese Christian Church will be appealing to the Chinese people.

The CICC defined the indigenized church in a clearer way, saying:

> The indigenized Chinese Church will not be exclusive, nor create any sects, nor found a national agency, nor set up any eclectic organization by syncretizing other religions. [As far as the meaning of an indigenized church is concerned, it has three points.] First, Christianity should be made more adaptable to the Chinese conditions and environment. Second, Chinese Christians should be taught what their personal and common responsibilities will be. Third, the Chinese Christian should make contributions to God and in doing so the Christian life will be extended and the role Christianity plays be expanded.

The aim of the CICC was threefold:

> First, the CICC studies how the Chinese Church can carry out God's orders in the most effective and most beneficial way. Second, the CICC pays attention to and reports the improvement of Chinese Church's

experiments. Third, the CICC illuminates Chinese Christians' aspirations for Western missionaries and free thinkers.

The CICC should carry out six responsibilities:

> First, it should study Chinese cultural elements that are perpetually valuable. Second, it should investigate thoroughly all religious groups' activities in modern times. Third, it should inquire into social movements criticizing religions such as the CCM. Fourth, it should study the situation of independent Christian churches in China. Fifth, it should study the relationship between Western missionary societies and the Chinese Church. Sixth, it should study various types of habitual practices of the Chinese churches.[45]

It should be pointed out that, although the CICC was formally set up, it failed to devote itself to the work mentioned above and its performance since the founding was actually not satisfactory. Even so, the influence of indigenization on the Church was still visible.

After the NCC, there were ongoing discussions of indigenization among Chinese Christians. Some Christian journals increased the number of articles focusing on indigenization of Christianity in China. For example, when Wang Zhixin started to lead the editorial board of *Theological Review* in the second half of 1922, he consciously published more articles respecting the Sinicization of Christianity in addition to those devoted to theoretical and intellectual studies. He specially pointed out:

> We preach Christian doctrines for the Chinese, don't we? We do hope that Christianity will occupy China, don't we? Thus, we should pay attention to all existing Chinese written materials in relation to indigenization. Are there not any useful materials in China's four-thousand-year history and immense number of books of *Four Treasures*? No. But nobody spends time and energy collecting these useful materials. For this reason, we specially stress Sinicization in the collection of primary sources for indigenization.[46]

In April 1923, Wu Zhenchun (i.e., Wu Leichuan), Bao Guanglin, Zhang Qinshi, Peng Jinzhang, Wu Yaozong, Chen Guoliang and Hu Xuecheng collaboratively published *Truth Weekly* after launching *The Life Monthly*. In the editorial of the debut edition, they said:

> The storm of reforming the Church and building a Chinese Church has been set off and grows increasingly strong. We, concerning ourselves with the future of the Church, feel obliged to study carefully and plan systematically and then carry out the programme as scheduled. We all sincerely share what we have learnt with comrades nationwide.

According to them, the aim of their *Truth Weekly* was as follows:

> On the one hand, *Truth Weekly* reviews the country's social problems and realities through the prism of Christianity and in doing so it cultivates the righteous public opinion. On the other hand, in the light of modern needs, it studies whether organizations, rules and inherited doctrines and their interpretations are proper and by doing so it helps the Chinese society grasp the true spirit of Christianity and makes attempts to reform the existing Church.[47]

The publication of *Truth Weekly* was really the icing on the cake of the discussion of indigenization of Chinese Christian Church. This journal, together with *The Life Monthly* and *Theological Review*, were the platforms, in which appeared the most intensive discussions of Chinese Church, in the period prior to 1924, when the second round of the CCM was launched.

Articles published by church-run journals in this phase could roughly be divided into several groups:

1. Some directly discussed the indigenized Christian Church, such as Zhao Zichen's "An Open Discussion of the Indigenized Church" (本色教会的商榷) and Xu Zuhuan's "How to Set up an Indigenized Chinese Christian Church?" (如何创造中国本色的教会).
2. A number of observers shed light on specific aspects of the indigenization of the Christian Church. Among them, some debated the issue of the reform of the Chinese Church, such as Luo Xigu's "How to Make Academic Theology More Socially Practicable?" (如何应用书本上神学到社会上), Wan Shanzhi's "Practical Theology" (实用神学), Zhao Zichen's "What Kind of Religion Do We Need?" (我们要什么样的宗教) and "Christian Preachers and Truth" (宣教师与真理), Hu Xuecheng's "What Should We Do?" (我们当作什么), Xiao Muxian's "What Does the Present-Day Church Desperately Need?" (教会今日的急需), Bao Zheqing's "Priests and Their Churches" (牧师与其教会), Liu Tingfang's "The Issue of Christian Preachers" (宣教师的问题) and "Tri-Benefit Society and the Church's Self-Support" (三益教会与教会的自养), Peng Jinzhang's "Opinions Respecting the Transformation of Missionary Societies into Independent Churches" (对于差会改建为自立会的意见), Jian Youwen's "Tri-Benefit Society and Christianity" (三益教会与基督教), Zhang Qinshi "What Should the Beijing Church Do?" (北京教会当作什么), Wu Yaozong "What Should Chinese Christian Students Do?" (中国的基督教学生应当作什么), Xinwu's "My Humble Opinion about the Church's Management of Talented People" (对于教会用人才的我见), Wu Zhenchun's "What Lies Ahead of the Chinese Church?" (论中国基督教会的前途), Wu Leichuan's "My Suggestions Regarding Reform of Church-Run Schools" (对于教会中学校改良的我见), Wang Qigang's "What Is the Church?" (教会是什么), Fan Bihai's "The Mission of

China Young Christians Association at Present" (中华基督教青年会今日的使命), Bao Guanglin's "Will the Status Quo of Chinese Students Association for Christian Propagation Meet the Needs of the Future?" (中华学生立志布道团的现状是否适合将来的要求), and You Shuxun's "The Rural Work of Propagating Christianity" (乡村布道谈).

3. Some discussed Christianity and the textual work, such as Zeng Yugen's "The Textual Work of Chinese Christianity" (中国基督教文字事业的问题), Liu Tingfan's "The Issue of the Christian Church's Textual Work" (教会文字事业的问题), Peng Changlin's "How to Improve the Chinese Christian Textual Work?" (中国基督教文字事业当如何改进？), Xu Guangdi's "The Question of Chinese Christian Textual Work" (中国基督教文字事业的问题), Zhefu's "A Preliminary Discussion of the Promotion of Christian Textual Work" (基督教提倡文字事业的刍议), Zhao Zichen's "The Future of Christian Textual Work" (基督教文字事业的前途), and Chen Guoliang's "The Chinese Church's Insufficient Knowledge Reserve" (中国基督教会的"学识盲").

4. Some discussed Christianity and traditional Chinese culture, such as Wu Leichuan's "Christian Canons and Confucian Classics" (基督教经与儒教经), "Christianity and Confucianism" (论基督教与儒教) and "What Lies Ahead of Christianity and Buddhism" (论基督教与佛教将来的趋势) and Wang Zhixin's "Christian Spirit and Neo-Confucian Sincerity" (中国理学家所言之"诚"与基督教所言之"灵"), "Christianity and Buddhist Study" (基督教与佛学) and his treatises comparatively analysing Christianity and philosophies developed by Chinese thinkers, such as Laozi, Zhuangzi and Liezi.

5. Some discussed the relationship between church, state and politics, such as Luo Yunyan's "Christianity and Politics" (基督教与政治), Bao Guanglin's "Faith and Politics" (信仰与政治) and "Christians and Political Parties" (基督徒与政党), Hu Xuecheng's "The Consciousness We Should Have in Perceiving State Affairs" (我们今后对于国事应有的觉悟), Chao Kunlin's "Patriotism, Internationalism and the Christian Church" (爱国主义国际主义和基督教教会), Wu Yaozong's "The Chinese National's Duty" (国民的责任), Liu Tingfang's "Patriotic Issues of Chinese Christians" (中国基督徒爱国问题评议), Zhao Zichen's "The Question of Nationality among Chinese Christians" (中华基督教的国籍问题), Chen Guoliang's "Foreign Missionaries and Extraterritoriality" (传教士与治外法权) and Lu Boheng's "Foreign Christian Preachers of Missionary Societies and Extraterritoriality" (外国差会的宣教师与治外法权).

6. Some penned articles respecting the unity of the Chinese Church.

Although these articles differed from one another in terms of the main arguments, they all advocated the idea that the Chinese Church should adapt itself to the Chinese culture and Chinese society and at the same time walk away from Western missionary societies. In comparison with similar writings produced in the MFM and the NCM, these articles were more intellectually extensive and profound. This progress should be attributed to the spiritual influence exerted by the CCM and the NCC.

In terms of the breadth of these articles, they discussed multiple aspects of the Church's organization. Some generally talked about churches and church-run schools. Some specifically analysed a local church, such as the Beijing Church and churches in the countryside. Some focused on the church-affiliated groups such as Young Christian Associations, student associations for Christian propagation and various Christian councils. The content of these articles was about the Church's own affairs such as organizations, the biblical theology, rituals, ethics, the textual work, believers and the clergy, as well as touching on the relationships between the Church and the Chinese culture, between the Church and the Chinese socio-politics, between the Church and education, and between the Church and other religions. These articles pioneered the exploration of new fields such as the relationship of Christianity and political parties and the relationship between missionaries and extraterritoriality. In terms of the depth of these articles, some furthered the academic argumentation and pioneered the theological indigenization by suggesting the unity of theology and Chinese social practice. Moreover, some Chinese Christians started to study Christianity from the perspective of traditional Chinese culture. For example, they made a comparative analysis of Christianity, three most basic Chinese teachings (i.e., Confucianism, Daoism and Buddhism), and the theories of the Chinese intellectual schools and in doing so they tried to find similarities and differences between these teachings and thus lay a foundation of indigenization of Christianity in China. Although these explorations were similar to the Confucian complement to Christianity advocated by Catholic missionaries such as Matteo Ricci and modern Protestant missionaries like Lin Lezhi and Li Timotai, in reality, Chinese Christians and Chinese Protestants in particular spent much less time and energy doing this study. After the NCC, Chinese Christians such as Wu Leichuan and Wang Zhixin began to explore this field further. In addition, many articles not only theoretically and theologically researched indigenization of Christianity but also made concrete suggestions regarding how to implement indigenization.

Some generalized these articles discussing the Chinese indigenization, concluding that their discussions focused on three topics, that is, "what is the indigenized Church?," "why must there be an indigenized Church?," and "how to create an indigenized Church?."

1 "What is the indigenized Church?"

There were a great variety of answers. The answer prepared by the NCC's *Chinese Manifesto* was:

> An indigenized Christian Church should, on the one hand, preserve the historical connection with other denominations worldwide and prevent

this connection from breaking; and on the other hand, truly assimilate the indigenous cultural and spiritual experience of the Chinese nation.

Cheng Jingyi's explanatory description of an indigenized Church was as follows:

> Now the indigenized Church has been known to the entire country. The indigenized Chinese Christian Church is also advocated by the National Christian Council of China. The indigenized Church requires that Chinese Christians should, on the one hand, take the responsibilities [demanded by Christianity], and on the other hand, carry forward the well-established Eastern [i.e., Chinese] civilization and help [the Chinese] Christianity get rid of the bad reputation as "*yangjiao*" (foreign religion).[48]

Evidently, Cheng placed emphasis on Chinese Christians' religious obligations and their endeavour to promote Chinese civilization and eliminate the excessive foreignness of Chinese Christianity.

Liu Tingfang held:

> The Chinese Christian Church is exactly the Church of Chinese nationals. The most important task of the Church lies in serving the Chinese and rehabilitating the Chinese society. The Church's organizations and programmes should all be based on the Chinese national spirit and adaptable to the Chinese national psychology. On the one hand, it should make an incessant effort to sort out and carry forward the essence of traditional Chinese culture. On the other hand, it should positively absorb good elements of civilizations all over the world.[49]

He stressed that the Chinese Church serves the Chinese society, adapts itself to the Chinese spirit, carries forward the national essence and remains open to world civilizations.

Zhao Zichen expressed his perception of an indigenized Church, saying:

> An indigenized Church should not be built on external non-Christian truths. But instead, it should be the defender of the truth revealed by Jesus Christ ... The indigenized Church should achieve the unity of truths embedded in Christianity and ancient Chinese culture, make the religious life and experience of Chinese Christians adaptable to Chinese conditions so that there will not be unnatural repercussions. After a certain time, which should be shortened by the love and cooperation of Chinese Christians, this indigenized Church will be economically owned by the Chinese, administratively managed by the Chinese, organizationally compatible with the Chinese character, and theologically digestible for Chinese thoughts ... Moreover, the indigenized Church will definitely prevent people of thought from being suspicious of Christianity and

must be fully patriotic and admit the mistakes [committed by this religion] at the national and international levels. The indigenized Church, enthusiastically and industriously, disseminates the gospels nationwide and selects love and care for the world as the only method [of propagating Christianity]. Although the indigenized Church has its own doctrines, it never partakes in the theological debate on the grounds that it is intellectually based on Chinese thoughts and holds that religious doctrines and theological debates should never be confused.[50]

Zhao's discussion referred to almost all the aspects of the indigenized Church, such as the economy, its organization, theology and Chinese culture and society.

Xu Zuhuan concluded the above-mentioned discussions, paraphrasing what Zhao Zichen had said:

An indigenized Church should not be built on external non-Christian truths. Rather, it aspires to achieve the unity of truths embedded in Christianity and ancient Chinese culture and make the religious life and experience of Chinese Christians adaptable to Chinese conditions, in case there will be unnatural repercussions.

2 "Why must there be an indigenized Church?"

In answering this question, Xu Zuhuan drew a three-point conclusion. First, the Church must be indigenized to be adaptable to the Chinese national character. In order that the excessive Western character could be eliminated, the Christian truth could take deep root in the Chinese cultural tradition and national characteristics, and the greatness and depth of the Chinese characteristics could be realized by means of Christianity, there must be an indigenized Christian Church in China. Second, the Church must be indigenized to achieve the national unity of Christian churches in China. Due to the influence exerted by Western sectarianism, the Chinese Church became highly divided. The reason for this should never be attributed to the Chinese. In order to gain power that was enough to perform the national salvation, there must be an indigenized Christian Church in China. Third, the Church must be indigenized to contribute to the development of free Chinese thoughts. Only when there was an indigenized Christian Church in China would the situation, in which the Chinese Church was oppressed by the established rites and doctrines of Western missionary societies and consequently Chinese free thinking was seriously restricted, be changed fundamentally and Chinese thoughts would be taken to new heights.

Zhao Zichen's relevant discussion was:

The reason why the Chinese Church must make the best use of its time to start afresh and walk a new path is complex. We Chinese Christians are

> born to love our customs and our traditional culture. [If] we are so lazy that we rely on others, we will definitely fear and tremble. Christianity, an imported religion from the West, still cannot take root in the Chinese society. Rather, it is protected [by foreign missionaries] and stays alive by manual infusion of nutrients. Under the circumstances, how can Christianity survive and keep growing in the Chinese land? Present-day Christianity has to face two conundrums. First, it must adapt itself to the new environment and respond to the social movement condemning Christianity and Chinese thinkers' critical spirit and reasonable attitude. Second, although the Chinese Church must have its own talented leaders, the personnel management adopted by the Church can neither increase the number of qualified candidates nor balance the supply and demand of talents. Due to these, the Chinese Christian Church is in a dilemma. At this moment, the Chinese people are being gradually awakened. As a consequence, people who truly love the country and God hold that founding an indigenized Chinese Christian Church is a matter of the utmost urgency.[51]

Not only did Zhao shed light on why there must be an indigenized Church in China but he also explained for what reason the creation of an indigenized Church for China was an urgent task.

3 "How to create an indigenized Church?"

Opinions regarding how to found an indigenized Christian Church in China varied. The *Chinese Manifesto* said:[52]

> We thus demand that all Chinese followers of Jesus Christ act with united strength to make the Church self-supporting by means of systematic donations, self-governing by means of resolute study, brave experiments and fearless spirit, and self-propagating by means of fully-fledged religious education, cultivation of leadership and cordial and ardent personal sermons. We declare that the time belonging to us has dawned. We Chinese Christians should carefully study Christian doctrines, boldly make experiments, and independently select and revise the Church's rites, ceremonies, organizations, systems and methods of propagation. In doing so, we benefit the Chinese Christian Church and finally make it a truly indigenized Christian Church. We sincerely invite leading Western missionaries working for the Chinese Church to give us practical advice, by which Chinese Christians can learn something and make themselves more competent. We also sincerely hope that Western missionaries would allow Chinese Christians to have full freedom in making their experiments.

To put it another way, just as Xu concluded, the Chinese Church should (1) boldly carry out its experiment; (2) bring a change to established Western

Christian rituals, ceremonies and doctrines; (3) overhaul all existing church organizations; and (4) have itself and truths embedded in the Chinese culture fused together.[53]

The afore-mentioned discussions could be regarded as the core content of indigenization. There were very extensive discussions that not only revolved around the core content but also inquired into specific aspects of indigenization of Christianity and Christian Church in China.

Digging into the reservoir of articles discussing the indigenization of the Christian Church in China, we find that many inherited the critical spirit of the NCM and exposed, one by one, the shortcomings of the Chinese Church in respect of indigenization. Some comparatively discussed Christianity and Buddhism, pointing out that, although both were imported religions, Buddhism had successfully indigenized itself and thus got rid of its bad reputation as a foreign religion. By contrast, inasmuch Christianity had failed to indigenize itself, it had always been a foreign religion. To be specific, Christianity had an almost ineradicable Western character, which was embodied in highly Westernized church buildings, interior settings, rituals and rules, in an ecclesiastical hierarchy in which the status of Westerners and Chinese were polarized and inequality predominated; in unduly repeated religious service which had caused strong negative feelings among followers; in Christianity's egregious exclusion of traditional Chinese teachings such as Confucianism, Daoism and Buddhism, which clashed with the established Chinese tolerant spirit and made the religion itself hardly ever compatible with the Chinese; in the inflexible handling of the Bible, which refused to make any changes to the biblical text and this backfired on the propagation work that turned out to be indigestible and unassimilable; and in the rigid sectarian divisions.[54] Some pointed out that urban Chinese churches were unable to cultivate leading Christians. The reasons were that young Christian students grasped neither general knowledge nor religious morality and that a small number of talented Christians found no way to communicate with the Church and felt very disappointed at the shortcomings of the Church that was less attractive to talented people. As far as rural churches were concerned, which had their vitality sapped, they were unable to meet the needs of the masses and what's worse, there were evil Christians who bullied villagers with the connivance of the Church. Consequently, rural residents thought there was an abominable overabundance of such churches.[55] Some fiercely criticized church-run schools and associations for young Christians. For example, Wu Yaozong pointed out that young Christian student associations such as the YMCA were not created out of students' natural, spontaneous needs but imported from the West. Therefore, these organizations were actually mechanically applied to the Chinese experience. When it came to church-run schools, Wu said the general atmosphere and management of these schools were too Western to lead China's student Christian movement to be truly Chinese and really vivid.[56] Echoing this, another article said, although church-run schools did make a significant contribution to Chinese education, most of them had already been unable to meet the social needs on the grounds that they were too conservative and too slow in making progress since modern schools had already been set up nationwide in China.[57]

Among the Chinese Church's problems, many were related to the Church's independence, the cultivation of clergy and the Christian textual work. In contrast, the issue of theological indigenization was often ignored by Chinese Christians. A journal entitled *Theological Review* (TR) was the pioneer in the exploration of indigenized Chinese theology. In the Spring of 1923, TR launched a general debate known as "how to make the academic theology socially practicable?," initiating the inquiry into the indigenization of Christian theology in China. Luo Xigu, one of the discussants, said:

> Recently, articles advocating the Sinicization of Christianity are published column after column in church-run newspapers and journals. Even so, there are not any pieces of writing discussing the Sinicization of theology that is used to protect and propagate the Christian religion. If the Westernized Church cannot work in China, how can the Western theology that defends and propagandizes the Westernized Church flourish alone in China? As we know, theology and religion are inseparably interconnected. Religion should be indigenized in China. In like manner, theology should be Sinicized, shouldn't it? Whenever theology is Sinicized, Christianity will naturally be indigenized in China.[58] [The most important task of theological indigenization is the combination of Christian theology and Chinese society.] Everybody knows that China and Western countries differ from each other in terms of national characters. Jesus attempts to save all humans on this planet, so that he chooses to live in this world and fulfil his ambition. For all theological threads in present-day China, they can neither save nor reform the society unless they are remade socially practicable. The socialized Christian theology can, on the one hand, cultivate people's devotion to public interests, make the society cohesive and solve social problems of all shades; and, on the other hand, nourish new lofty beliefs guiding the society to uproot bad common practice.[59] [But unfortunately, the textbook adopted by seminaries are] either theoretically too abstract or epistemically too old, consisting of either extremely awkward translations or highly lengthy originals, none of which are suitable for social practice.[60] [Therefore, how can we make theology more socially practicable? Simply speaking, there should be] such a Christian theology that it can be mutually helpful and intrinsically related to Chinese society. This new theology does not obstinately follow ancient or modern Western theologies; nor does it proceed from religion and end in religion, remaining totally irrelevant to the society. Rather, it is the ferryboat interconnecting Christianity and the Chinese society. This new [Sinicized] Christian theology is created against the backdrop of Chinese society, as well as being conducted to have the Chinese society religionized.[61]

In the meantime, Luo suggested seminaries should reform their basic systems and research methods. According to him, if theologians wanted to make theology more socially practicable, they should accomplish three tasks. First, they should achieve enlightenment. To be specific, theologians should completely understand written works, thoroughly explore them, fully grasp the essence, and freely and comprehensively investigate all things from theological perspective. Second, they should liven up the theology. That is to say, theologians should vividly represent truths in the Bible and disseminate them as extensively as possible. In doing so, the personality of Christ would melt into their own lives. If done, the soul of people would be revived and society would be rehabilitated. Third, they should do propaganda work, which was comprised of text, language and the personality [of Christ].

Unlike the above-mentioned Luo, who theoretically discussed how to combine theology with social practice, Wang Shanzhi and Sha Yalun make specific suggestions as to how Christians could apply theology to social practice. Wang mentioned the Christian ritual ceremony, saying:

> When a priest is lecturing from the Bible, he should put on formal attire; when praying, he should bend his knees; when listening to sermon, he should stand; and when receiving donations, he should make a bow with hands folded in front. Within the church, it is better not to offer seats, which should be replaced with clean carpet and well-arranged rush cushions.[62]

Moreover, the interior settings of a Chinese Christians' family should be in accordance with the Chinese psychology. For example, the traditional Chinese painting known as *One Hundred Galloping Horses* should be replaced with the shepherd image and the traditional Chinese painting of beauties be replaced with the Christian one portraying Jesus and a Samaritan woman at the well. In preaching Christianity, Christians should adopt songs and poems that were popular among the Chinese. For example, hymns could be sung with popular Chinese tunes such as Lady Meng Jiang. Wang, in one of his articles, even advised the Church to follow the settings of Buddhist sermon, such as incense burners and candleholders, and in doing so the indigenization of the Church could be well shown. According to Wang:

> [Within the Church, there can be a wooden tablet dedicated to God, on which] four words "God, The Heavenly Father" are inscribed. In front of the wooden tablet, there is an incense burner table [on which] a cross, the Crucifixion of Jesus, or one painting of Jesus are displayed and placed on the right of the tablet. This display is in line with what the Bible records. All utensils such as communion cups, kettles and plates, water pot for baptism and bag of donations are all placed on the table. In addition, a small incense burner and a pair of candleholders are provided for burning incense and lighting candles.[63]

The lectern was located at the lower right corner of the incense table; and musical instruments and the place for the choir, at the lower left corner. When the religious service was being performed, it must be conducted in an orderly manner. For example, the preachers must wear formal attire and the followers must be marshalling as flying geese. As soon as Wang's article was published, there was a heated debate within the Church. Some agreed with him; some recognized parts of his suggestion; and the majority of clergy dismissed it. Among those who supported Wang, a few put his suggestions into practice. For instance, a Christian centre in Xiaguan of Nanjing adopted some Buddhist forms. No matter whether or not these Christians agreed with Wang's suggestions, the debate itself and a few churches' praxis demonstrated that indigenization did draw attention to itself in the Chinese Church.

Among debates on the indigenization of the Christian church in China, the independence of the Chinese Church was always the focus. According to *The Christian Occupation of China*:

> The annual cost of the propagation of Christianity in China is 12,000,000 dollars, among which Chinese Christians can only afford less than 1,000,000 dollars. [Even so,] there is one paid Christian professional in every fourteen Chinese followers. By contrast, there is no such thing in Europe and America.[64]

How could the Chinese Church become truly independent? How could the Church in China transform itself from being a missionary society's appendage to an independent Chinese Christian institution? In short, how to fulfil the self-governing, self-supporting and self-propagating ambitions of the Chinese Church? Therein lay the most important question respecting the indigenization of the Christian Church in China. Many held that, although economic independence was the first step of indigenization, it was very hard to achieve. Quite a few leading Chinese Christians did worry about this. Zhang Qinshi, for instance, discussed the true situation, saying:

> [Every year the administrative organs of Beijing-based Christian churches spent 3,000,000 dollars, among which] the amount afforded by Chinese Christians is less than one-twelfth. The ultimate goal of the Christian movement in China is to create an indigenized Chinese Church and change the Chinese society by means of the spirit of Jesus, isn't it? But how many people would like to be self-sacrificing for the Church at any time among Christians in Beijing? Are these Christians strongly united? Are they sharing the same aspiration? If the donations of Western missionaries and their governing countries are all revoked tomorrow, will Christians in Beijing be able to carry forward the mission and help all the organs of the Beijing churches run as usual?[65]

Some went further, pointing out:

> The cry for the Chinese Church's to be self-supporting has always lingered in our ears for years. But so far, the endeavour to realize self-support is still in its infancy. As a matter of fact, the Chinese Church is still slavishly dependent on Western missionary societies. Indeed, there are a few independent and self-supporting churches. But among these independent churches, some are actually independent and self-supporting in name only. They do not have the independent spirit at all. But instead, they angle for reputation and take an exclusive stand on the pretext of self-government and self-support.

The reason why there was such a phenomenon was Western missionaries. It was these foreign missionaries who manipulated the Chinese Church through money and thus held in their hands immeasurable power. In these circumstances, Chinese Christians had no alternative but to be absolutely obedient to Western missionaries. With the passing of time, the Chinese Church became known for its lack of responsibility.[66]

In order to be self-supporting, many clergy contributed ideas and exerted efforts for this cause. Their efforts could be divided into four groups. First, the missionary society reduced their funds annually and this would force the Chinese Church to be gradually economically independent of Western missionary societies. If the reduction plan could last for one decade, viz., that the missionary society cut down one-tenth of the fund every year, the final result would be that Chinese Christians could be able to afford the entire expenses of the Church. Second, donations were encouraged. In doing so, the Church's independence could be, at least to a certain extent, achieved. Independent churches could be sorted into the fully independent ones, the half-independent ones and the much less-independent ones. Regardless of the degree of independence, these churches were all allowed to employ their own priests and given honour. Third, the Chinese Church, following Buddhist monasteries purchasing immovable property, tried its best to gain a regular income, whereby it could feed itself. Fourth, if a local church was really unable to be economically independent, it could ask for help from other churches. By doing so, this church could be less dependent on foreign missionary societies, even though it was not truly independent. Some investigated the economic activities of churches in a certain region, probing into the ways the Chinese Christian Church could be self-supporting of. For example, Jian Youwen conducted a survey of Jia'nan (i.e., Canaan) Hall (a real estate company) and the Tri-Benefit Society (TBS) affiliated to a Protestant church in Dongshan. The TBS pooled money from its followers and then invested the money in building houses in Guangzhou, the provincial capital. It profited from these built-for-rent houses. The 20 per cent of profits was reaped by the church, so that the church could be self-supporting and the followers who bought a share could earn profit, too. Soon, churches of Guangdong and beyond were choosing to follow the example of TBS. But some disagreed with TBS's *modus operandi*, pointing out that this would make the church too materialistic and the religiousness of the church would be diluted. In a word, what TBS did was, overall, harmful to the Christian Church. Jian Youwen specially wrote a 10,000-word article discussing TSB and its attempt to be self-supporting.[67] Jian's article initiated a wide debate on the self-supporting concept for the Chinese Church. Liu Tingfang reviewed Jian's paper, saying:

> The motive, purpose and attitude of Mister Jian, who authored this paper, are appropriate. Tri-Benefit Society's praxis, in which it is able to support itself, is worth being deeply studied. Although the Society's praxis is provincial, there is indeed the possibility to promote it nationwide. In this sense, the effort made by the Society matters not only to churches in Guangdong but also to churches all over China.[68]

The above-mentioned praxes were all efforts to make the Chinese Church self-governing and self-supporting by economic means. But some held that these could not solve the root of the problem, on the grounds that the independence of the Chinese Church was not an economic issue but an issue related to the ecclesiastic organization and system. Take Peng Jinzhang, for example. He pointed out that, normally, the founding of a church was premised on the unity of comrades having common goals, which laid the foundation of the Christian Church. This could be corroborated by churches in the Apostolic Age and (modern) Europe and America. Contrary to this,

> The situation in present-day China is very different. First of all, there are the Christian Church's houses and organizations. Then, there are followers, who join the church. After converting to Christianity, followers abide by the regulation requiring that they come to a specially-built house, in which they worship, pray and sing hymns on schedule. Leaders of the church do not tell followers that they should shoulder responsibility for the church; nor do followers feel obliged to do anything for the church. But now, you tell them that they should be self-governing and self-supporting. The answer you will receive from them might be that "we will not go to church!" For the followers, it is not the church, for which they desire.[69]

In view of this, Peng suggested new local churches give up constructing new church buildings, saying:

> It is better for the Church to send only preachers to disseminate Christian truths. When the number of Christian converts is large enough, there will naturally be external things embodied in buildings and ritual systems, which conform with general human nature and meet the needs of the

society. Herein lies an ideal indigenized Christian Church. This church is what Chinese Christians really want and can build. The holy hall, in which the Christians worship God, is either their home or under the tree or on the riverbank. Neither do they need to pay clergy nor will they spend any money repairing church buildings. Is it necessary for such a church to be independent?

In other words, this church was not self-supporting but completely natural. That is to say, it was fully owned by Christians themselves. For churches managed by foreign missionary societies, transformation into truly independent churches was almost an impossible mission. Even so, the churches run by missionary societies must be transformed. Churches should not sacrifice quality to quantity. In other words, the churches that were unable to adapt to the change would be abandoned rather than be kept. There was a specific plan. Preachers would not be sent to the churches that did not have preachers yet. The churches that did not have buildings should give up their building plans. Only when their followers really wanted a church building would they raise money and work out a plan of construction. For existing churches, if they felt unable to pay professional preachers, they should cut down the number of paid clergy; or, they could rent the building out to local followers, who would be fully responsible for running the church. The Church should teach followers what worship and the Church itself actually mean and grant them the right to formulate ritual codes and handle church affairs.[70] In the meantime, some suggested the Church, on the one hand, should train enterprising talented people who would in turn help the Church grow by itself; and, on the other hand, it should encourage follower to be unpaid volunteers working for the Church, so that bad practices would be corrected.[71] To sum up, far-sighted people within the Chinese Church did try their best to find feasible programmes whereby the Church could achieve independence and be self-supporting.

In addition, some concerned themselves with the Chinese Church's cultivation of talented people and regarded this cultivation as the most important job of the Church. For example, Cheng Jingyi said: "Only when we have a large number of well-educated and well-trained talented people will we be able to set out on the grand cause."[72] Zhao Zichen systematically discussed the relationship between leaders of Chinese Church and indigenization, pointing out that the Chinese Church desperately needed two types of talented people, that is, indigenized clergy and indigenized writers. As far as the existing personnel trained by the Church were concerned, many of them were actually unsuitable for the cause. Zhao explained this, saying:

> The reason is that the Church hardly ever takes into consideration the issue of indigenization. Exactly because of this, the Church makes no attempt to build a pool of leading indigenized talented Christians, which can be used to handle the changing situation. [Under the circumstances,]

the Church never finishes training such people, who not only fully respect the traditional Chinese culture but also completely grasp the essence of the Chinese spiritual heritage. Rather, the Church has turned Chinese Christians into quasi-foreigners. [If] there is not any leading Chinese Christians, there will not be any indigenized Chinese churches; nor will Chinese churches be economically independent, self-governing and self-propagating. On the other hand, if Christian leaders do not know much about the essence of Chinese culture and fail to well perceive the nature of the Chinese spiritual heritage, there can by no means be truly indigenized leading Chinese Christians.[73]

Zhao particularly stressed that leaders of the Chinese Church must well understand Chinese culture and Chinese psychology, because this understanding was the foundation stone of the indigenization of the Christian Church in China. In this regard, Zhao said:

If the leaders of the Chinese Christian Church are unable to fully understand and really appreciate Chinese psychology, that is deeply embedded in the Chinese history and customs, the Chinese Church cannot be truly indigenized. If there is no indigenized Christian Church, which leads the Chinese to be Christians, living their religious life in Chinese social customs and habits, Christianity will find no way to take deep root in the country. If the life of Chinese Christian converts cannot adapt to the inherent character of the Chinese, then Christian China and the Christian Chinese will be nonexistent.[74]

Zhao's analyses indicated that, for the indigenized Church, the cultivation of talented people serving the Church was a matter of life and death.

In the NCM, both Christians and free thinkers were increasingly concerned with issues such as the leadership of the Chinese Christian Church and foreign missionaries in particular. The reason was twofold, according to Liu Tingfang. First, due to external stimulation and epistemic progress, Christians gradually became consciously concerned with the Church and as a consequence, there were criticism of the Church and foreign missionaries in particular. Second, thanks to the NCM, which encouraged people to ask questions, religion became one of the research objects of philosophers, anti-religionists and political commentators, all of whom would naturally pay attention to the issue of foreign missionaries in their discussions.[75] According to his conclusion, there were two points in free thinkers' criticism of foreign missionaries. "First, Christian preachers' acts belie their words. Second, what Christian preachers say contradict what modern philosophy teaches."[76] Critics from the Church held that, because missionaries had neither ability nor knowledge and repeated what was already stereotyped and outdated, Christian converts felt so disappointed that they could not be spiritually enlightened. Some, who worked for the Church and at same time were influenced by the CCM, scorned Western missionaries and Chinese clergy. Take Xinwu, for example. He said:

> Leaders of the Chinese Church really do not have either knowledge or experience, just like those who have no backbone. They are always servile to Westerners, hoping that by doing so they will be given an important position in the Church. This can be seen everywhere in the Chinese Church ... [Such servility and utilitarianism are] really huge hindrances to the development of the Chinese Church. The reason for such a mistake should be attributed not only to the Chinese but also to Westerners, among whom some came to China for personal gain and colonial power of their governing countries rather than for the propagation of Christianity and to benefit the Chinese substantially. Therefore, the leaders of the Chinese Church and especially those who fall within of the orbit of the Western churches must clearly realize that they will be deprived of their freedom if they bend their knees to the West's money and colonial power.

In addition, Xinwu pointed out that some leaders of the Chinese Church were totally passive and fully under Westerners' control. Chinese Christians and free thinker disliked this very much. At this point, he said:

> First, others tell them that their true mission is not disseminating the gospel but making money. Second, others tell them that they are nothing more than slaves of foreigners. Take the extremely unpleasant manifesto prepared by the alliance condemning religions, for example. It is brought about by the afore-mentioned servility [of the leadership of the Chinese Church], isn't it?[77]

Echoing Xinwu, some criticized that the Western missionaries appointed people on the basis of favouritism. To be specific, foreign missionaries did not assign to positions those who were trained by the Church but their henchmen and even their servants, who were actually poorly educated. Some went further, pointing out:

> [Chinese] priests of the Church are all under Western missionaries' control. Due to the Westerners' domination, Chinese priests have no chance to carry out their aspirations and work. As a result, many people of thought and ability cannot realize their dream to be good priests. It is true that these Chinese Christians still lack boldness, patience and stamina. It is also true that Western missionaries are far from being inclusive and tolerant.[78]

All these indicated that those missionaries who sought only personal gain were nothing more than obstacles to the indigenization of the Chinese Christian Church.

Among a huge number of papers discussing the issue of missionaries, Zhao Zhichen's "Christian Preachers and Truth" was the most theoretical. In this article, Zhao asked the most fundamental question—what was the most important character of a missionary? Liu Tingfang, introducing this article to readers, said:

> Taken together, what a missionary preaches is the most fundamental question in relation to the issue of missionaries. To put it another way, whether or not what a missionary preaches is the truth? [Moreover,] all appointed preachers should use this paper as a ruler measuring to what degree they are worthy of their job, that is, propagating Christianity. [Even] for those Christians who are not clergy, they should carefully study this paper, on the grounds that the Church is not owned exclusively by preachers but by all Christians.[79]

Zhao's article was originally a draft of a speech written for the national Christian propagation meeting, which was held in the summer of 1922 at Guling in Jiangxi. Zhao did not attend this meeting due to illness. Soon this draft was fully reprinted by *The Life Monthly*. Zhao's paper did not literally discuss the issue of missionaries. Rather, it shed a philosophical light on this issue from the perspective of truth. In other words, profoundly, it discussed philosophical and theological questions. Analysing this article, we can grasp how Zhao helped religion, or the Christian truth, harmonize with the new cultural movement in China.

Zhao's article was divided into four sections: (1) how people could obtain truth; (2) what the scope of truth was; (3) what the authority of truth was; and (4) how Christian preachers could practise truth. When it came to the question of how people could obtain truth, Zhao contended that there was actually not any fixed path or time regarding the perception of truth, which required that people thirst for and be spiritually well prepared for the truth. Neither an individual nor a generation could produce truth. "The human truth is not unchangeable but instead it is a concept that keeps evolving." Therefore, there were not any fixed, established rules applied to the perception of truth. A qualified Christian preacher should realize: "The myriad things—cloth, silk, bean, millet, birth, senility, illness, death, heaven, earth, writings, and so on—all can be placed nestling truth or the cradle of truth." The scope of truth could be as extensive as the human life. Whether or not religion contradicted science? Zhao answered:

> All elements must harmonize with one another and finally be united within the realm of truth. [As far as] the nature of science [is concerned], it aspires to find the causality reigning over all phenomena. Religion, on the other hand, resolves to preserve the value of human life. [In terms of method and results, science and religion differ from each other. Even

so,] religion and science do not conflict with each other. Rather, each has its own realm. Indeed, possibly both religion and science could co-exist, where the truths of the two complement each other and are bound to achieve a perfect unity.[80]

The expectation of harmonization involving religion, reason and science was an important aspect of the Chinese Christianity's adaption to the Chinese society witnessing a new culture movement. In addition to this article, other articles penned by Zhao emphasized that a religion holding firmly to the truth should constantly improve itself and evolve. Religion should accord with the progress of knowledge, have reason, and never run counter to the most valuable facts in the thoughts of the times. In this sense, the Christian religion was such a religion that not only conformed to ethics and society but also respected personality.[81] Only this religion was able to grasp the truth. In many aspects, Zhao's paper was directly related to the indigenization of Christianity in China. As for the question what the scope of truth was, this article set forth:

> The scope of truth must be expanded. If a state was obstinately governed by established classics, it would definitely grow weak. In like manner, if a religion propagated itself by means of well-established canons, theology, rites and rules, it would irrevocably decline.

Therefore, Zhao said Christianity was not the religion that was exclusively based on an established canon but such a religion that was centred on Christ and built on life. He contended:

> When Christianity was introduced into Greece, there was a fusion of the Hebrew ethical spirit and Greek philosophy, by which [the content of] Christianity was greatly enriched. At present, Christianity has been in China for over one hundred years. Therefore, whether or not Christianity should accommodate its doctrines to the Chinese culture and finally change itself into an indigenized religion has become an important issue. If Chinese Christians decide to carry out this accommodation, existing Christian truths must be reformulated. For Christian preachers, the reformulation of Christian doctrines is really a difficult job. Even so, they should never impede the progress of this transformation.[82]

Moreover, Zhao critically reexamined the relationship between Christian preachers and the external environment, saying:

> [In the face of a new environment, some Christian preachers choose to be] closed and even obstinately resist, retreat, wallow in fantasy, resent and vainly disdain [others]. They think they are defending the Christian truth. But actually, they are slandering and even destroying the religion.[83]

He suggested Christian preachers should listen to free thinkers' opinions, read nonreligious books, communicate with persons outside the Church, do research, investigative work, and in doing so they could explore truths in diverse ways. In a word, the exploration of truth should never be carried out irrespective of external circumstances. Zhao advised Christian preachers instead:

> If they really want to save people, they must, first of all, save themselves. If they really want to disseminate Christian truths, they must, first of all, grasp the truths and make themselves embodiments of truth. [And,] if they really want to propagate the gospel, they must make the gospel concrete. If they really want to preach Christ, they must personalize Christ. Only by doing so will there be true, substantial God's decrees that can be announced publicly. Otherwise, they have nothing to say; nor is what they say truth; nor are they true Christian preachers ... Looking back at history, one finds that Christ was concretized or personalized by apostles such as John and Paul and thus thousands upon thousands of Christian saints made remarkable contributions [to the religion]. Moreover, Christianity had been indigenized in Greece, the Roman Empire and modern Europe and America, so that there were Greek, Roman, European and American understandings [of the Christian truth] and propagation work. But in China, where Christianity [i.e., Protestantism] has been there for over one hundred years, the Christian religion is not yet indigenized to adapt itself to Chinese preachers, culture and psychology. Thus, how can China assimilate the life of Christ and become a Christian state?[84]

Zhao's elaboration had Christian truths advocated by missionaries and Sinicization closely interconnected. In other words, if what missionaries preached could not be adaptable to the Chinese social culture or failed to be Sinicized, Christian truths would not be successfully disseminated among the Chinese. In many papers, Zhao repeatedly said Christian preachers must be morally good, if they wanted to spread truths among the Chinese. For example, he suggested preachers "be well-behaved and fair-minded and not afraid of failure, which might be the starting point of future success."[85] Zhao pointed out that, if a preacher acted arbitrarily, his understanding of Christian truth would be doubtful. Not only did Zhao's article require Christian preachers to improve their moral quality but it also demanded that the dissemination of Christian truth must be Sinicized.

Another important aspect of debates on indigenization was the integration of Christianity and Chinese culture, which includes questions such as how to reform the textual work respecting Christianity and how to combine the propagation of Christianity with the traditional Chinese culture. Many articles mentioned that the Christian textual work played a crucial role in the survival and development of the Chinese Church. But, as far as the textual work itself was concerned, it had serious problems. For example, some pointed out that the Church actually did not realize the importance of textual work; nor did they try to train people for this work, let alone prepare adequate Chinese reference books. In practice, there were many restrictions imposed on the Church's freedom of speech and their publications had to be economically dependent on Western missionaries, who were completely ignorant of Chinese customs and feelings and thus could not judge what a good Chinese Christian text was.[86] Inasmuch as church-run schools did not pay enough attention to the Chinese education, Christian reading materials were notoriously known for their coarseness, inarticulateness and inability to meet the needs of the time and accord with the psychology of the Chinese people.[87] In order to improve the situation, many proposed reform programmes, such as attaching greater importance to the Chinese language in church-run schools, prioritizing Chinese education, and inviting renowned men of letters to deliver speeches. Moreover, some suggested that there should be standard Chinese textbooks and Chinese libraries in church-run schools; that the Western and Chinese learning be equally valued by missionary colleges and universities; and that Christian educational institutes specializing in Chinese be set up.[88] Moreover, some advised the Church to found well-organized and powerful institutions promoting and carrying out the Christian textual work, to train talented people for the textual work, and to encourage those who loved the work, such as teachers and students of seminaries, to competitively practise writing Chinese by organizing seminars and essay contests. A discussant straightforwardly said:

> Henceforth the organ in charge of Christian textual work must be managed by the Chinese. The reason is that, even though there are Westerners who know Chinese customs and practices well, they hardly ever really grasp the Chinese characters. Furthermore, Westerners and the Chinese all have a hand in the textual work, so that the procedure became complicated and disorderly and the result of this work was actually unsatisfactory.[89]

Reading through piles of writings discussing the Christian textual work in China, we find one of Zhao Zichen's articles was the most theoretically outstanding.[90] In this article, first of all, he shed light on the relationships between the Chinese culture and Christianity and between the Christian textual work and the Sinicization of Christianity, saying:

> When an organic creature is transplanted from original land to new surroundings, whether or not it can survive is fully dependent on its adaptability to all elements of the new surroundings. If it is able to adapt to the new surroundings, it survives. If it is unable to adapt itself to the new surroundings, it perishes. This creature adapts to the new surroundings; and the new surroundings will, in turn, accept this creature. The cultural transplantation is done in much the same way. Take the Western culture's infiltration into the Eastern (/Chinese) culture, for example. If the two

cultures can adapt to each other, the result of their integration must be a new culture mixing Western and Eastern (/Chinese) elements together. Since Christianity's (i.e., Protestantism) first arrival in China, there have been one hundred and fifteen years. At the very start, Christianity, a purely Western religion, invaded the life of ordinary Chinese. Then, this imported Western faith and the enlightening Chinese culture looked face to face. It is in this course that the question that whether or not Christianity can survive and grow in China is raised. Far-sighted members of the Christian Church not only gain clear insight into this question but also find the only solution. Specifically, there is no other way but gathering together all awakened talented Chinese Christians and asking them to find difference and similarity in Christianity and China and make both adaptable to each other by abandoning prejudice and sincerely working together. In doing so, the teachings of Jesus will not be rejected and complete Chinese Christian doctrines will be created. Christianity must experience such a course in which it adapts to the new surroundings and the new surroundings adapt to Christianity. To put it another way, Christianity must penetrate into the kernel of Chinese culture, so that it can simultaneously Sinicize itself and Christianize China. This becomes more explicit and more agreeable in an era witnessing national consciousness and cultural awakening. If Christianity passes this test, it will flourish in China. If it fails, it will grow weak and finally perish in this land. The key to this religion's success lies in whether or not the Chinese Christianity has methods and a pool of talent that can provide proper guidance for this religion. The textual work is an important method, to which we Chinese Christians should pay much attention.

Zhao held that the textual work and the foundation and future of the Church were inseparably interconnected. That is to say, "Each paragraph of Christian text is woven in the context combining Christianity with the Chinese culture, then brought into full play and finally able to convey the meaning." Zhao mentioned that, in its early phase, Christianity grew strong due to the integration of Greek and Roman cultures. Later, new elements such as the Crusades, the Renaissance, the Reformation and the scientific revolution were added to this religion in its further development. Now in China, it was by means of the textual work that Christianity and the Chinese culture, consciously and automatically, assimilated each other.

Zhao argued that then the domestic situation of China was most suitable for the reconciliation of Christianity and Chinese culture, saying:

[Present-day China is witnessing its modern Renaissance (i.e., the New Culture Movement).] Under such circumstances, Christianity, on the one hand, is being severely criticized by the Condemning Christianity Movement; and on the other hand, is being culturally awakened to accept the Chinese tradition. Moreover, Christianity has realized that it is better

National Congress of Christianity in 1922   71

for itself to rehabilitate its propagation work, educational effort, social service, medical work and textual work and that by means of the intellectual penetration, it could relocate itself in the heart of Chinese life. Take the Christian textual work, for example. This work has laid an unprecedentedly extensive foundation of indigenization of Christianity in China ... If we miss this golden opportunity close at hand, I cannot find any excuses for our stupidity and stubbornness.

The above discussion was succeeded by a detailed proposal regarding what the Christian textual work should do. Zhao's six-point proposal was as follows:

First, the Chinese Christianity should publish essays and books advocating a new society, by which the standard of an ideal society and farsighted social movement can grow so strong that they are able to lead a new society to become true. All Chinese Christian texts should be orientated to present-day Chinese society, judge the true situation, and find feasible solutions to social problems ... The Chinese Christian texts should aspire to disseminate the social gospel, purify the people's mind, and reform the social environment[.] Second, the Christian Church should find a place in the cultural movement, [where] it trains talented people and invests them in studying the national essence for the movement and exploring the spiritual heritage and religious experience of the Chinese nation. Then, the Church should go further, having what it has discovered in the Chinese tradition and basic Christian doctrines fused into rich, beautiful elements of life, by which the Church will be able to carry forward the Chinese culture and lead Christianity to flourish in this land. Third, the Chinese Christian texts should immediately contribute to China's endeavour to rehabilitate declining morality by providing ethics, an outlook on life, a view of society and a world-view. Fourth, the Chinese Christian texts should play a significant role in refining human nature and feelings. Christian music, hymns, translations, public prayers, all of which should be correctly beautified. [The Church,] taking a look at the present-day cultural movement, should realize that literature and art really matter. Under the circumstances, the Chinese Christian texts should never focus exclusively on content, meanwhile paying no attention to form. In other words, if the writing of the Chinese Christian texts is poor and broken, it will be much less spiritually attractive. Fifth, the Chinese Christian texts should be more creative in developing Christian doctrines and theology ... The role that the Chinese Christian theological texts can play is twofold. First, they help the Chinese people to understand the profundity of Christian theology. Second, they create Chinese theological theories, through which the Chinese can incorporate their own philosophies and religious experience into established Christian doctrines. In doing so, the Chinese Church can be well-prepared to meet Chinese Christians' need to understand their religion. Sixth, the Christian texts and the free thinkers' texts should work cooperatively together ... As far as the life itself is concerned, it has multifarious aspects. For this reason, it is necessary for religion and [free thinkers'] scholarship to complement each other. For example, science and religion [are actually] not in conflict; and philosophy and religion [are in fact] closely interconnected ... We Chinese Christians should break all barriers [existing between Christianity and free thinkers' scholarship] and lead [both] to freely communicate with each other. We do believe that, by doing so, there will be brilliant achievements illuminating the history of culture.

If the above six points were all accomplished, the Chinese Christian text work would be fully indigenized.

But Zhao himself knew very well that his six-point proposal was merely theoretical and it would be really difficult to put it into effect. Therefore, he went further, pointing out the existing problems facing the Chinese Church and made some suggestions regarding how to solve these problems. First, although the number of talented people devoting themselves to the Christian textual work was very few, the Chinese Church should never be dependent on Westerners, whose ignorance of Chinese society determined that they could neither do excellent external work nor improve the work from within. In a word, the Chinese Church must find qualified Chinese candidates who could play a leading role in the textual work and it must be able to find, train and recruit more talented people and invest them in the work. Second, there should be a Chinese Christian literature department consisting exclusively of Chinese Christians. This department would be fully independent of official Christian associations, so that the disadvantages caused by barriers existing between the Christian leaders and the Chinese culture and spirit would be avoided. Third, economic factors should not be neglected in promoting the textual work. Specifically, people who specialized in this field and those who had funds should communicate and understand each other and in doing so, the textual work could be sufficiently funded. At this point, Zhao said:

> If the Chinese can raise enough money by themselves and carefully spend all the money developing the Chinese Christian culture, Christianity will have firmly established itself in this country and make itself very trustworthy. Thus, Western comrades would like to give substantial help to their Chinese counterparts. [And,] as soon as the Church becomes economically independent, the Chinese Christian literature department can be set up. The department will be the pivot of the entire Christian textual work.

The above three suggestions were actually feasible. Later, the creation of the Christian Literature Department corroborated this point.

Moreover, Wu Leichuan (i.e., Wu Zhenchun) and Wang Zhixin did an outstanding job in discussing the integration of Christianity and traditional

Chinese culture. Both did a series of studies of leading thinkers of ancient Chinese intellectual schools. Their achievements indicated that the Church was paying increasing attention to the Chinese culture in the course of indigenization.

Wu Leichuan held:

> In all cases, only when a popular religion, which is introduced from one place to another, mutually assimilates and accepts an indigenous culture will it continue to grow. [It thus can be concluded that the integration of Christianity and Confucianism epitomizing the Chinese culture is very important.] In present-day China, there are two popular world religions. One is Buddhism and the other is Christianity. If we do hope that the two religions can develop well in China, we must admit that both do need to blend into Confucianism.[91]

According to Wu, there were, at least, three similarities between the Christian canons and the Confucian classics. First, the creation of man that was recorded by Genesis in the Holy Bible and the beginning of *The Doctrine of the Mean* related the same thing. To be specific, the author of Genesis said: "And the Lord God formed man of the dust of the ground, and breathed into his nostrils the breath of life; and man became a living soul" (Genesis 2:7).[92] *The Doctrine of the Mean* began with the assertion that "[w]hat Heaven has conferred is called The Nature."[93] Zhu Xi (1130–1200), a renowned Confucian philosopher in the Southern Song, annotated this assertion, writing:

> "Ming" (conferment) is "ling" (order). "Xing" (Nature) is "li" (Principle). Heaven, by means of the *yin-yang* (positive and shaded) forces and Five (quintessential) Elements, creates the myriad things, among which there is the well-shaped *qi* (vital breath) and *li* (Principle). This course is precisely like the course of implementing order. As a result, the created human beings and matters all have their own properly-given principle and are all directed to smoothly conform with the correct virtues of the Five Elements. This is thus called Nature.

In this sense, both Genesis and *The Doctrine of the Mean* worked on the same question. As far as the difference existing between the two ancient texts was concerned, it merely referred to the discrepancy of two writing systems, which accorded with the early or late development of culture. Second, the "root of Jesse" predicting Christ (Isaiah 11:1–10)[94] coincided with the Confucian expectation of people in possession of all sagely qualities (*The Doctrine of the Mean*: Chapter 31). Third, the Holy Spirit mentioned by the Bible was similar to *ren* (benevolence), one of the key concepts embedded in the Confucian classics. Wu thus said: "What is called 'the Holy Spirit' in Christianity is exactly the Confucian *ren* (benevolence). In many cases, a comparative interpretation of the Holy Spirit in the New Testament and the *ren* of Confucian classics are viable."

After analysing these similarities, Wu concluded:

> First, there are a large number of realistic texts in Christian canons. Readers can grasp the spirit of these texts, so long as they can overcome the barrier created by the form of writing. Second, among Christian doctrines, some can be proven by Confucian classics, so that many superstitions handed down from the past will be dispelled. Third, not only can Christianity be disseminated in the circle of Confucian scholars but Confucianism itself can be carried forward [with the help of Christianity].[95]

In discussing whether or not Christianity and Confucianism could successfully fuse together, Wu laid stress on the dissimilarity between *jiao* (religion/teaching) and *dao* (the Way or grandest principle of a religion/teaching). He pointed out that the fusion of Christianity and Confucianism did not denote the integration of the two types of *jiao* but the blend of Christian and Confucian *dao*. Wu said:

> The is only one *dao* (the Way) in the entire universe. By contrast, there are innumerable *jiao* (religions). [Inasmuch as] *jiao* is always created out of the practice of *dao*, there are many man-made elements in *jiao* and particularly factors such as the time, locality, and human relationships are unavoidably incorporated into *jiao*. As a consequence, the true *dao* will be gradually masked. [Just like] the ritual system of Confucianism, which originally has heavenly regulations embodied in human affairs and leads people to abide by them, has no alternative but to face an embarrassing fact that, as time goes by, people have forgotten the refined meaning of rites and merely observe them in form. The ritual system itself is castigated in the end. In like manner, the Christian Church, a mechanism designed for propagating the true *dao* invented by Jesus, has to provide followers with formalistic belief, because it pays undue attention to personnel management and obstinately adheres to established dogmas and hermeneutic tradition. The Church is thus ridiculed for this mistake, which is compared to the story where one pays too dear for a glittering casket without any jewels. This is the disadvantage brought about by the excessive stress on *jiao* and undue ignorance of *dao*. [It should be pointed out that *jiao* is general and *dao* is not easily understandable for common Christians. In this world, most people live a mediocre life. Consequently, the *dao* developed by Confucius and Jesus is encumbered to such an extent that it has become unduly formalistic and less spiritual.] Even so, no matter how *jiao*, which is built on *dao*, grows weak and decadent, the base of *dao* will never be destroyed. Therefore, if Christians really want to save *jiao*, they can only resort to rehabilitating the true essence of *dao*.

The above discussion was followed by a comparative study of Christian and Confucian trustworthiness, sincerity, adherence to principles and benevolence. Wu held that the Christians' purest belief was centred on the personality of Jesus. He proved that wisdom, benevolence and bravery elaborated in *The Doctrine of the Mean* were consistent with the trustworthiness, expectation and love advocated by Christianity. For Wu, those who achieved all these virtues were perfect beings. Similarly, sincerity mentioned in *The Doctrine of the Mean* generally conformed to Christian discourses on God. In this regard, Wu explained:

> The general principle of Christianity is the love for God and man. The Way penetrating entire Confucianism lies in adherence to principles and benevolence. Obviously, there is a commonness in terms of the most basic tenet reigning over the creation of Christianity and Confucianism.[96]

Furthermore, Wu contended:

> Not only Christianity and Buddhism but also Christianity and Confucianism should integrate with each other. Metaphorically speaking, among three persons known as A, B and C, not only A makes friends with B and C but at the same time B and C also need to strike up a friendship with each other. Only when these three people all become friends will a solidarity group be created.

Wu quoted "Buddhist Sutra Reveals Strong and Weak Points of Christianity," written by Zhang Chunyi, who converted to Buddhism from Christianity, in its entirety. Zhang numerated 10 facts and 14 examples in this essay. He suggested Easterners should grasp the 10 facts, such as the discrepancy between the ancient Hebrew culture and its Chinese counterpart before doing a study of Christianity. Moreover, Zhang, illustrating 14 examples, argued that Christianity should rehabilitate itself by assimilating the valuable Eastern culture. For example,

> People should know that, all the while Jesus realizes that the epistemic foundation of Europeans and Americans is not well established, thus they cannot understand the profound Way of Buddhism and Daoism. Precisely for this reason, Jesus voluntarily chose to be born in the land of the Jews and was ready to turn the Wheel of Dharma for Westerners.

Zhang praised Buddhist doctrines and at the same time he criticized Christianity imported from the West. He pointed out that Westerners showed contempt for all Eastern buddhas, bodhisattvas and sages and treated them as nothing more than mortals and even strangled many true cultures in the East. Their Christianity was not true Christianity at all. For Zhang, the true Christianity was essentially consistent with Buddhism. It was preachers of Christianity who betrayed the grandest principle of true Christianity and turned Christianity into a foreign religion. At the end of his article, Zhang wrote:

> China proudly has the most complete religiousness. Now that we are Chinese and we attempt to find and disseminate *dao* (the Way or the grandest Principle) in China, it is better for us to grasp all religious essence contained in subtle philosophic theories of Confucian classics, such as *The Book of Changes*, *The Book of History*, *The Book of Poetry* and *The Book of Rites*, in Daoist thoughts elaborated by great thinkers such as Laozi, Wenzi, Zhuangzi and Liezi, in inward intellectual refinement performed by statesman-thinkers, such as Guanzi, and in legalist interpretations of Daoist thinking, such as Han Fei's treatises on Laozi. Besides, the universal love developed by Mozi was almost a precursor of Jesus's teaching and worthy of being carefully studied. After studying all these intellectual threads, the propagation of Christianity can be carried out. This course accords with what Paul said: "If thou, being a Jew, [should live] after the manner of [the Jews]" (Galatians 2:14).[97] But in present-day China, the Christian preachers are not at all like the Chinese but like foreigners instead. It is really a shame.

After introducing Zhang's article to his readers, Wu concluded: "Zhang's sharp-minded criticism of the Chinese Christianity is really a blow and a shout to wake Chinese Christians up from the mistakes they are committing." Moreover, he cited "Postscript to Anecdotes of *Vimalakirti Sutra*", authored by a Buddhist known as Li Jinxi, saying: "In the light of the author's explanation of Buddhist doctrines, we can draw a conclusion that the essence of Buddhism perfectly harmonizes with that of Christianity."[98] To sum up, Wu did his best to intellectually integrate Christianity with traditional Chinese culture by stressing the *dao* underpinning a common ground.

Wang Zhixin, adopting a method similar to that of Wu Leichuan, made a comparative study of Confucian *cheng* (sincerity) and Christian *ling* (spirit). His conclusion was as follows:

> *Cheng* (sincerity) set forth by neo-Confucian thinkers of the Song dynasty (960–1279) has very profound meanings. Not only does this concept completely illuminate the creation of the universe, but it also teaches people how to improve their morality in a concise way. *Cheng* is indeed similar to *dao* (the Way) of Christianity. If we are able to grasp the true meaning of "God is Spirit" by consulting one of the Confucian assertions that "the individual possessed of the most complete sincerity is like a spirit,"[99] we will understand more than half of the essence of the Christian *dao*.[100]

The above citation repeated Christianity's harmonization with Confucianism advocated by missionaries in favour of the indigenization of Christianity in

China. In addition, Wang inquired into Buddhism, explaining why he turned to the study of Buddhism. There were three general points in his explanation. First, next to the fact that Buddhism was renowned for its profound scholarship and abundance of academic writings, Christianity really paled in terms of the literature. Many academic celebrities had studied Buddhist teachings, meanwhile disdaining Christianity. Therefore, only when Christian scholars had a good command of Buddhist doctrines and highlighted the strong points of Christianity through a comparative study would free thinkers know the Christian religion well. Second, Buddhist thinking had been well established in the Chinese intellectual world and most Chinese people, directly or indirectly, believed in some Buddhist doctrines. The reason was that Buddhism had long been successfully Sinicized and intellectually approximated to the spirit of the new culture and science. Further Christian study of Buddhism would help Christianity gain a firm foothold in China. Third, since it was a time of open scholarship, Christianity should neither be parochial and sectarian nor aggrandize itself. Buddhism was a powerful rival of Christianity. In order to prevent Buddhism from overshadowing Christianity, Christian scholars must conduct an in-depth study of Buddhism and in doing so they would be able to counteract the Chinese intelligentsia favouring Buddhism.[101]

In light of the above discussions, we can conclude that the purpose of Wang's study of Buddhism was to help Christianity become more acceptable to Chinese society and the Chinese people. For him, if Chinese Christian scholars did not study Buddhism well, the propagation of Christianity would not be carried out smoothly. Explaining why he studied Buddhism, Wang pointed out that, although Christianity did meet the needs of converts, it needed some Buddhist materials to better itself and make itself more notable. In other words, Christianity manifested its strong points through a comparative study of Christianity and Buddhism. Even so, Wang candidly admitted that there were indeed Buddhist truths, to which Christianity could not turn a blind eye. For example, when Wang was discussing the Buddhist morality, he pointed out that there were both positive and passive elements. When it came to the Buddhist alms giving, he held that it was actually an element of charity and propagation (of religion). Wang particularly said the Buddhist endurance in practice was really worth being adopted as the Christians' model. Overall, his attitude towards traditional Chinese culture was similar to that to Buddhism.[102] In a word, Wang remained intellectually open to the traditional Chinese culture and Buddhism that had integrated itself into Chinese culture. Although Wang's aim was to make the strong points of Christianity more remarkable through a comparative study, he did further Chinese Christians' understanding and acceptance of traditional Chinese culture. This helped Christianity extricate itself from its bad reputation as "*yangjiao*" (a totally negative foreign religion).

The relationship between Christianity and patriotism was another popular topic. Liu Tingfang, responding to some free thinkers' criticism that Chinese Christians were unpatriotic, specially wrote an article.[103] He analyzed why people thought Chinese Christians did not love their country. Liu mentioned that, between Chinese Christians and Western missionaries there was an intimate connection, which inevitably impeded the growth of patriotic feeling of Chinese Christian converts. The reason for this intimacy was that some Chinese Christians gained benefits from Western missionaries and thus felt very grateful to the latter. But some argued instead that there were plenty of Chinese Christians who were intellectually independent of Westerners. They said:

> In the Church, [the intellectually independent] Chinese Christians never act as yes-men; nor are they afraid to confront Western missionaries. Not only do they hardly ever blindly follow the West but they also have the guts to stand up against [foreign missionaries]. When it comes to international issues, [the intellectually independent] Chinese Christians never make any concessions to Westerners. In dealing with matters related to China, they will, first of all, fulfil their duty as Chinese nationals. The number of such Chinese Christians is increasing with each passing day with the Church.

In the end, Liu concluded:

> Those critics say Chinese Christians are unpatriotic. Such criticism is insufficiently grounded, neither accurate, nor fair. [It should be pointed out that] among 360,000 Chinese Christian converts, there are a huge number of ardent patriots. We should never simplistically say those who are not strongly interested in state affairs are unpatriotic. In actuality, the number of Christians who do not love the country is very small.

Of course, Liu admitted that, because the patriotic feeling was closely related to people's level of knowledge and degree of education, some Chinese Christians were indeed poorly educated when considering their complicated background. For the country's future, the quality of these poorly educated Christians must be improved. At the end of his article, Liu placed emphasis on the indigenization of the Christian Church in China. He stated:

> It is inevitable that Chinese Christians will be denounced as unpatriotic in a Church ruled by foreigners. In order to avoid being treated unjustly, Chinese Christians must create the Church owned by the Chinese themselves. [Such a] Church must be truly Sinicized, so that, on the one hand, Chinese Christian converts could develop a pure personality, holding fast to the most basic Christian doctrines and, on the other hand, they will not live a life that is neither Western nor Chinese but sociopathic. [It is recommended that Christianity should], in the light of the Chinese culture and advantages of Western culture, bring into play again Christ's most basic ideas respecting the handling of national questions. In doing so, Christianity leads the entirety of Chinese converts to love their country and compatriots in accordance with the true spirit of Christ.

Herein lies the Chinese Church's bounden duty to reform [the established Christianity]. Only when this duty is fulfilled, will the Church be truly indigenized.

To put it another way, according to Liu, only indigenization could protect Christianity from being condemned by free thinkers. In like manner, only indigenization could lead Chinese Christians to develop an independent personality. The ultimate goal of indigenization was to guide all Chinese Christian converts to love their country and love their people.

Some argued against the idea that Chinese Christians should not talk about the love for their country because Christianity advocated the great harmony of the entire world, which prevailed among some Christian communities,[104] saying:

It is a huge mistake. God's decree is that loving the country wherein we are living is our bounden duty. Loving one's own country never means the resentment of others' countries. Such a love is congruous with the Christian harmony of the world.[105]

Agreeing with this, Zhao Zichen echoed:

Those who do not love their own countries but love the world are ignorant and presumptuous. What they say is nonsense. Those who love their own countries in a narrow-minded way and treat other countries and their cultures as worthless straw dogs are despicable and pernicious. What they say is destructive.[106]

Some discussed how to carry out the Christian national salvation. Compared to the discussions conducted in the May Fourth era, these were more feasible. Some said:

At present, China needs a powerful national group supervising the central government and putting into effect the people's demands and expectations. [To be specific,] on the one hand, such a group urges the government to implement [programmes]; on the other hand, it tries its utmost to lead the people to improve themselves to such an extent that they have the ability and knowledge to participate in politics. If this is done, almost all the problems will be solved gradually.

This was a golden opportunity for Christianity, which should actually assume such a great responsibility.[107] Some advocated the idea that patriotism should start with the individual. Wu Yaozong, for instance, said:

[The most basic duty of a citizen was not to supervise or urge the government] but, above all, to focus on her or his own work, into which the person should throw her/himself according to the most virtuous principles. At the same time, the person should treat the life of the country as something indispensable to her or his own life and sincerely pay close attention to the sufferings of the country and everything taking place in the country. [In order to do this, there must be citizenship education.] With citizenship education, even though we do not convene the national congress, true popular patriotic activities will be naturally carried out. Neither is the national salvation a burst of enthusiasm nor can it be fulfilled by merely following the procession, waving flags and shouting slogans. Saving the nation is no more than the common things done by ordinary citizens at the normal time.[108]

Some proposed concrete methods of implementing patriotism from the perspective of Christian groups. For example, Fan Bihai set forth three points respecting the tasks of the YMCA. The first was universal fraternity, which stressed that associations for young Christians should serve society and help the country in crisis. The second was Christian egalitarianism, which emphasized that Christianity was not a religion of capitalists, on the grounds that Jesus himself was a worker. Therefore, associations for young Christians should serve the ordinary people by setting up educational institutions, such as half-day and night schools. The third was patriotism, which should be revived by young Christians. As far as patriotism was concerned, it was, according to Fan, the global harmony advocated by Jesus, who actually had an ardent love for his country. Precisely for this reason, Fan suggested:

> The patriotic work should be used to guide the young people. Neither are young Chinese Christians redolent with odours of political factions; nor are they partial to any political parties; nor are they obsessed with politics. But they are eager to cultivate the pure, strong patriotic feelings in their hearts. That is to say, these young souls want to develop love for their country in their moral, academic, physical and communal education. Patriotism developed in this way is substantial and reliable. These young Christians' love for their country is not the love in spoken or written words only; but instead, it is from the heart and has been translated into quiet, hard work.[109]

Some enlightened Chinese Christians, encouraged by the patriotic spirit, questioned and argued against the extraterritoriality grabbed by foreign missionaries and their societies. This intellectual campaign against (foreign missionary societies') extraterritoriality was triggered by the Lincheng Incident that occurred in May 1923 in Shandong. At that time, there were rumours that missionaries had been kidnapped by bandits. The missionary societies availed themselves of this opportunity to ask their governing regimes to increase their military presence in China and send soldiers to the Church on the pretext of protecting life and property. These missionaries claimed that nothing except extraterritoriality could provide them with protection.[110] The

Washington regime planned to send armed forces to suppress the bandits at the behest of the foreign missionaries in China. This aroused intense discontent among patriotic Chinese Christians, one of whom was Chen Guoling. Chen, in his article epitomizing this discontent, pointed out:

> In this day, when the indigenization of the Christian Church in China is being enthusiastically promoted, the handling of the issue [of extraterritoriality] will exert a tremendous influence on the future. The correct solution lies in consulting primarily the opinion of the Chinese Christians. [Since] the outbreak of the Boxer Uprising, Westerners [and Western missionaries in particular] have become increasingly powerful. It is not unusual for some Christians in China to take advantage of foreign missionary societies' power to bully local residents. In most cases, the local authorities have given unprincipled protection to missionaries and their underlings due to the fear of foreign powers. Even those missionaries, who did not behave that badly, are often out of line. With the lapse of time, missionaries have changed into a privileged higher caste in Chinese society. The missionary caste is even more privileged than the Manchu aristocrats in the Qing dynasty that no longer exists. Some envy it. Some resent it. Is it a blessing for the Church in China? [Observers, rethinking the situation in which the Washington regime is attempting to send troops to China merely because of a conflict involving a few missionaries and local bandits, may have the guts to point out that] it is so ridiculous that China will be deprived of its sovereignty at the behest of a handful of foreign missionaries! [We have to say] Western missionaries having an unduly privileged position in Chinese society is against normal practice. If things continue this way, missionaries, using foreign forces far superior to China, easily pose a threat to the peace of the state. This brings shame to the sacred mission of propagating Christianity and exerts a pernicious influence on China, Chinese society and the Chinese people. [At this point, we should cry:] "Where are you, the fair, just treaties?"[111]

The above words perfectly voiced patriotic Chinese Christians' strong desire to abrogate unequal treaties.

Precisely inspired by the patriotic spirit, some suggested Chinese Christians should be enthusiastic about society and politics. Not only was this enthusiasm, as they pointed out, required by the basic Christian doctrines, but it also directly mattered to whether or not the Chinese Church could survive. Luo Yunyan, for instance, held that Christianity was not merely such a realm, in which individuals could do nothing except their personal spiritual cultivation, but an institution directly serving society, on the grounds that the individual and society were inseparable. Thus, he said:

> If society is trapped in bad practices, all individuals will be seriously affected. Therefore, Christianity should, first of all, reform society and

in doing so it lays the foundation of the work of building a paradise on Earth. [At present,] the life and efficiency of Christianity depend on whether or not it is able to meet what China now needs most. Will Christianity survive in China? Will this religion perish here? The answer depends fully on whether or not Christianity can provide the country with a large number of talented Christians who truly love their country, remain loyal to their country, serve their country and even sacrifice themselves for their country.[112]

The unity of all Christian churches in China was a hot topic at that time. In 1923, a theological conference was held at the Nanjing-based Jinling Seminary. The seventh panel of this conference focused on the unity of Chinese churches. There was a heated debate on this issue. An article penned by Jiong is worthy of mention here.[113] First, Jiang discussed both the necessity and unnecessariness of Christian sectarianism from the perspectives of faith, ecclesiastic administration and geography. His conclusion was that sectarianism was completely unnecessary. Second, Luo analyzed what prevented the unity of church. The first obstacle was Westerners themselves. It would not be very difficult for the Chinese Church to unite various Christian sects. But it was really hard for Western missionary societies of all shades to abandon their hereditary sectarianism and entrenched discrimination against (non-Western) other countries. For Western missionary societies, "There are not only sectarian strains but also inter-state competition. Western missionaries are responsible for the mixture of unnecessary beliefs and parochial nationalism in the Chinese Church."[114]

The second obstacle was the minister. In practice, the vast majority of ordinary Christian converts were in favour of the unity of the Church; but in contrast to them, most ministers turned a cold shoulder on unity, because they regarded this issue in the light of their own power, position and turf rather than of the teachings of the Bible. In the circumstances when the Church was still ruled by these ministers, how could the Church be truly united? Even so, Jiong proposed a three-point solution. First, unity could be achieved by creating a ritual system in accordance with the principle of freedom. In other words, the Church did not expect a highly uniform system regarding religious ceremonies. For example, the Christian ceremony of baptism could be freely made according to local conditions. Nanjing's Christian Centre was another example. Some said the Centre followed the example of Buddhist institutions in adapting itself to the Chinese psychology and arousing converts' religious piety. But at the same time, some were opposed to the Nanjing praxis. Jiong personally held that Christians could accept it, as well as rejecting it. For those who turned it down, there was no need to prevent others from following it. If Christian sects were all truly tolerant towards one another, the issue of a ritual system would not be an impediment to the unity of the Church. Therefore, it was not necessary for a united Church to formulate a uniform ritual system. Rather, the Church should let this be wide open to Christians themselves. Second, the unity could be fulfilled by cooperation. Specifically,

> First, the role that National Christian Council of China (NCCC) plays in the Christian mission should be accorded great importance. We should always bear in mind that the NCCC is an organization serving the mission but not a megachurch. The task of the NCCC is that it should attempt to unite all Christian churches in China. The NCCC should manage to apply a uniform name to all churches, such as Christian Church, and at the same time persuade churches to abandon their sectarian titles. Moreover, the NCCC should, regardless of their sectarian origins, select members and delegates in strict accordance with their true abilities. Otherwise, the sectarian barrier can never be removed. Second, churches should make a concerted effort to propagate Christianity nationwide. The best practice of unity of the Church is the domestic propagation of Christianity. [But it should be pointed out that some Western missionary societies—the Methodist Episcopal Church, for instance—do not act cooperatively but use their own title instead in the Northeast. Consequently], the pure land of the Northeastern provinces of China is tainted by Western Christian sectarianism. [In view of this], we must uphold the idea that the concerted effort made by churches in propagating Christianity in China is exactly the foundation of the unity of the Church. Third, all Christian schools should be run jointly by different churches. [One decade ago, many sneered at] Jinling Seminary [because it gathered together many students from different churches. But by now, all parties have recognized the Jinling praxis, on the grounds that] the numbers of students studying there and member churches joining the seminary have multiplied several times. [So far, this mode has been followed by a number of Christian schools in Nanjing.] Other provinces have made remarkable achievements in promoting an integrated Christian education, too. As far as Jinling Seminary is concerned, the student body is known for its diverse sectarian origin. Despite this, young students, studying together in the same school for years, develop a solid friendship that is definitely conducive to the unity of the Church.

Fourth, unity could come true if the Chinese Church accomplished economic independence. The unity of the Chinese Church must be based on economic independence. Just like Buddhist monasteries, which had their own estates and other properties, Christian churches in China must have their own funds to meet their own self-supporting needs. Overall, Jiong's article shone a light on the relationship between the Church's unity and indigenization by combining ecclesiastical unity with multiple issues such as the religious ritual system, the propagation of Christianity, the NCCC, Christian education and the Church's economic independence.

In addition to the above issues, the Chinese Church then started to pay special attention to the propagation of Christianity in China's countryside, because it had realized that the vast majority of the Chinese population and the "genuine China" were actually not found in large cities but in the countryside. For this reason, the NCCC made a positive effort to develop Christianity in the rural areas.[115] The Chinese Christianity (i.e., Protestantism) distinguished itself from Catholicism, which conducted its work mainly in the countryside, in focusing on the urban area. Now, the situation changed due to the ongoing indigenization of Christianity in China. As a consequence, the Chinese Church understood the importance of the rural church in the country, realizing:

> The Chinese cultural spirit lasting for thousands of years actually nestles in the countryside. It is the reason why in ancient times there were laws prioritizing agriculture over commerce. In present-day China, there are one million villages, in which land is generally owned by the peasants. China has three hundred million peasants, who make up three-quarters of the entire population. This reality is so well established that it cannot be ignored.[116]

Therefore, the NCCC set up a standing committee devoting itself to rural churches and peasant life. The committee dispatched cadres to provinces such as Guangdong, Sichuan, Hubei, Jiangxi, Zhejiang, Shandong and Zhili (present-day Hebei), where they made an inspection tour in various villages and tried their best to improve local churches. According to *Annals of the Chinese Christian Church*, published in 1925, the committee produced a series of reports, which included Chinese ones such as *The Rural Church and the Indigenization of Christianity*, *Rural Christian Movement*, *Churches in Chinese Countryside* (volume one) and *The Committee Bulletin and Five Suggestions*, and English ones, such as *The Church and the Agricultural Experiments*, *The Church and Peasants' Life* and *The First Step of Christian Occupation of the Chinese Countryside*.[117] The committee's concrete suggestions regarding the development of the rural church were as follows:

> First, rural churches and schools affiliated to them must serve the countryside. Second, rural churches should recruit volunteers for the Christian mission and encourage them to work more enthusiastically. Third, seminaries and Bible schools must make an effort to train people working for the rural churches. Fourth, the churches must launch a public health campaign in rural areas.[118]

In addition, the Christian Education Society specially set up a department of rural education. Quite a few associated agencies of the Christian Church founded special groups studying the rural propagation of Christianity and many church-run newspapers and magazines published articles intensively discussing the reconstruction of rural churches and how to improve the propagation of Christianity in the countryside. Some renowned journals, such as *The Life*, *The Christian Occupation of China*, and *The Chinese Recorder and Missionary Journal*, published special issues reporting on the rural churches. Associations for young Christians set out to study how to develop Christianity among the rural youth. The Chinese Church suggested that, in the rural Christian movement, there were five matters needing attention:

> First, the biggest task of the mission propagating Christianity in China is the fulfilment of the Christian occupation of the Chinese countryside and it is not yet complete. Second, Christian preachers working in the countryside must fully adapt themselves to rural conditions and they must be specially trained to be able to meet the needs of the peasants. Third, from the word go, rural churches must be independent, self-supporting and fully indigenized. Fourth, rural churches must help peasants acquire literacy, by which peasants will be able to read the Bible and improve their common sense. Fifth, rural churches must find ways to gradually improve the peasants' everyday life, on the grounds that only when life is stable and prosperous will people be willing to refine their spiritual life.[119]

These five points were precisely the foundation of the indigenization of the rural Christian churches. Moreover, many articles made specific analyses of the status quo of the rural churches and proposed programmes to improve the rural Christian institutions. You Shuxun did an excellent job in this field.[120] First, his article examined the true situation of the Chinese countryside, particularly mentioning the strong and weak points of the rural residents. Then, it suggested those who were propagating Christianity in the countryside should adopt measures to suit the local conditions, such as disseminating Christian doctrines through seven methods based on individuals, families, the temple fair, waterway, texts, shadow figures and random choices. Moreover, You advocated that Christian social work should consist of popular speeches, mass education, agricultural knowledge, public undertakings, medical care, disaster relief, poverty reduction, local councils and community clubs. He also mentioned things, to which Christian preachers working in the countryside should pay attention. For example, he suggested that, when preachers were spreading Christianity, they should use popular language, tell vivid stories, lecture on ethical lessons, preach auspicious gospels, pay close attention to local customs, speak cautiously, and gain insight into popular religious psychology. In addition, You talked about the proper attitude that Christians should assume towards rural residents' practice in which they ask supernatural beings to perform healing and exorcism and pray that Heaven would bless them with good weather for the crops. When it came to *jiaoan* (disputes involving local residents and foreign missionaries), You made a fair, objective observation. His article ended by discussing how to train people for the propagation of

Christianity in the countryside. Overall, You's article was full of rich content and made very practical suggestions suitable for the rural reality. It should be pointed out that there were actually a batch of articles with similar themes, which did make a contribution to the development of the rural church. Last but not least, inasmuch as rural churches had the closest relationship with indigenization, they, in turn, forced the Chinese Church to be indigenized in the course of indigenizing themselves.

In brief, comparatively speaking, the theoretico-practical exploration of indigenization of Christianity in China in the MFM and the NCM was outstripped by that done in this period in terms of breadth and depth. Chinese Christians' critiques of the Church's education, extraterritoriality, and quality of Christian converts actually constituted free thinkers' criticism of Christianity in the next stage of the Condemning Christianity Movement. This indicated that people of good sense within the Church had perceived the problems existing in this institution. At the same time, the ongoing social movement criticizing Christianity compelled the Church and Chinese Christians to more deeply understand these problems and take action to correct them.

Notes

1. Chen Hongjun 陈鸿钧, "The 1922 National Congress of Christianity" (民国十一年基督教全国大会), *Annals of the Chinese Christian Church*, No. 7 (1924), 62.
2. Anon. "Issues Concerning the National Congress of Christianity" (基督教全国大会的个问题), *Progress of the Youth*, No. 52 (April 1922), 59.
3. Anon. "Special Issue Devoted to the National Congress of Christianity" (大会报告号), *The Christian Occupation of China* (中华归主), No. 23 (10 June 1922), 7.
4. Ibid.
5. Anon. "Issues Concerning the National Congress of Christianity," op. cit., 59.
6. See: Anon. *The Christian Occupation of China*, No, 18 (10 January 1922), 2.
7. Cheng Jingyi 成静怡, "The Chinese Christian Church" (中国的教会), *Progress of the Youth*, No. 52 (April 1922), 25.
8. Liu Tingfang, "The National Congress of Christianity" (基督教全国大会), *The Life Monthly*, Vol. 2, No. 3 (October 1921), 1.
9. Ibid., 2.
10. Ibid.
11. Ibid.
12. See: *The Christian Occupation of China*, No. 18 (10 January 1922), 3.
13. Cheng Jingyi, "The Chinese Christian Church," op. cit., 17.
14. Ibid., 18.
15. Jian Youwen, Part One of "The National Church", *Progress of the Youth*, No. 52 (April 1922), 41–44.
16. For a detailed discussion, see: Tianxie 天协, "The Development of Sinicized Christianity" (中国化基督教的发展), *Progress of the Youth*, No. 52 (April 1922), 49–51.
17. *Lunyu*, or *The Confucian Analects*, trans. James Legge, available at: https://ctext.org/analects/shu-er/ens.

18 For Xingwu's detailed discussion, see: Xingwu 惺吾 (i.e., Jia Yuming贾玉铭), "The Present-Day Chinese Christian Church" (今日之中华基督教会), *Theological Review* (神学志), Vol. 8, No. 1 (Spring, 1922), 23–25.
19 For Shen's detailed discussion, see: Shen Sizhuang 沈嗣庄, "Three Manifestos" (宣言三种), *Theological Review*, Vol. 8, No. 1 (Spring, 1922), 57–59.
20 For Zhenru's detailed discussion, see: Zhenru 真如, "Four Suggestions Respecting the Chinese Christian Church in the Future" (关于明日教会的四个建议), *Theological Review*, Vol. 8, No. 1 (Spring, 1922), 33–48.
21 See: Gu Ziren 顾子仁, "My Attitudes towards the National Congress of Christianity" (我对于基督教全国大会的观念), *Theological Review*, Vol. 8, No. 1 (Spring, 1922), 12–21.
22 For a detailed discussion, see: Peng Changlin 彭长琳, "Discussions Concerning Leadership of the Chinese Christian Church" (教会领袖问题的讨论), *Theological Review*, Vol. 8, No. 1 (Spring, 1922), 90–97.
23 Ibid., 98.
24 See: Luo Zhang 罗章, "The Future Leadership of the Chinese Christian Church" (将来之领袖), *Theological Review*, Vol. 8, No. 1 (Spring, 1922), 98.
25 See: Peng Changlin, "Discussions Concerning the Leadership of Chinese Christian Church," op. cit., 97.
26 Liu Nanshan 刘南山, "Discussions Concerning the Leadership of Chinese Christian Church" (教会领袖问题的讨论), *Theological Review*, Vol. 8, No. 1 (Spring, 1922), 100–101.
27 Situ Leideng 司徒雷登 (John Leighton Stuart), "The Independence of the Chinese Christian Church" (中国教会的自立), *Progress of the Youth*, No. 52 (April 1922), 45–48.
28 Zhao Zichen 赵紫宸, "Advantages and Disadvantages of the Chinese Christian Church" (中国教会的强点与弱点), *The Life Monthly*, Vol. 3, No. 5 (January 1923), "Treatises" (著论), 1–8.
29 Quoted in Xu Zuhuan 许祖焕, "How to Set up an Indigenized Chinese Church?" (如何创造中国本色的教会), *Theological Review*, Vol. 10, No. 4 (1924), 95.
30 Liu Tingfang 刘廷芳, "The Chinese Christian Church" (中国的基督教), *The Life Monthly*, Vol. 2, Nos. 9–10 (June 1922), 1–10.
31 Quoted in Xu Zuhuan, "How to Set up An Indigenized Chinese Church?", op. cit., 95.
32 Yi Wensi 易文思 (Robert K. Evans), "What Is the Proper Attitude of Western Missionaries towards the Chinese Church?" (西宣教士对于中国的基督教会应取的态度), *The Life Monthly*, Vol. 2, Nos. 9–10 (June 1922), 1–7.
33 Liu Tingfang ed., *Discussions on the Chinese Christian Church* [中国教会问题讨论] (Shanghai: National Publication Centre of the YMCA 中华基督教青年会全国协会书报部, 1922), 14–16.
34 Shao Yuming 邵玉铭 ed., *The Chinese Christianity in the Twentieth-Century China* [二十世纪中国基督教问题] (Taibei, Taiwan: Cheng Chung Group, 1980), 519–520.
35 Ibid., 523.
36 Fan Yurong 范玉荣, "The National Christian Council of China" (中华全国基督教协进会), *The Young Women* (女青年报) (December 1922), 11–12.
37 See: *The Christian Occupation of China*, No. 23 (10 June 1922), 3.
38 Chen Hongjun 陈鸿钧, "The 1922 National Congress of Christianity," *Annals of the Chinese Christian Church*, Vol. 7 (1924), 63.

39. Quan Shaowu 全绍武, "What Is the National Christian Council of China?" (甚么是中华全国基督教协进会), *Annals of the Chinese Christian Church*, Vol. 7 (1924), 66.
40. Ibid.
41. Wang Zhixin 王治心, "The National Congress of Christianity and Its Follow-up" (聚过基督教全国大会以后), *Theological Review*, Vol. 8, No. 2 (Summer, 1922), 1–8.
42. Zhang Junjun 张君俊, "An Appraisal of the National Congress of Christianity" (评基督教全国大会), *The Life Monthly*, Vol. 2, Nos. 9–10 (June 1922), 3–5.
43. Wang Zhixin, "The National Congress of Christianity and Its Follow-up," op. cit.. 6.
44. Ibid., 4–5.
45. For a detailed discussion of the CICC, see Li Zeling 李则灵, "Review of the National Christian Council of China's Three-Year Work since Its Founding" (中华全国基督教协进会三年以来之回顾), *Annals of the Chinese Christian Church*, Vol. 8 (1925), 98–99.
46. Wang Zhixin, "The Journal's Contribution to the Propagation of Christianity" (本志对于传道部的贡献), *Theological Review*, Vol. 8, No. 4 (Winter, 1922), 3.
47. Anon. "Editorial for Debut Edition of *Truth Weekly*" (《真理周刊》发刊词), *Truth Weekly* (真理周刊), No. 1 (April 1923), 1.
48. Quoted in Wang Zhixin, *A Historical Sketch of Chinese Christianity* [中国基督教史纲] (Hong Kong: Chinese Christian Literature Council, 1993), 274.
49. Quoted in Xu Zuhuan, "How to Set up an Indigenized Chinese Church?", *Theological Review*, Vol. 10, No. 4 (1924), 95.
50. Zhao Zichen, "An Open Discussion of the Indigenized Church" (本色教会的商榷), *Progress of the Youth*, No. 76 (October 1924), 8–9.
51. Ibid., 9–10.
52. Quoted in Xu Zuhuan, "How to Set up an Indigenized Chinese Church?", op. cit., 97.
53. Ibid., 95–97.
54. Xiao Xuan 萧暄, "The Indigenized Christianity" (中国化的基督教), *The Life Monthly*, Vol. 3, No. 5 (January 1923), 1–3.
55. Wu Zhenchun 吴震春, "What Does Lie Ahead of Chinese Church?" (论中国基督教会的前途), *Truth Weekly*, No. 11 (10 June 1923), 2.
56. For the detailed discussion, see: Wu Yaozong 吴耀宗, "What Should Chinese Christian Students do?" (中国的基督教学生应当作什么), *Truth Weekly*, no. 10 (3 June 1923), 1.
57. For the detailed discussion, see: Wu Leichuan 吴雷川, "My Suggestions Regarding the Reform of Church-Run Schools" (对于教会中学校改良的我见), *Truth Weekly*, no. 16 (15 July 1923), 1.
58. Luo Xigu 罗锡嘏, "How to Make Academic Theology More Socially Practicable?" (如何应用书本上神学到社会上), *Theological Review*, Vol. 9, No. 1 (Spring, 1923), 11–12.
59. Ibid., 12.
60. Ibid., 11.
61. Ibid., 16–17.
62. Shen Yalun 沈亚伦, "How to Make Academic Theology More Socially Practicable?" (如何应用书本上神学到社会上), *Theological Review*, Vol. 9, No. 1 (Spring, 1923), 23.

63 Quoted in "Discussions of Liturgical Ceremony" (关于礼拜仪式的讨论), *Theological Review*, Vol. 9, No. 2 (Summer, 1923), 168.
64 Bao Guanglin 宝广林, "Will the Status Quo of Chinese Students Association for Christian Propagation Meet the Needs of the Future?" (中华学生立志传道团的现状是否适合于将来的要求), *The Life Monthly*, Vol. 3, no. 5 (January 1923), 1.
65 Zhang Qinshi, "What Should the Beijing Church Do?" (北京教会当作什么), Truth Weekly, no. 9 (27 May 1923), 1.
66 Xiao Muxian 萧慕先, "What Does the Present-Day Church Desperately Need?" (教会今日的急需), *The Life Monthly*, Vol. 3, no. 5 (January 1923), 3.
67 Jian Youwen 简又文, "Tri-Benefit Society and Christianity" (三益会与基督教), *The Life Monthly*, Vol. 4, no. 6 (February 1924), 1–17.
68 Liu Tingfang 刘廷芳, "Tri-Benefit Society and the Chinese Church's Self-Support" (三益会和教会自养), *The Life Monthly*, Vol. 4, no. 6 (February 1924), 1–3.
69 Peng Jinzhang 彭锦章, "Opinions Respecting the Transformation of Missionary Societies into Independent Churches" (对于差会改建为自立会的意见), Truth Weekly, no. 7 (13 May 1923), 1–2.
70 Peng Jinzhang, "A Sequel to 'Opinions Respecting Transformation of Missionary Societies into Independent Churches'" (对于差会改建为自立会的意见（续）), Truth Weekly, no. 8 (20 May 1923), 1.
71 Bao Guanglin, "Will the Status Quo of Chinese Students Association for Christian Propagation Meet the Needs of the Future?", op. cit., 1.
72 Quoted in Xu Zuhuan, "How to Set up an Indigenized Chinese Church?", *Theological Review*, Vol. 10, no. 4 (1924), 96.
73 Zhao Zichen, "An Open Discussion of the Indigenized Church," *Progress of the Youth*, no. 76 (October 1924), 11.
74 Ibid., 12.
75 Liu Tingfang, "The Issue of Christian Preachers" (宣教师的问题), *The Life Monthly*, Vol. 3, no. 3 (November 1922), 1.
76 Ibid.
77 Xinwu 心悟, "My Humble Opinion about the Church's Management of Talented People" (对于教会用人才的我见), Truth Weekly, no. 9 (27 May 1923), 3.
78 Bao Zheqing 鲍哲庆, "Priests and Their Churches" (牧师与其教会), *The Life Monthly*, Vol. 3, no. 5 (January 1923), 1–2.
79 Liu Tingfang, "The Issue of Christian Preachers,", *The Life Monthly*, Vol. 3, no. 3 (November 1922), 2.
80 Zhao Zichen, "Christian Preachers and Truth" (宣教师与真理), *The Life Monthly*, Vol. 3, no. 3 (November 1922), 7–8.
81 Zhao Zichen, "What Kind of Religion Do We Need?" (我们要什么样的宗教), *The Life Monthly*, vol. 3, no. 9 (1923), 1.
82 Zhao Zichen, "Christian Preachers and Truth", op. cit., 10.
83 Ibid., 14.
84 Ibid., 17.
85 Ibid., 18.
86 Peng Changlin, "How to Improve Chinese Christian Textual Work?" (中国基督教文字事业当如何改进？), *The Life Monthly*, Vol. 3, no. 2 (October 1922), 4–5.
87 Zeng Yugen 曾郁根, "The Textual Work of Chinese Christianity" (中国基督教文字事业的问题), *The Life Monthly*, Vol. 4, nos. 9–10 (July 1924), 9.
88 Ibid., 10–12.

89 Xu Guangdi 许光迪, "The Question about Chinese Christian Textual Work" (中国基督教文字事业的问题), *The Life Monthly*, Vol. 3, no. 2 (October 1922), 11.
90 Zhao Zichen, "The Future of Christian Textual Work" (基督教文字事业的前途), *Rejuvenating China* (兴华报), Special Issue Commemorating the Twentieth Anniversary of Publication (特刊》（20周年纪念）) [January 1924], 112–118.
91 Wu Zhenchun 吴震春 (i.e., Wu Leichuan 吴雷川), "Christianity and Confucianism" (论基督教与儒教), *Truth Weekly*, no. 43 (20 January 1924), 1.
92 See: *King James Bible*, available at: www.kingjamesbibleonline.org/Genesis-Chapter-2/#7.
93 *Liji*, or *The Book of Rites*, trans. James Legge, available at: https://ctext.org/liji/zhong-yong/ens.
94 See: *King James Bible*, available at: www.kingjamesbibleonline.org/Isaiah-Chapter-11/.
95 Wu Leichuan, "Christian Canons and Confucian Classics" (基督教经与儒教经), *The Life Monthly*, Vol. 3, no. 6 (March 1923), 1–6.
96 Wu Zhenchun (i.e., Wu Leichun), "Christianity and Confucianism," op. cit., 1–2.
97 See: *King James Bible*, available at: www.kingjamesbibleonline.org/Galatians-Chapter-2/#14.
98 Wu Zhenchun (i.e., Wu Leichuan), "What Lies Ahead of Christianity and Buddhism" (论基督教与佛教将来的趋势), *Truth Weekly*, no. 44 (27 January 1924), 1–3.
99 *Liji*, or *The Book of Rites*, trans. James Legge, available at: https://ctext.org/liji/zhong-yong/ens.
100 Wang Zhixin, "Christian Spirit and Neo-Confucian Sincerity" (中国理学家所言之"诚"与基督教所言之"灵"), *Theological Review*, Vol. 9, no. 3 (Autumn, 1923), 8–15.
101 Wang Zhixin, "Christianity and Buddhist Study" (基督教与佛学), *Theological Review*, Vol. 9, no. 2 (Summer, 1923), 69–86.
102 Ibid., 86–100.
103 Liu Tingfang, "A General Discussion of Chinese Christian Patriotism" (中国基督徒爱国问题平议), *The Life Monthly*, Vol. 4, nos. 9–10 (June 1924), 1–8.
104 See: Fan Bihai (范皕海), "The Mission of China Young Christians Association at Present" (中华基督教青年会今日的使命), *Progress of the Youth*, no. 55 (July 1922), 91–92.
105 Ibid.
106 Zhao Zichen, "The Question of Nationality among Chinese Christians" (中华基督教的国籍问题), *Progress of the Youth*, no. 73 (May 1924), 15.
107 Hu Xuecheng 胡学诚, "The Consciousness We Should Have in Perceiving State Affairs" (我们今后对于国事应有的觉悟), *Truth Weekly*, no. 46 (10 February 1924), 1.
108 Wu Yaozong, "The Chinese Nationals' Duty" (国民的责任), *Truth Weekly*, no. 46 (10 February 1924), 1.
109 Fan Bihai, "The Mission of China Young Christians Association at Present," op. cit., 92–93.
110 Lu Boheng 陆伯衡, "Foreign Christian Preachers of Missionary Societies and Extraterritoriality" (外国差会的宣教师与治外法权), *The Anglican Church News* (圣公会报), Vol. 16, nos. 23–24 (October 1923), 16.
111 Chen Guoliang 陈国梁, "Missionaries and Extraterritoriality" (传教士与治外法权), *Truth Weekly*, no. 35 (25 November 1923), 1.

112 Luo Yunyan 罗运炎, "Christianity and Politics" (基督教与政治), *The Life Monthly*, Vol. 3, no. 3 (December 1922), 4.
113 Jiong 炯, "The Unity of the Church" (教会之统一), *Theological Review*, Vol. 9, no. 1 (Spring, 1923), 45–57.
114 Ibid., 47.
115 Quan Shaowu, "What Is the National Christian Council of China?", *Annals of the Chinese Christian Church*, Vol. 7 (1924), 65.
116 Zhong Ketuo, "Chinese Christian Churches: A Survey," *Annals of the Chinese Christian Church*, Vol. 8 (1925), 14.
117 Li Zeling, "Review of National Christian Council of China's Three-Year Work since Its Founding", *Annals of the Chinese Christian Church*, Vol. 8 (1925), 93.
118 Ibid.
119 Zhong Ketuo, "Chinese Christian Churches: A Survey," *Annals of the Chinese Christian Church*, Vol. 8 (1925), 14.
120 You Shuxun 尤树勋, "*The Rural Work of Propagating Christianity* (乡村布道谈), *Theological Review*, Vol. 10, no. 1 (Spring, 1924), 53–67.

Bibliography

Anon. *The Christian Occupation of China* (中华归主). No. 18 (10 January 1922).
Anon. "Issues Concerning the National Congress of Christianity" (基督教全国大会的个问题), *Progress of the Youth* (青年进步). No. 52 (April 1922).
Anon. "Special Issue Devoted to the National Congress of Christianity" (大会报告号). The Christian Occupation of China (中华归主). No. 23 (10 June 1922).
Anon. "Editorial for Debut Edition of *Truth Weekly*" (真理周刊》发刊词). *Truth Weekly* (真理周刊). No. 1 (April 1923).
Anon. "Discussions of Liturgical Ceremony" (关于礼拜仪式的讨论). *Theological Review* (神学志). Vol. 9, No. 2 (Summer, 1923).
Bao, Guanglin 宝广林. "Will the Status Quo of the Chinese Students Association for Christian Propagation Meet the Needs of the Future?" (中华学生立志传道团的现状是否适合于将来的要求). *The Life Monthly* (生命月刊). Vol. 3, No. 5 (January 1923).
Bao, Zheqing 鲍哲庆. "Priests and Their Churches" (牧师与其教会). *The Life Monthly* (生命月刊). Vol. 3, No. 5 (January 1923).
Bihai, [Fan] 范苾海. "The Mission of China Young Christians Association at Present" (中华基督教青年会今日的使命). *Progress of the Youth* (青年进步). No. 55 (July 1922).
Chen, Guoliang 陈国梁. "Missionaries and Extraterritoriality" (传教士与治外法权). *Truth Weekly* (真理周刊). No. 35 (25 November 1923).
Chen, Hongjun 陈鸿钧. "The 1922 National Congress of Christianity" (民国十一年基督教全国大会). *Annals of the Chinese Christian Church* (中华基督教会年鉴). No. 7 (1924).
Cheng, Jingyi 诚静怡. "The Chinese Christian Church" (中国的教会). *Progress of the Youth* (青年进步). No. 52 (April 1922).
Fan, Yurong 范玉荣. "The National Christian Council of China" (中华全国基督教协进会). *The Young Women* (女青年报), December 1922.
Gu, Ziren 顾子仁. "My Attitudes towards the National Congress of Christianity" (我对于基督教全国大会的观念). *Theological Review* (神学志). Vol. 8, No. 1 (Spring, 1922).

Hu, Xuecheng 胡学诚. "The Consciousness We Should Have in Perceiving State Affairs"(我们今后对于国事应有的觉悟). *Truth Weekly* (真理周刊). No. 46 (10 February 1924).

Jian, Youwen 简又文. "The National Church"(民族的教会). *Progress of the Youth* (青年进步). No. 52 (April,1922). Part One.

Jian, Youwen 简又文. "Tri-Benefit Society and Christianity" (三益会与基督教). *The Life Monthly* (生命月刊). Vol. 4, no. 6 (February 1924).

Jiong 炯. "The Unity of the Church" (教会之统一). *Theological Review* (神学志). Vol. 9, No. 1 (Spring, 1923).

Li, Zeling 李则灵. "Review of the National Christian Council of China's Three-Year Work since Its Founding"(中华全国基督教协进会三年以来之回顾). *Annals of the Chinese Christian Church* (中华基督教会年鉴). Vol. 8 (1925).

Liu, Nanshan 刘南山. "Discussions Concerning Leadership of the Chinese Christian Church" (教会领袖问题的讨论). *Theological Review* (神学志). Vol. 8, No. 1 (Spring, 1922).

Liu, Tingfang 刘廷芳. "The National Congress of Christianity" (基督教全国大会). *The Life Monthly* (生命月刊). Vol. 2, No. 3 (October 1921).

Liu, Tingfang刘廷芳. ed. *Discussions on the Chinese Christian Church* [中国教会问题讨论] (Shanghai: National Publication Centre of the YMCA 中华基督教青年会全国协会书报部, 1922).

Liu, Tingfang刘廷芳. "The Chinese Christian Church" (中国的基督教会). *The Life Monthly* (生命月刊). Vol. 2, Nos. 9–10 (June 1922).

Liu, Tingfang刘廷芳. "The Issue of Christian Preachers" (宣教师的问题). *The Life Monthly* (生命月刊). Vol. 3, No. 3 (November 1922).

Liu, Tingfang刘廷芳. "Tri-Benefit Society and the Chinese Church's Self-Support" (三益会和教会自养). *The Life Monthly* (生命月刊). Vol. 4, No. 6 (February 1924).

Liu, Tingfang刘廷芳. "A General Discussion of Chinese Christian Patriotism" (中国基督徒爱国问题平议). *The Life Monthly* (生命月刊). Vol. 4, Nos. 9–10 (June 1924).

Lu, Boheng 陆伯衡. "Foreign Christian Preachers of Missionary Societies and Extraterritoriality" (外国差会的宣教师与治外法权). *The Anglican Church News* (圣公会报). Vol. 16, Nos. 23–24 (October 1923).

Luo, Xigu 罗锡嘏. "How to Make Academic Theology More Socially Practicable?" (如何应用书本上神学到社会上). *Theological Review* (神学志). Vol. 9, No. 1 (Spring, 1923).

Luo, Yunyan 罗运炎. "Christianity and Politics" (基督教与政治). *The Life Monthly* (生命月刊). Vol. 3, No. 3 (December 1922).

Luo, Zhang 罗章. "The Future Leadership of the Chinese Christian Church" (将来之领袖). *Theological Review* (神学志). Vol. 8, No. 1 (Spring, 1922).

Peng, Changlin 彭长琳. "How to Improve Chinese Christian Textual Work?" (中国基督教文字事业当如何改进？). *The Life Monthly* (生命月刊). Vol. 3, No. 2 (October 1922).

Peng, Changlin彭长琳. "Discussions Concerning the Leadership of the Chinese Christian Church" (教会领袖问题的讨论). *Theological Review* (神学志). Vol. 8, No. 1 (Spring, 1922).

Peng, Jinzhang 彭锦章. "Opinions Respecting the Transformation of Missionary Societies into Independent Churches" (对于差会改建为自立会的意见). *Truth Weekly* (真理周刊). No. 7 (13 May 1923).

Peng, Jinzhang 彭锦章. "A Sequel to 'Opinions Respecting Transformation of Missionary Societies into Independent Churches'" (对于差会改建为自立会的意见). *Truth Weekly* (真理周刊). No. 8 (20 May 1923).

Quan, Shaowu 全绍武. "What Is the National Christian Council of China" (甚么是中华全国基督教协进会). *Annals of the Chinese Christian Church* (中华基督教会年鉴). Vol. 7 (1924).

Shao, Yuming 邵玉铭 ed. *The Chinese Christianity in the Twentieth-Century China* [二十世纪中国基督教问题] (Taibei, Taiwan: Cheng Chung Group, 1980).

Shen, Sizhuang 沈嗣庄. "Three Manifestos" (宣言三种). *Theological Review* (神学志). Vol. 8, No. 1 (Spring, 1922).

Shen, Yalun 沈亚伦, "How to Make Academic Theology More Socially Practicable?" (如何应用书本上神学到社会上). *Theological Review*(神学志). Vol. 9, No. 1 (Spring, 1923).

Situ, Leideng 司徒雷登 (John Leighton Stuart). "The Independence of the Chinese Christian Church" (中国教会的自立). *Progress of the Youth* (青年进步). No. 52 (April 1922).

Tianxie 天协. "The Development of Sinicized Christianity" (中国化基督教的发展). *Progress of the Youth* (青年进步). No. 52 (April 1922).

Wang, Zhixin 王治心. "The National Congress of Christianity and Its Follow-up" (聚过基督教全国大会以后). *Theological Review* (神学志). Vol. 8, No. 2 (Summer, 1922).

Wang, Zhixin王治心. "The Journal's Contribution to Propagation of Christianity" (本志对于传道部的贡献), *Theological Review* (神学志). Vol. 8, No. 4 (Winter, 1922).

Wang, Zhixin王治心. "Christianity and Buddhist Study" (基督教与佛学), *Theological Review* (神学志). Vol. 9, No. 2 (Summer, 1923).

Wang, Zhixin王治心. "Christian Spirit and Neo-Confucian Sincerity" (中国理学家所言之"诚"与基督教所言之"灵"). *Theological Review* (神学志). Vol. 9, No. 3 (Autumn, 1923).

Wang, Zhixin王治心. *A Historical Sketch of Chinese Christianity* [中国基督教史纲] (Hong Kong: Chinese Christian Literature Council, 1993).

Wu, Leichuan 吴雷川. "Christian Canons and Confucian Classics" (基督教经与儒教经). *The Life Monthly* (生命月刊). Vol. 3, No. 6 (March 1923).

Wu, Leichuan吴雷川. "My Suggestions Regarding Reform of Church-Run Schools" (对于教会中学校改良的我见). *Truth Weekly* (真理周刊). No. 16 (15 July 1923).

Wu, Zhenchun 吴震春 (i.e., Wu Leichuan 吴雷川). "What Does Lie Ahead of Chinese Church?" (论中国基督教会的前途). *Truth Weekly* (真理周刊). No. 11 (10 June 1923).

Wu, Zhenchun吴震春. "Christianity and Confucianism" (论基督教与儒教). *Truth Weekly* (真理周刊). No. 43 (20 January 1924).

Wu, Zhenchun吴震春. "What Lies Ahead of Christianity and Buddhism" (论基督教与佛教将来的趋势), *Truth Weekly* (真理周刊). No. 44 (27 January 1924).

Wu, Yaozong 吴耀宗. "What Should Chinese Christian Students Do?" (中国的基督教学生应当作什么). *Truth Weekly* (真理周刊). No. 10 (3 June 1923).

Wu, Yaozong吴耀宗. "The Chinese Nationals' Duty" (国民的责任). *Truth Weekly* (真理周刊). No. 46 (10 February 1924).

Xiao, Muxian 萧慕先. "What Does the Present-Day Church Desperately Need?" (教会今日的急需). *The Life Monthly* (生命月刊). Vol. 3, No. 5 (January 1923).

Xiao, Xuan 萧暄. "The Indigenized Christianity" (中国化的基督教). *The Life Monthly* (生命月刊). Vol. 3, No. 5 (January 1923).

Xingwu 惺吾 (i.e., Jia Yuming 贾玉铭). "The Present-Day Chinese Christian Church" (今日之中华基督教会). *Theological Review* (神学志). Vol. 8, No. 1 (Spring, 1922).

Xinwu 心悟. "My Humble Opinion about the Church's Management of Talented People" (对于教会用人才的我见). *Truth Weekly* (真理周刊). No. 9 (27 May 1923).

Xu, Guangdi 许光迪. "The Question about Chinese Christian Textual Work" (中国基督教文字事业的问题). *The Life Monthly* (生命月刊). Vol. 3, No. 2 (October 1922).

Xu, Zuhuan 许祖焕. "How to Set up an Indigenized Chinese Church?" (如何创造中国本色的教会). *Theological Review* (神学志). Vol. 10, No. 4 (1924).

Yi, Wensi 易文思 (Robert K. Evans). "What Is the Proper Attitude of Western Missionaries towards the Chinese Church?" (西宣教士对于中国的基督教会应取的态度). *The Life Monthly* (生命月刊). Vol. 2, Nos. 9–10 (June 1922).

You, Shuxun 尤树勋. "The Rural Work of Propagating Christianity" (乡村布道谈). *Theological Review* (神学志). Vol. 10, No. 1 (Spring, 1924).

Zeng, Yugen 曾郁根. "The Textual Work of Chinese Christianity" (中国基督教文字事业的问题), *The Life Monthly* (生命月刊). Vol. 4, Nos. 9–10 (July 1924).

Zhang, Junjun 张君俊. "An Appraisal of the National Congress of Christianity" (评基督教全国大会). *The Life Monthly* (生命月刊). Vol. 2, Nos. 9–10 (June 1922).

Zhang, Qinshi 张钦士. "What Should the Beijing Church Do?" (北京教会当作什么), *Truth Weekly* (真理周刊). No. 9 (27 May 1923), 1.

Zhao, Zichen 赵紫宸. "Christian Preachers and Truth" (宣教师与真理), *The Life Monthly* (生命月刊). Vol. 3, No. 3 (November 1922).

Zhao, Zichen 赵紫宸. "Advantages and Disadvantages of Chinese Christian Church" (中国教会的强点与弱点). *The Life Monthly* (生命月刊). Vol. 3, No. 5 (January 1923).

Zhao, Zichen 赵紫宸. "What Kind of Religion Do We Need?" (我们要什么样的宗教). *The Life Monthly* (生命月刊). Vol. 3, No. 9 (1923).

Zhao, Zichen 赵紫宸. "The Future of Christian Textual Work" (基督教文字事业的前途). *Rejuvenating China* (兴华报). Special Issue Commemorating Twentieth Anniversary of Publication (特刊》（20周年纪念） [January 1924].

Zhao, Zichen 赵紫宸. "The Question of Nationality among Chinese Christians" (中华基督教的国籍问题). *Progress of the Youth* (青年进步). No. 73 (May 1924).

Zhao, Zichen 赵紫宸. "An Open Discussion of Indigenized Church" (本色教会的商榷). *Progress of the Youth* (青年进步). No. 76 (October 1924).

Zhenru 真如. "Four Suggestions Respecting the Chinese Christian Church in the Future" (关于明日教会的四个建议). *Theological Review* (神学志). Vol. 8, No. 1 (Spring, 1922).

Zhong, Ketuo 钟可讬. "Chinese Christian Churches: A Survey" (中国教会概况). *Annals of the Chinese Christian Church* (中华基督教会年鉴). Vol. 8 (1925).

Internet resources

King James Bible. Available at: www.kingjamesbibleonline.org.
The Book of Rites. Trans. James Legge. Available at: https://ctext.org/liji/.
The Confucian Analects. Trans. James Legge. Available at: https://ctext.org/analects/.

3 The Campaign for Taking Back the Right of Education and Christianity

The background to the second round of the Condemning Christianity Movement

The vast majority of participants of the first round of the Condemning Christianity Movement (hereinafter referred to as the 1st CCM) were young students. For this reason, the 1st CCM lasted merely several months. It started in March 1922, reached a climax in April and May, and then lay low in July and August, when schools closed for the summer holidays. By the end of 1922, the 1st CCM had almost completely disappeared from the scene.

In the summer of 1924, a student alliance devoting itself to the CCM was set up again, marking the beginning of the second round of the Condemning Christianity Movement (hereinafter referred to as the 2nd CCM). The organizers of the 2nd CCM, witnessing the Shanghai Massacre in China, perpetrated by the forces of imperialist Japan and its running dogs on 30 May 1925, decided to further their campaign and did not give up fighting until 1927, when the National Revolution failed. The 2nd CCM had two distinguishing features. First, the criticism of Christianity was closely combined with efforts to take back the right of education and the abrogation of unequal treaties. Second, the 2nd CCM had a clear political appeal. Not only was this embodied in political parties' direct participation, as practised by the Communist Party of China (CPC), the factions of the Guomindang, and the Chinese Youth Party (CYP, which was founded in December 1923. and consisted of a few members of the Society for Young China), but it was also reflected by the combination of criticism of Christianity and the anti-imperialist struggle, which was articulated in critics treating Christianity as the running dog of the capitalists and the lackey of imperialism. The present author divides the 2nd CCM into three phases, namely, Phase I (from the summer of 1924 to the eve of the Shanghai Massacre in May 1925), Phase II (the post-Massacre phase) and Phase III (also known as the Northern Expedition phase extending from the autumn of 1926 to the Spring of 1927).

The present chapter discusses why the 2nd CCM had the above-mentioned two features.

DOI: 10.4324/9781003345169-3

96 *Campaign for Taking Back Right of Education*

1   The dissemination of Marxism-Leninism and Lenin's theoretical discussions of imperialism in particular exerted an increasing influence on well-educated Chinese. There were three key reasons for this. First, a socialist government was founded in Russia immediately after the successful October Revolution in 1917, which introduced China to Marxism-Leninism. In 1919 and 1920, Soviet Russia declared that all China's unequal treaties with the tsarist Russia were abolished. This exerted a tremendous influence on Chinese intellectuals. Second, the CPC was founded in 1921. Moreover, early Chinese Marxists such as Chen Duxiu and Li Dazhao did their best to vigorously spread Marxism-Leninism among the Chinese. Third, a large number of patriotic intellectuals, together with the left wing of the Guomindang (the Nationalist Party of China), showed a strong aversion to the bullying tactics of the imperialist Western powers and accepted Lenin's anti-imperialist theories instead. Take Sun Yat-sen, for example. Originally, Sun nurtured an illusion that Western powers would like to help China. But his illusion was destroyed by the brutal reality, in which these rogue powers not only completely ignored Chinese delegates' just demands at the Paris Peace Conference (1919–1920) and coercively transferred colonial Germany's unlawful interests in China to imperial Japan but also refused to support the Guangdong revolutionary government led by Sun himself, meanwhile giving a hand to the corrupt warlord known as Cao Kun who put the Beijing government under his control. Sun, being fully disappointed in the Western powers, turned to the CPC and formed an alliance with Soviet Russia and the Communist Party in 1924. By then, Sun had politically accepted anti-imperialism. As a consequence, Lenin's anti-imperialist theories started to prevail in China. These were particularly attractive to young students, who attempted to launch again a society-wide criticism of Christianity and set up a greater anti-imperialist league. Anti-imperialist patriotic activities grew increasingly intense in the wake of the Shanghai Massacre. All these movements were closely related to the campaign for taking back the right of education. The patriotic teachers and students used the theory respecting the imperialist cultural invasion to justify their criticism of Christianity.

2   The scientific spirit advocated by the New Culture Movement (NCM) had become deeply rooted in the hearts of the Chinese people, and thus people were increasingly disgusted with church-run schools and demanded that the right of education must be taken back. The NCM led the people to understand how modern education greatly mattered to Chinese society. Consequently, the Chinese people held that only when the country's education was substantially improved would there be a powerful and prosperous China. Education was one of the keys of the mission extricating China from poverty and backwardness. If education could not be improved, the people would be ignorant and benighted forever and the country would forever be bullied by foreign powers. Now

that education was so relevant to the national welfare and the people's livelihood, the Chinese naturally turned against missionary schools ruled by foreigners. To make matters worse, students in church-run schools were frequently forced to pray and read the Bible. This increased Chinese intellectuals' antipathy towards Christian schools, on the grounds that the well-educated Chinese were deeply influenced by the NCM. This antipathy was intensified in the 1st CCM. For example, in 1922, Cai Yuanpei, a leading Chinese educator, said in the national alliance criticizing religions that universities and colleges should abandon the Department of Theology; that all schools should ban the propagation of Christian doctrines and prayer sessions; and that those who lived by preaching Christianity should refrain from participating in education. Cai's suggestions were based on the worry about religion's interference in education. In the same year, when the first annual meeting of the China Association for Improving Education (CAIE) was being held in Ji'nan, a number of intellectuals, such as Hu Shi, Tao Menghe and Ding Wenjiang penned a resolution on primary education. According to this resolution:

> All schools, including kindergartens, are not allowed to teach any religions, religious theories and religious rituals. The reason is as follows. Children of that age have the strongest perceptivity; but at the same time, their judgement is the poorest. For this reason, educators should never make use of this to inculcate children with stories—such as "there is God governing the entire universe," "God creates the world" and "spirits do exist and are able to let the poetic justice come true"—that are unprovable or still not yet proved. Nor they should avail themselves of this opportunity to preach religion by teaching children how to perform religious ceremonies such as prayer, solution, meditation and incantation. In a word, school and primary schools in particular are not the place for propagating any religions. For those who exploit children's lack of sophistication, weakness and innocence to preach Christianity, they perpetrate a crime.[1]

3   The patriotic spirit and nationalist awakening achieved in the NCM and the 1st CCM made the Chinese people's aversion to church-run schools stronger. Many Chinese people and especially those who disliked religion very much were really disgusted with church-run schools' goal of Christianizing the whole of China. The China Continuation Committee (CCC) mentioned in previous chapters had set up missionary societies in China and conducted a survey of the mission propagating Christianity in the last two decades (1900–1920). It finally finished a comprehensive report entitled *The Christian Occupation of China*. According to this report, in 17 years (1900–1917), the number of church-run schools had tripled to 240,000. In 1921, sponsored by the Rockefeller Financial Group, educators from America, Britain and China formed a Chinese Education Mission

(CEM), which carried out a four-month survey of over 500 schools in 36 mainland Chinese cities, Hong Kong and Manila. The report entitled, *The Christian Education in China*, was finished in the next year. It pointed out that, if schools run by missionary societies or Christian churches really wanted to continue to exist in China, they would have to reform themselves to meet the needs of the Chinese people and the Chinese Christian Church, as well as making clear proposals whereby church-run schools could be more efficient, more Christianized and more Sinicized. The Sinicization required that courses taught in universities or colleges must be adaptable to the real Chinese conditions. In order to achieve this, the tertiary educational institutions affiliated to missionary societies or Christian churches should pay greater attention to vocational courses in fields, such as sociology, pedagogy and business administration and, at the same time, they should increase the number of Chinese teachers and executive staff. The improvement of efficiency required that there be uniform regulations, such as standards regarding admission and graduation that could be applied in all church-run schools; and that schools of the same nature in the same region be merged. Foreign missionaries should study dialects and be trained professionally. The missionary societies should allow colleges to be financially independent. The Christianization meant that the best teachers in a school should teach religious courses; that there should be a small number of required religious courses and the majority of religious courses should be left optional; and that the most important thing was that the spirit of Christ should be diffused into the entire school and all fields. Christianization was based on the CEM's observation that religious rituals and religious courses in many church-run schools had become merely a formality and were used to meet the needs of missionaries and their governing churches. But for those who criticized Christianity, they emphatically said the proposal of Christianization was nothing more than the direct or indirect religious propagation done by Christian schools and its ultimate goal was still to turn the whole of China into a Christian state. At the same time, imperial Japan had set up a huge number of schools in the Northeast. To be specific, by 1920, there were 459 schools ranging from kindergartens to colleges. Courses offered by these schools were used not only to peddle the Japanese culture but also to preach Japan's colonial interests in China. All these were daggers in hearts of Chinese intellectuals, who were so eager to take back China's own right of education from foreigners. They pointed out:

> Setting up schools in China is a right grabbed by foreigners through [unequal] treaties. Just like extraterritoriality and [forced] tariff agreements, it is a humiliation for China. Foreigners firmly believe that the Chinese people are barbarians or semi-civilized and China is a virgin land waiting to be cultivated by them. Because their most basic idea about China is fundamentally wrong, all their measures and attitudes can by no means be correct. Education in their mind

is no more than a tool for preaching Christianity. [Moreover], they attempt to create an educational system that is fully independent of the existing Chinese system of education. The ultimate goal of their endeavour lies in creating a church-run system of education, whereby China will be fully Christianized.[2]

On 13 October 1923, the Society for Young China (SYC) passed its constitution. The fourth article of the *SYC Constitution* was as follows:

The Society advocates the nationalist education, by which the spirit of loving the country and defending the nation will be nurtured. At the same time, the Society is strongly opposed to the missionary education, which not only is devoid of the national character but also is essentially similar to an invasive cultural policy.[3]

Yu Jiaju, one of the members of the SYC, specially wrote an article arguing against Christian education from the nationalist perspective. First, Yu pointed out that China's loss of the right of education was brought about by Western powers' aggression by force and priests preaching Christianity in China acted as a spearhead of the invasion. As far as the goal of Christian education was concerned, it was, just as mentioned above by the CEM, the full Christianization of the whole of China. But did China really need Christianity? Yu refuted the CEM's various attacks on China, contending that the Christian education did show an utter lack of substance in itself. He said the Christian education was actually pernicious. First, it was of an invasive, aggressive nature. Second, it created a religious caste. Third, it impeded the unity of Chinese education. In view of this, Yu suggested that education in China must be neutral and fully independent of any religions, including Christianity. He proposed specific measures by which educational neutrality could be obtained. First, the national constitution should stipulate that education must be independent of all religions. Second, all schools must be officially registered. Third, the law stipulating the qualification of teachers must be enforced. Fourth, the compulsory education law must be strictly implemented. Fifth, students and graduates of schools that are not officially registered should not be allowed to have the same rights as those from officially registered schools. There were detailed rules and regulations of these five measures. Generally, all schools should be prohibited from preaching any religions.[4]

The above-mentioned discussions and debates laid an intellectual foundation for the 2nd CCM.

The second round of the Condemning Christianity Movement: taking back the right of education

It could be convincingly argued that the 2nd CCM began with the endeavour to take back the right of education from missionary societies. The start of this educational endeavour was found at the Guangzhou-based Holy Trinity School (HTS), which was managed by the Episcopal Church. In March 1924, some students of HTS, influenced by free thinkers' school, made an attempt to found a Student Union and implement student autonomy. The school authority thwarted the students' endeavour by declaring the summer vacation in advance and expelling a few students. Infuriated by this, the vast majority of HTS students appealed to the society for support, awakening the public by saying: "We should rise up and resist the slavish education [imposed on us by the Church] and the imperialist oppression and invasion."[5] HTS students' struggle won wide support and sympathy from the public. The journals of the CPC, the CYL (Communist Youth League) and the Guomindang published articles expressing their support for the HTS students. These journals went further, bringing forward proposals objecting to the education manipulated by Christian churches and suggesting the Chinese government take back the management right of schools affiliated to missionary societies and Christian churches.

HTS students were followed by their counterparts in the Public Health School and the Sacred Heart Institute, both of which were located in Guangzhou. Consequently, the idea of fighting against the imperialist cultural invasion was well known to people there. On 18 June of the same year, the Guangzhou Students Association (GSA) published "The Declaration of the GSA Committee of Taking Back the Right of Education," which pointed out:

> The invasion taking the shape of education is much more pernicious than any other forms of invasion. [This education] turns young Chinese students into slaves of foreign masters and has them brainwashed to forget the Chinese race, country, history, politics and society. [In view of this], we demand that the right of setting up schools must be taken back from foreigners in China. [Specifically, there are four minimum requirements.] First, all schools under foreigners' control in China must be officially registered as required by the Chinese government. Second, the Chinese education authorities have the right to recognize or remove courses offered by these schools. Third, all schools affiliated to foreigners or foreign agencies are not allowed to preach any forms of Christianity by means of courses and lectures and they are strictly prohibited from forcing any students to worship Christian deities and read the Bible. Fourth, under no circumstances can these schools oppress students and deprive students of their freedoms of assembly, association, speech and publication.[6]

In addition to missionary schools in Guangzhou, their counterparts in large and medium-sized cities, such as Xuzhou, Changsha, Hankou, Chongqing, Kaifeng, Fuzhou, Nanjing and Xiangtan soon witnessed student protests. Chinese educators paid attention and gave support to the students' endeavour. Many of them, such as Cai Yuanpei and Hu Shi, were originally against the religious education conducted in Christian schools. Some—Yu Jiaju, for instance—were radically opposed to the Christian Church's involvement in education. Therefore, they all enthusiastically supported the campaign for taking back the right of education. The CAIE convened a special meeting in Ji'nan in July 1924. The number of participants, including visitors, was unprecedentedly high, amounting to 1,040 in total. Among these participants, there were radical critics, such as Yu Jiaju and Wang Jingwei, and mild liberalists, such as Hu Shi and Zhang Taiyan. The two wings launched a heated debate on how to take back the right of education. Finally, they all made concessions and adopted a compromised resolution. Even so, the final resolution still seemed reserved. This was embodied in the resolution's fifth article. The full text of this resolution was as follows:

> First, we request the government formulate stricter registration regulations, by which all schools in China must strictly abide. Second, the registration is divided into two types. All schools and similar educational institutions must be officially registered as Type B. And, the schools, which offer courses meeting the government's minimum requirement, do not impede the basic political system of China, and have passed the government's inspection, should be officially registered as Type A. Third, students of schools that have not been officially registered as Type A schools are not allowed to have any rights given to students of registered schools. Fourth, schools, in which there are foreigners scheming a cultural invasion, will be ordered to close immediately, as soon as it is proven true. (Reserved) Fifth, the Type A registration application of kindergartens, primary schools and secondary schools, in which there are courses preaching religion and religious ceremonies, will be officially rejected. The fifth article has been discussed and it is left to the Directorate for further investigation.
> (The Third Annual Conference held in July 1924)[7]

Soon after the close of the CAIE's annual meeting, a new wave of nationalism surged in China. Greater anti-imperialist alliances were founded in Beijing, Shanghai, Wuhan, Tianjin, Hunan and Shandong. Inspired by this, there was a louder appeal for taking back the right of education in the educational world of China. In October 1924, the National Association for Education (NAE) convened a conference in Kaifeng. It was attended by 35 delegates from 19 provinces. Many draft resolutions were discussed at the conference and two of them were adopted. One was *Resolution on Prohibiting Foreigners from Founding Educational Institutions in China* (hereinafter referred to as *Prohibition*). The other was *Resolution on Banning Propagation of Religion in All Schools* (hereinafter referred to as *Ban*). *Prohibition* explained why foreigner-run educational institutions must be banned, saying:

> So many abuses have been committed by foreigners, who manage educational institutions in China. Overall, there are four types of abuses. [Type

A.] Education is one of the most significant domestic affairs. But now, foreigners are free to set up schools in China. Neither are these schools under foreigners' control officially registered in relevant government departments; nor will they be examined and evaluated by the Chinese government. This is actually an infringement on China's education sovereignty. [Type B.] Education in different countries has its original intention. The national characters and situations of foreigners are different from that of China. For this reason, the education managed by foreigners cannot be compatible with the Chinese education. This is actually a violation of the original Chinese education. [Type C.] As far as the education managed by foreigners is concerned, it is similar to a market deal, as well as assimilating to colonization. It exerts subtle influence on the educated. As a consequence, those who are educated in Japanese schools will love Japan; and those who are educated in British schools will love Britain. So will those who are educated in American, French and German schools love America, France and Germany respectively. The independent spirit of these students is thus destroyed completely. This is a harm done to the patriotic feeling of young Chinese students. [Type D.] Digging into the content of education manipulated by foreigners in China, we find that what interests sponsors is either religious propagation or political invasion. For them, education is nothing more than an appendage. When it comes to the management of schools, courses are offered and arranged as foreigners please and none of them measure up to the Chinese standard. This is actually a deliberate negligence of obligatory subjects for Chinese students.

Moreover, there were 11 specific regulations, which were as follows:

First, schools and other educational institutions managed by foreigners must report to the government and be officially registered. Second, only when the founding of foreigner-run schools and institutions is up to the central government's specifications for schools and to educational regulations promulgated by provincial governments, will they be allowed to be registered. Third, all schools managed by foreigners must be under the local education authorities' supervision and direction. Fourth, the qualification of teaching stuff of schools managed by foreigners must meet the standard required by Chinese educational laws and regulations. Fifth, the tuition of foreigner-run schools cannot exceed that of private schools of the province wherein they are located. Sixth, students of unregistered foreigner-run schools cannot enjoy the same treatment as that of students of officially registered Chinese schools. Seventh, all unregistered foreigner-run schools will be ordered to close within a time limit. Eighth, the ceremonies held by foreigner-run schools must comply with the Chinese regulations applied to all schools. Ninth, all foreigner-run schools are not allowed to make use of school and other educational institutions to preach any religions. Tenth, all foreigner-run schools and educational institutions must be taken back and then run by the Chinese at a certain time. Eleventh, there should never be new foreigner-run schools and educational institutions from the day when this resolution comes into effect.

In like manner, *Ban* shed light on why it was adopted, pointing out:

> There have always been well-established approaches regarding how a school selects subjects and offers relevant courses, by which the healthy personality and republican spirit of young students can be properly nurtured. But recently, some mediocre persons preach Christianity, force students to read the Bible and hold religious ceremonies in the campus on the pretext of managing a school. What they do is confusing and disorganized, running counter to the original goal of school education and causing social disputes. If we cannot put a strict ban on them, the malpractice will not be fundamentally corrected and the school cannot be put on the right track.

Specific measures that should be taken to implement *Ban* were as follows:

> First, schools at all levels are strictly prohibited from preaching any religions and (mis)leading students to pray, worship supernatural beings and recite religious canons. Second, the local education authorities should strictly inspect all schools at any moment in case schools preach and propagate any religions. For schools acting against the ban, their registration must be revoked and schools themselves be dissolved. Third, teachers and students, regardless of their religious background, are fairly and equally treated in schools.[8]

But, in fact, although there were the above-mentioned resolutions, none of them came into effect due to the opposition of many parties. According to an observer's analysis, there were four groups of opponents. The first group consisted of foreigners such as headmasters, teachers and priests of missionary schools, foreign secretaries of the YMCA, and other foreign nationals; the second group, Chinese Christian converts; the third group, educators who had been educated in missionary schools; and the fourth group, the educators, who originally had nothing to do with missionary schools but now increased their own strength by colluding with foreigners through educational institutions affiliated to Christian churches.[9]

In order to push forward the campaign taking back the right of education, a journal entitled *The Educational World of China* published a special issue dedicated to this campaign. An array of educators' treatises setting forth why and how to take back the right of education were published in this issue. Among them, Chen Qitian's article was worthy of mention.

Chen contended that there were five reasons why the right of education must be taken back. First, it was required by the education sovereignty, which was one of the parts of national sovereignty. As we know, education, which greatly mattered to the national sovereignty and national life, could by no means be grabbed by foreigners. The education sovereignty was made up of three parts, that is, the national education fulfilling the country's ideal of education, the non-governmental education that should be under the state's supervision and administration, and the prohibition of foreign nationals from setting up schools and educating the Chinese. Such education sovereignty had already been realized in countries such as Britain, America, Germany, France and Japan. Second, taking back the right of education accorded with the original goal of education. In this regard, Chen said:

> The most basic goal of education in a country lies in cultivating the citizens of the country, prolonging the life of the country, and brightening up the fate of the country. In no way are any special goals of education allowed to contradict this basic goal of national education. Otherwise, the national education will be less efficient and the foundation of national education be undermined. At present, the Christian education nakedly parades its goal of propagating Christianity [through educational methods]. It has overstepped the boundary of education. Moreover, the Christian education is actually conducted to create a community of Christian converts rather than to cultivate ordinary Chinese nationals; and it aims at having China and the Chinese Christianized, meanwhile it is not inclined to educate the Chinese. In a nutshell, the Christian education, which is created to breed the Chinese counterparts of foreign Christians, and the national education of China are as incompatible as water and fire. If the Christian education is recognized, there must be impediments to the development of national education. For this reason, we must stand up against missionary schools and uncompromisingly take back the right of education.

Third, laws and regulations promulgated by the Chinese government required that the right of education must be taken back. In fact, since the late Qing, when modern schools began mushrooming in China, the identity of students educated in schools under foreigners' control had been not legally recognized. Even for a missionary school operated by the Chinese, its operation was premised on the truth that it should never obstruct the implementation of public education. But in reality, neither did missionary schools obey the basic tenet of national publication; nor did they make any concerted efforts and accept the government's supervision. In other words, the Christian education invisibly wreaked havoc on the Chinese education. To be specific, in Christian schools ranging from primary schools to universities or colleges, there were religious ceremonies that should be strictly forbidden in accordance with the principle of Chinese education. Obviously, Christian schools under the

Church's control always defied Chinese laws and regulations. Specifically, as evidenced by *The Christian Education in China*, Christian schools did not carry out the national standard of education. Rather,

> Selectively, Christian schools follow those that are conducive to themselves meanwhile acting against those that are unconducive to themselves. As everyone knows, for a country, its most basic national spirit is inseparable from the national standard of education and the fulfilment of the goal of national education. Therefore, for private education, it must comply with the national standard of education when it comes to matters of importance. It can be more autonomous only in dealing with matters of insignificance. But, at present, Christian schools are completely against the national standard of education. If we let this go unchecked, how can the national education survive? If we continue to give up taking back the right of education, what will happen to the national education?

Fourth, the freedom of religious belief required that the right of education should be taken back by China. The freedom of religious belief was a general rule adopted by modern countries. The most basic guarantee of this freedom was the education that was fully independent of all religions. In other words, under no circumstances would any religions be allowed to make use of education to preach religious beliefs, offer religious courses and hold religious ceremonies. But, in China, Christian schools, breaching the national constitution, tried every means to force and seduce young students to believe in religion. In view of this, the right of education must be taken back from schools ruled by missionaries and their governing churches. Fifth, in order that education could achieve more, the right of education must be taken back. The result of education could be evaluated by examining whether or not it benefitted Chinese society and the Chinese state. There were two criteria respecting this. First, whether or not education could inherit the established cultural tradition. Christian schools were all set up by foreigners, who did not have any Chinese cultural roots and thus were completely unable to impart the traditional Chinese culture. In schools under missionaries' control, foreigners and Chinese Christians were the people in power, none of whom were able to teach the Chinese culture on the grounds that they worshipped the Western culture and had a very poor command of traditional Chinese culture. Most fundamentally, the *raison d'être* of Christian schools lay in the propagation of Christianity. Thus, the Christian education would never inherit the traditional Chinese culture. Second, whether or not education could facilitate or impede the national consciousness. The key of nurturing the national consciousness was the common, consistent goal and spirit shared by all schools ranging from primary school to tertiary institutions through the national education. Contrary to this, the tenet of Christian education was to create Chinese counterparts of foreign Christians. By contrast, the Chinese education aimed at cultivating the Chinese nationals. The two types of education were entirely different from each other. Different goals resulted in different spirits. In many cases, students educated in Christian schools were nothing more than quasi-foreigners, who might damage the national consciousness. Generally, there were two consequences generated by Christian schools. One was the repudiation of the traditional Chinese culture. The other was the complete extermination of consistent Chinese national consciousness. In the light of the five reasons, it can thus be concluded that, inasmuch as schools affiliated to missionary societies and Christian churches were entirely harmful to China, or at least the disadvantages of Christian schools outweighed the advantages, undoubtedly the country needed to take back the right of education as soon as possible.

In addition, Chen proposed several approaches whereby the right of education could be taken back. First, the spirit of non-cooperation should be adopted. Specifically, neither should the Chinese work for missionary schools; nor should the young Chinese attend missionary schools; nor should students who were studying in missionary schools take part in religious activities; nor should the government give any financial aid to missionary schools; nor should Chinese educational groups cooperate with missionary schools. Second, the special organ responsible for taking back the right of education should be set up. It could be nongovernmental organizations freely created by Chinese nationals, such as the Kaifeng-based Council of Taking Back the Right of Education. It could be government agencies, too, such as the central and provincial committees for taking back the right of education. There would be a careful division between the governmental and nongovernmental organizations. Detailed regulations were set out in Chen's treatise. At the end of his article, Chen wrote a 15-item draft resolution regarding how to take back the right of education. For example, he suggested that the Chinese government should forbid foreigners without official approval from running any schools within the territory of China; should prohibit all schools from setting up any religious courses and holding any religious ceremonies; should order all kindergartens, primary schools, secondary schools and normal schools to be run by the Chinese; should demand missionary universities and colleges merge with Chinese tertiary education as much as possible and with no religious conditions attached; should order all unregistered private schools to close within a definite time; and explicitly should stipulate that Christians are debarred from heading the central and provincial education authorities and holding presidencies of national and provincial universities.[10]

Compared to Chen, Hu Shi took a moderate line on the church-run schools. He held that there were three barriers facing the Christian education in China. The first barrier was the nationalist countermove against Christianity. Due to the feeling of rising nationalism, the Chinese demanded that the tariff agreement coerced by foreign powers be abolished so that Chinese industry and commerce could develop in a fair, equal environment; that extraterritoriality which was grabbed by foreign powers be taken back; that the right of education be returned to China; that the foreign propagation of Christianity be banned; and foreigners' prerogatives in China be abrogated. These countermoves were responses to the past 80-year-history, in which the Chinese people were incessantly bullied by foreign powers and foreigners grabbed various prerogatives and built foreign settlements at will on Chinese territory. As long as the injustice perpetrated by the foreign powers on China was not wiped out and the inequality imposed on China continued to exist, the Chinese would not stop resisting the perpetrators. The second barrier was the rise of rationalism. Rational thinkers believed that the universe and all the myriad things ran and changed naturally and there was grim competition for survival in the biological world. Therefore, they did not think there was *a* God that was supernatural and benevolent. For them, man was no more than one of the animals and would definitely decompose after death. This was a natural phenomenon that was the least of our worries. The basic attitude of this new rationalism was suspicion. In other words, man must cast doubt before choosing to believe. Their challenge was: "Show me your evidence, please." As a consequence, religions, including Christianity and its doctrines, were inevitably severely criticized. The third barrier lay in the missionaries' easy, comfortable life in China. To put it politely, foreign missionaries in China were a mixture of both good and bad people. Those who should come and those who should not come all actually arrived in China, in the end. The future of the Christian education in China was dependent on whether or not it could overcome the three barriers. Hu thus made two suggestions, saying:

> First, the Christian education should centralize its financial and human resources and then invest them into building a small number of outstanding schools rather than disperse them in building a large number of medium- and low-level schools. [The reason is that, only when one or two extraordinary schools run by Christian churches emerge, thanks to the centralization of financial and human resources, can the Christian education stand firmly in China.] Second, Christian schools should focus exclusively on education meanwhile giving up propagating the Christian religion. [The reason is that], in present-day China, where the awakened nationalism and new rationalism prevail nationwide, it is impossible for schools to engage in education and at the same time remain a staunch servant of religion. Christian schools aiming at the propagation of Christianity can hardly survive, [because,] on the one hand, it is immoral for Christian schools to avail themselves of children's inability to think to force them to perform religious rites and seduce them into believing in religious doctrines, and, on the other hand, it is better for Christian preachers not to recruit a large number of young, gullible followers but to attract a small number of mature believers, who are true Christians worthy more than one hundred and even thousand [unsteady believers] on the grounds that they have had the opportunity to think freely and then gradually realize their need for religion and grasp the meaning of religion in their life experience.

Hu further explained his suggestion that the Christian education should abandon religious propagation and concentrate on education itself and proposed several methods of achieving this. His methods were as follows:

> First, Christian schools should never force students to worship God. Second, Christian schools should never have the religious education embodied in their curricula. Third, Christian schools should never seduce children and their parents to believe in Christianity. Fourth, Christian schools should never be megaphones for Christian doctrines. Fifth, Christian schools should be open to both Christians and free thinkers and evaluate all candidates in strict accordance with their true scholarship. Sixth, Christian schools should always, fairly and equally, treat children of Christians and free thinkers. Seventh, Christian schools should always promote the freedoms of thought, speech and faith.[11]

Hu's words indicated how liberal Chinese intellectuals treated the Christian education. These liberals did not lay stress on the demand that all Christian schools must be run by the Chinese but on the expectation that Christian schools would be renowned for their academic excellence, freedom from religious propagation, and equal treatment of children of both Christians and free thinkers.

Although there were different understandings of the endeavour to take back the right of education in the educational world of China, most people agreed with the idea that the Christian education should not be the tool inculcating students with religion. Moreover, they suggested that all Christian schools must be officially registered and approved by the government. It was after the Shanghai Massacre that these suggestions came into effect.

The founding and activities of the Second Condemning Religion Alliance

As indicated above, the 2nd CCM began with missionary-school students' attempt to take back the right of education. This student-initiated endeavour soon triggered the founding of the greater Second Condemning Religion [i.e., Christianity] Alliance (SCRA). In August 1924, the SCRA was officially founded in Shanghai. Ke Bainian, Gao Erbo and others were elected the executive members of the SCRA. General regulations compiled by Wu Zhihui were adopted. And the SCRA's *Manifesto* (hereinafter referred to as the *1924 Manifesto*) was published. Compared with the *1922 Manifesto* prepared by the first Condemning Religion Alliance (CRA), the *1924 Manifesto* intensively highlighted the stand against the imperialist colonial invasion and combined the critique of Christianity and the political movement fighting against imperialism and struggling for national liberation.

According to the *1924 Manifesto*:

> [The reason why we are against Christianity and other religions in the general sense is that all these religions preach hypocritical concepts of peace and happiness and despise the realistic, material (/corporal) struggles. They dissuade people from fighting against oppressors and plutocrats and] lead the toiling masses on the planet to blindly worship God and yield themselves to the alleged predestined fate. As a consequence, some religious followers [are brainwashed to] care only for the Heavenly Kingdom, while believing that there is no harm even in extreme misery. ... Religions of all shades commit the same sin. Among them, Christianity, which is known for its extensive and powerful organization, perpetrates crimes in a deeper and greater way. For this reason, we are particularly opposed to Christianity. [Moreover], in a certain sense, we have no alternative but to turn against Christianity. Looking back at history, Christianity was positioned in the privileged caste in the feudal age [and then] the bourgeoisie rose to prominence and metamorphosed into the class in possession of prerogatives. The capitalist class preserves and makes full use of Christianity. First, it uses Christianity to narcotize the working class. The narcotized workers will believe that the rich and the poor are foreordained by the divine will. So that they will never disobey the divine will nor will they make any attempts to destroy the established social system through the class struggle. Second, it uses Christianity to narcotize the people living in colonies and the semi-colonies and by doing so they mislead these people to believe that foreign powers' gunboats and armed forces are not used to plunder their fortunes but to send them God's gospels, education and culture. If Christianity works, the colonized people will be deeply grateful for the colonizers' goodness and give up their resistance forever. Capitalists and imperialists keep using Christianity to benumb the colonized peoples. Herein lies the most important reason why we Chinese must be against Christianity. [The truth is that] Christian priests are parading in advance and following after are [foreign powers'] gunboats and armed forces. On every page of the Bible, there are such words: 'We are giving you guns and money!' In the past eight decades, there have always been such missionary work and trades conducted in this way. How can we forget these! [However], in recent years, Christianity is propagated in a much subtler way. Specifically, the missionary work is being carried out through churches, schools, hospitals, youth groups, social service corps, children scouts, mass education, and so on. By doing so, the true goal—propagating Christianity—is successfully concealed, so that Christianity is being increasingly embedded in the Chinese society and the young Chinese people are more and more captivated by this religion. Due to its camouflage, people can only see Christianity spending money building schools and hospitals, but meanwhile failing to see this

religion investing dozens of times or even hundreds of times as much money in more profitable business. Worst of all, as soon as hordes of priests or pastors returned to their countries, they dehumanize the Chinese to the extreme by portraying the Chinese as a creature that is stupid, uncivilized and gullible. In this sense, Christianity plays quite a significant role in fomenting anti-Chinese racism. When missionaries arrive in China, no matter what they do—propagation of Christianity or education, they all, consciously or unconsciously, engage in destroying the nationalist awakening and the Chinese people's love for their country by advertising the alleged cosmopolitanism pandering to international capitalism. For all these reasons, we are particularly against Christianity among all the religious faiths.

The aim of the SCRA was as follows: "The Alliance, driven by the ardent love for the country and equipped with the scientific spirit, does its utmost to use every positive means to object to all undertakings carried out by Christianity and the religion itself."

The specified work of the SCRA included:

First, the textual publicity work, that is, the publication of various written materials; second, the oral publicity work, that is, the organization of public lectures and speeches; and third, the research work, that is, academic inquiries into Christianity and its undertakings.[12]

Next to its predecessor written in 1922, the *1924 Manifesto* underlined nationalism. Organizationally, the SCRA was more complete than the first alliance had been. For example, it set up an executive committee consisting of five persons. The tenure of office of an executive member was one year. The SCRA formulated detailed regulations respecting the fund management. As required, it should convene a conference every year. Following Shanghai, many cities and provinces in China and even Chinese students studying in Japan set up an alliance condemning Christianity. Finally, a large-scale national campaign criticizing Christianity was launched in China. Shanghai, Guangzhou, Changsha and Wuhan were the four centres of the 2nd CCM.

Yang Tianhong analysed the 2nd CCM in his monograph entitled *Christianity and Modern China*, pointing out that critics of Christianity focused on three issues. "First, they continue to study, investigate and criticize Christianity and its missionary work in China and in doing so the criticism of Christianity will be led to new heights." Participants of the 2nd CCM, such as student associations, the SCRA, the CYL, the Guomindang, the CPC and anarchists, all used their own publications such as *The Young Chinese*, *Awakening*, *The Guide*, *New Students*, and *The Republican Daily*, to vehemently criticize Christianity. Thanks to the effort made by these publications, the public opinion generally supported and sympathized with the 2nd CCM. "Second, they realize that the surge of students' participation in the criticism against Christianity will facilitate the campaign of taking back the right of education." By publishing articles in the *Special Issue of Condemning Christianity Movement*, critics brought to light what truly took place in Christian schools and what these schools' true goal was. In the meantime, they called on young people studying in Christian schools to discontinue their schooling or refuse to work there after graduation. "Third, they make efforts to organize a 'Condemning Christianity Week' around Christmas." This activity made the 2nd CCM more influential in the society.

The 2nd CCM was more political and less intellectual-cultural than the 1st CCM in 1922. Not only did the 2nd CCM openly attack imperialism, demand the abrogation of unequal treaties with China, attempt to take back the right of education, and resist the cultural invasion perpetrated by foreign powers, but it also was much better organized. This improvement was closely related to political parties' direct participation and the CPC's support in particular. According to Yang's study, at that time, dozens of leading members of the CPC, such as Chen Duxiu, Qu Qiubai, Deng Zhongxia, Yun Daiying, Xiao Chunü, Cai Hesen, Mao Zedong, Zhou Enlai, Zhang Qiuren, Tang Gongxian, Li Chunfan and Shi Cuntong, directly or indirectly, participated in the 2nd CCM. Among them, some, such as Tang Gongxian, Ke Bainian (i.e., Li Chunfan), Zhang Qiuren and Shi Chuntong, even played a leading role in the executive committee of the SCRA. A series of resolutions adopted by the CPC's Fourth National Congress, which was held in January 1925, expressed the Party's enthusiastic support for youth groups partaking in the 2nd CCM, such as the New Students Society. In August 1923, the CYL, led by the CPC, decided to set up organizations criticizing Christianity in campuses. Then, in January 1925, the CYL's third national congress passed a resolution encouraging young Chinese people to devote themselves to taking back the right of education, calling for the abolition of missionary schools, and facilitating the development of the 2nd CCM. *The Young Chinese*, the CYL's official publication, published a great number of articles reporting and guiding young students' effort to criticize Christianity. In the meantime, many senior members of the Guomindang, such as Cai Yuanpei, Wu Zhihui, Liao Zhongkai, Dai Jitao, Wang Jingwei, Zou Lu and Zhang Zhou, voiced their critique of Christianity. Contrary to them, Jiang Jieshi (Chiang Kai-shek) and Sun Yat-sen supported Christianity and disapproved of the 2nd CCM. It should be pointed out that, although Sun Yat-sen himself was a Christian, he strictly held fast to the principle of separation of religion from politics throughout his life. An observer said:

> [Mister Sun] believes in Christianity. But he pays attention to spirit rather than form. He is never interested in the restrictive Christian doctrines and ecclesiastical rites. [Moreover, Sun is strongly against foreign powers that oppress China while parading their Christian faith. In one of Sun's letters to a friend, he voices his idea. Relevant words read:] Westerners had believed that Christ was a revolutionary aspiring to eliminate inequality

entirely. But at present, Western countries, which are self-proclaimed Christian states, actually treat China as a slave and oppress their own people. Personally, I think what they are doing is neither different from the historical cannibalism in which self-styled followers of the teaching of Jesus destroyed each other in the name of Christianity nor from the modern atrocity in which the Jews are burned in the name of the highest lord of Jewish people.[13]

Therefore, Sun remained neutral in the face of the 2nd CCM. That is to say, neither was he opposed to the movement; nor did he interfere in it. Sun's attitude determined that some Guomindang members' criticism of Christianity was merely an individual behaviour and could by no means express the attitude of the party. Even so, a few Guomindang members, such as Wu Zhihui, did play a great role in the 2nd CCM.

The SCRA published a huge number of critical essays on Christianity, in which Christianity and imperialism were inseparable. The authors of these essays had this inseparability corroborated by the world and Chinese history. Two treatises—Li Chunfan's "The Christian Missionary Work and Imperialism" and Mei Yunlong's "Christianity and China"—are worthy of discussion here. In his treatise, Li, first of all, enumerated historical cases revealing the interrelation of Christian missionary work and imperialism, such as imperial Spain's colonization of foreign lands with the help of Christianity and the British and French colonialism spearheaded by missionaries. Then, Liu made an analysis of China's diplomatic history extending from the trade treaty signed by Russia and Emperor Kangxi, which allowed Russian missionaries to reside in Beijing, to Western powers' partition of China by reason of handling disputes involving Christian missionaries and local residents, and down to the Boxer Uprising in which China was bled for huge indemnities. All these demonstrated that the Christian missionary work was exactly an imperialist tool of plunder. This analysis was followed by Liu's discussion of Western powers' keen competition for *baojiaoquan* (the alleged right to protect missionary work in China), which further proved that the missionary work was a means of aggression. Liu's final conclusion was as follows:

> It is, historically, factually and unambiguously, proven that Christianity is the spearhead of imperialism and a tool of imperial powers' aggression against China. If Christians attempt to deny this, please refute these historical facts first. If Christians are unable to do so, please eat your empty fine words. In no way are we fooled by you![14]

Mei divided the history of Christianity since the time of Matteo Ricci into three stages. The first stage started from 1582 (the tenth year of the Wanli reign of Emperor Shen of Ming) and ended in 1841, when the First Opium War was still going on. In this stage, Christianity was on the wane and exerted little influence on China. The second stage began with the end of the First Opium War in 1842 and ended in the appearance of the brute Eight-Power Allied Forces in 1900. The third stage extended from 1901 to 1924. In the second and third stages, Christianity in China was gradually rehabilitated. It was in this period that whenever China suffered a diplomatic defeat, Christianity experienced a significant growth. Mei made an attempt to explain this. Since the seventeenth and eighteenth centuries, when the West witnessed the Industrial Revolution, some Western countries had started to expand overseas and occupied South America and Oceania one after another. At that time, these colonial powers were not yet strong enough to invade the East. But by the mid-nineteenth century, when the West had grown into economic imperialism, the colonial powers held that the existing market was not big enough and thus they expanded eastward and intruded into China. This imperial, colonial expansion was spearheaded by Christianity. For this reason, Christianity mushroomed in China in the wake of the First Opium War (1840–1842). The Christian missionary work was indispensable to the imperial powers' economic invasion. At this point, Mei said: "Foreign firms' plunder in the treaty ports cannot satisfy [their governing regimes'] greed. [These colonial powers] still need Christian missionaries to help them exploit the inland area of China and bleed people there white." This point could be corroborated by unequal treaties, through which the imperialist powers exert themselves to the utmost to protect Christianity and its agencies in China.

> The expansion of imperialism and the growth of Christianity in China are inseparable. Disputes and conflicts between Christian missionaries and local residents are perfect excuses, by which imperialism could substantially increase its presence in China. Christianity and imperialism perfectly harmonize and walk in step with each other.

For example, in 1858, the Anglo-French army, using the death of two missionaries as an excuse, captured Tianjin and then stormed Beijing, where they barbarously destroyed by fire the incomparably beautiful Yuanmingyuan (the Old Summer Palace) and coerced China into ceding territory and paying indemnities. In 1897, Germany, using the same excuse, grabbed Jiaozhou Bay from China. Three years later, imperial powers availed themselves of the Boxer Uprising to force China to sign the *Boxer Protocol* demanding China pay staggeringly huge reparations. Mei finally pointed out:

> China has had enough of Christianity! Humiliations such as China being forced to cede territory and pay indemnities are all brought about by Christianity! In order to save our country, we have no alternative but to stand up against Christianity! Oh compatriots! Please do not forget every alarming scene in which Christianity assisted imperialist countries to invade China in the past eight decades![15]

Not only was the 2nd CCM against Christianity in accordance with the anti-capitalist and anti-imperialist stand and against the Christian education from the perspective of national education, but it also was discontent with the Christian religion from the angle of Buddhism and Confucianism. Nie Yuntai and Zhang Chunyi did an excellent job in their papers discussing the inter-relationship of Christianity, Confucianism and Buddhism. In his "Setting Doubts about Religion," Nie said:

> Christianity teaches people to serve Heaven. But the Christian Heaven is not the practical, immediate benefit but remote, vain glory. In like manner, the rewards of God are not for righteous actions but for the undivided faith. In other words, Christianity thinks highly of externality rather than internality, as well as attending to superficial things rather than to essentials. Moreover, the Christian God arbitrarily blesses or curses people in accordance with whether or not people believe in him rather than on the basis of their merits and faults. By contrast, Confucianism and Buddhism all value the internal work, despise external forces and attach importance to self-cultivation and sincere confession. In other words, the two teachings guide people to manage to do difficult jobs. Unlike Confucianism and Buddhism, Christianity merely leads people to do easy things, such as believing in the name of Jesus in exchange for salvation and atoning their own crimes by the sacrifice of Jesus, all of which are nothing more than rewards for fraudulence and punishment against sincerity.[16]

Zhang Chunyi wrote "Buddhism Refines Christianity," saying:

> At present, Christianity is the most formidable force attempting to eliminate the entirety of Eastern culture. For this reason, Chinese clergy working in Christian churches and Chinese students studying in missionary schools are the most wretched people. Westerners are almost completely ignorant of Buddhism, so that they have a kaleidoscopic array of prejudices that have been handed down generations after generations. Sadly, Chinese Christians dogmatically treat these prejudices and misinterpretations as golden rules, meanwhile they know nothing at all about the errors and absurdities in the Old Testament and the New Testament, all of which should be deleted immediately. From the Buddhist perspective, leading Christians are really miserable and ordinary Christians who blindly follow them are more unfortunate. In view of this, I cannot bear to abandon the idea that Buddhism should be remoulded by means of Buddhist doctrines and turned into a branch of Buddhism. If this works, my dream will come true, finally.[17]

It should be pointed out that Nie and Zhang were both originally Christians, both of whom later converted to Buddhism due to their exposure to Buddhism and criticism of Christianity. Therefore, the two Christians-turned-Buddhists' critique of Christianity was really well grounded.

The Church's response to the Condemning Christianity Movement and its indigenization before the Shanghai Massacre

The Christian Church did not respond promptly to the 2nd CCM. It was not until the end of 1924 that the Church published a number of articles answering the criticism. On 21 January 1925, the Executive Committee of the National Christian Council of China (NCCC) convened a meeting and set up a task force to intensively study the 2nd CCM. This task force was headed by Yu Rizhang. This indicated that the Chinese Church had become more mature. Yu's team, inviting Christian leaders from the YMCA, the YWCA, the SDCK and the Society for Christian Education (SCE), organized a serious of symposia. At the meeting, Cheng Xiangfan introduced the convention participants to various criticisms against the Church and Christian education. Pan Shaotang discussed how to respond to the new round of CCM and what kind of attitude Christians should have towards these criticisms. In response to the four types of criticism of Christianity, there were four discussion panels, namely, (1) the panel of Christian life and thoughts; (2) the panel of Christian organization; (3) the panel of Christian schools; and (4) the panel of missionary societies. Also, Yu's team prepared 21 questions regarding the essentials of the critique of Christianity and mailed them to leaders of local churches, who studied them carefully and contributed their wisdom. Some questions were insightful. For example, what was the difference between the NCM and the CCM? What was the most noticeable point of the CCM's observation of the Christian Church? Did the misapprehension of the Christian Church create the CCM? Did we Christians need to make some explanations? What was the main object of the CCM's criticism against the Christian schools, organizations and management? What was the essence of the criticism against the Christian leaders, missionaries, churches and faith? What was Christian leaders' own critique of Christianity? Did Christians understand the CCM's intellectual and philosophical systems criticizing Christianity and grasp the key points of the CCM's criticism against the Christian organization and view of life? Was the 2nd CCM created by the intellectual enlightenment or by people's discontent with specific problems in relation to Christianity? Was the CCM's criticism of Christianity and the Christian Church grounded? If so, should Christianity and the Church make a correction? For what reason had Christianity failed to arouse enthusiasm among students just as communism did?[18] These questions demonstrated that the Chinese Church did study the 2nd CCM and at the same time performed a self-examination of problems existing within the Church.

Overall, Chinese Christians' attitude towards the 2nd CCM was not very different from that in the first round of the CCM. Some were strongly averse to the CCM, taking an apologetic stand against all criticisms. Some defended their religion, meanwhile rethinking profoundly the Church's own problems. Quite a few essays responded to criticisms by suggesting the Church further its indigenization and lead Christians to behave well. Take Wang Wenxin's article, for example. Wang, first of all, divided reasons why there was severe criticism of Christianity into several groups. First, in some cases, Christianity was the enemy of sovereign countries. In other words, Christianity was a stooge, which played quite a significant role in the cultural invasion, of imperialism and capitalism. Second, Christianity was, to some extent, an enemy of knowledge. That is to say, Christianity was the foe of science and a superstition, impeding progress. Third, up to a certain point, Christianity was an enemy of society. This point was embodied in Christians' rampant hypocrisy, bullying people, and their slavish dependence on Christian churches. Wang contended that the first group was caused by misunderstanding; the second, by prejudice; but the third, grounded in fact. He further generalized these reasons into Westernized Christianity and the (bad) behaviour of Christians. Therefore, he suggested Chinese Christians make two efforts so that they could eliminate the reasons for anti-Christian criticism. The two efforts were as follows:

> Organizationally, the Chinese Christianity should be, in all aspects, accordant with the Chinese ethics, dispositions, customs and habits. It is unnecessary for it to blindly follow Western rules and habits acting against the Chinese ones. It is true that in many aspects, the modern Christianity is suspiciously capitalist and imperialist. In fact, this disadvantage can be attributed to the Christian Church's organizational defects causing misunderstanding. Therefore, Chinese Christians should do their best to clear the air. To do this, the Chinese Christian Church should have the entirety of its organizations fully indigenized. [When it comes to the behaviours of Chinese Christians, it is strongly suggested that] Chinese Christian converts should truly emulate Jesus Christ. [That is to say, we Christians are not followers of Christ in name, but instead we should practise what we preach. Mister Cheng Jingyi has said:] "The object of criticism of Christianity can be a Christian school, an organization of the Church, a historical figure of Christianity, or one piece of history of Christianity. But few criticisms are directed at Jesus himself." [It thus can be seen that even critics think highly of Jesus. Therefore, we Christians should do our utmost to emulate Christ and in doing so we can put an end to criticisms. At this point, the words of L. J. Birney, the Bishop of the Methodist Episcopal Church, should be quoted:] "The most critical matter of the present-day Church does not lie in converting thousands of or even tens of thousands of people to Christianity but in cultivating those who have joined the Church and call them followers of Christ to be true Christians."

The quoted words indicated that the true behaviour of Christians did matter to this religion. Only when Chinese Christians substantially improved their own behaviour and the Church's organizations would critics' doubts about Christianity be eliminated.[19]

Wu Leichuan was tolerant of free thinkers' criticism of Christianity. Most obviously, he welcomed the afore-mentioned critical re-examination of Christianity from the Buddhist perspective by Zhang Chunyi and Nie Yuntai and even recognized some parts of their arguments. Wu said:

> It is true that Christianity is being vehemently criticized by both free thinkers and Christians. It is also true that such criticism gives Christianity an opportunity to improve itself. For those who are criticized, they should not feel angry but critically rethink themselves; nor should they feel panic but be more prudent. Digging into Mister Nie's treatise, we find that the author obviously thinks highly of Christianity, even though it sets doubts about Christianity in name. As for Mister Zhang Chunyi's open correspondence with reporters, in spite of severely rebuking the Christian Church's mistakes and absurdities, it still attempts to create a Christian branch of Buddhism and in doing so it proves the imperishableness of Christianity. To be honest, we Christians do need to immediately improve those aspects that are criticized by free thinkers and at the same time make a great effort to carry forward the imperishableness of Christianity. By doing so, the Christian truth will be made more brilliant and more remarkable. With the lapse of time, the criticism of Christianity will subside. I do sincerely hope that leading Chinese Christians and all followers will make a well-concerted effort to improve this religion.[20]

But at the same time, some Christian apologists defended the entirety of Christianity, refuting item by item criticisms of the religion in the hope that they could dispel all misunderstandings of Christianity. For example, Tu Zheyin argued against accusations such as Christianity was the spearhead of imperialist invasion, a shield of capitalism and a superstition, Christianity was unpatriotic, and the propagation of Christianity was an act of invasion. Finally, Tu sincerely advised:

> [Chinese Christians should] raise up their spirit and make corrections to their defects, such as the erroneous faith, meaningless rituals, disorderly organizations and corrupt personalities. [In the meantime, free thinkers should] concentrate themselves on various constructive undertakings, such as promoting the national unity and peace, transferring military expenditure to industry and agriculture, raising money to build railways, defending and taking back national sovereignty, and rehabilitating the national education.[21]

As we can see, among Chinese Christians responding to the 2nd CCM, some had a very positive attitude and some put themselves on the defensive. But even for those who felt an antipathy towards the criticism, they did, due to the CCM's influence, admit that there were indeed many problems besetting the Christian Church. To put it another way, the criticism of the criticism of Christianity had some positive elements.

Exactly because of the close relationship between the 2nd CCM and the Christian education, how to treat free thinkers' critique of Christian education became an important issue. In fact, those who engaged in the Christian education had very different ideas respecting the campaign for taking back the right of education. Some unambiguously objected to the resolution attempting to put a ban on teaching religion in all Christian schools, contending that this would shake the foundation of education. Li Denghui, who then presided over the Shanghai-based Fudan University, explicitly said:

> If the government allows this resolution to come into effect, young Chinese people in the general sense will be directly affected. Those who put forward such a proposal can by no means be blameless. [The student movement is by nature negative. Because among] such students, more than half of them are academically poor and interested in nothing else but making trouble. [For these trouble-makers,] their only goal is creating a disturbance in the campus. [Frankly,] they are not that harmful. But if teachers, who have been intellectually mature and academically play a leading role, participate in the student movement, there will be serious and even unimaginable results.[22]

Li himself fully recognized the Christian education, arguing that both the world and Chinese history had proved that, so long as the method of education was right and effective, religion could not destroy the national character, nor could it jeopardize patriotism. Li wrote: "Christianity's greatest contribution is the role it plays in refining the patriotic spirit and disseminating patriotism. Moreover, it leads patriots to love the entirety of humankind, so that internationalism is pushed forward."[23]

For Li, the danger was not Christianity but materialism and the radical Bolshevism. The nationalism could be used to cope with the two isms. The May Fourth Movement (MFM) had dealt a heavy blow to the moral basis, lasting for thousands of years in China. As a consequence, the Chinese youth had no moral codes and thus could do as they pleased. Under such circumstances, only when the religious morality was restored would China be saved. Therefore, Li wrote:

> I profoundly realize that Christianity is the best method of saving present-day China. Of course, other religious ethics are not unconducive to the country ... For Christianity, which has taken root in China, first, it can have improper superstitions replaced with a healthy outlook on life; second, it can eliminate selfishness and corruption by means of fraternity and justice; and third, it can rectify the all-pervading indifference by the spirit of service.[24]

It thus can be concluded that Li was a representative figure who totally repudiated the 2nd CCM and the campaign for taking back the right of education.

Contrary to Li, some, overall, affirmed the national campaign aiming to take back the right of education. Take Wang Biting, for example.[25] Wang said:

> The spirit driving the effort to take back sovereignty and fight against oppressive foreign powers is really more than 100 per cent admirable. In comparison with meaningless and blind actions conducted in the past, this spirit is much more valuable.

Of course, Wang knew very well that gaining such spirit was a hard job, on the grounds that there were four difficult problems that must be overcome. First, the corrupt government manipulated by warlords was completely unable to take back the right of education. Second, public schools were being plagued by economic panics, shortages of talented people, lack of teaching devices, incessant strikes by students and teachers, and so on, so that they could not be substitutes for Christian schools. Third, if the state suddenly took back the right of education from Christian schools, which were widely dispersed and had taken root in many poor rural areas and had found a solution to many rural children's lack of education, there would be a large number of boys and girls who would have to discontinue their schooling in the event of the local governments' inability to set up alternative schools. Fourth, courses taught in foreign languages and the Western way of life in campuses of Christian schools were popular among some young Chinese people, who worshipped almost everything foreign. In view of these points, Wang concluded that the opportunity to take back the right of education had not yet arrived. Some raised similar questions, suggesting that Christian schools be supervised by the government and at the same time the government refrain from taking part in the school management except for evaluating a school's performance and formulating the curriculum standard. For them, Christian schools did make a contribution to the national education and thus were really worth preserving. Taking back the right of education could not be done by empty talk. Rather, whether or not this endeavour could succeed depended on many factors such as the economic strength and pool of talented people.[26] Some held that taking back the right of education would be an impetus to the reform of Christian schools. Dong Jianwu, for instance, proposed four points regarding this:

> First, all Christian schools should be registered at the Ministry of Education. Second, all Christian schools should pay enough attention to the traditional Chinese scholarship. Third, all Christian schools should appoint Chinese people to important posts. Fourth, all Christian schools managed by missionaries and their governing churches should be turned over to the Chinese Church, when the time is right.[27]

Among the published articles, the one by Liu Tingfang epitomized enlightened Chinese Christians' attitude towards the 2nd CCM and the campaign for taking back the right of education.[28] Overall, Liu himself was tolerant of the criticism of the Christian education. He held that, in comparison with the Boxer Uprising, the 2nd CCM was more thoroughly critical of foreign forces and churches and at the same time less averse to foreigners and Christianity. Therefore, he suggested the Chinese Church should take a sober, steady attitude towards this movement. When it came to essays criticizing the Christian education, Liu said Christians should make a concrete analysis of them and admit that some were indeed fair and grounded and voiced what members of the Church were promoting. For those that were sophistical, groundless and even abusive, Christians should not treat them in a general way but instead try to prove clear relevant facts and ascertain whether or not they were written on impulse. In any case, Christians should not engage in a public verbal battle. He strongly advised the whole of Chinese Christianity to always be tolerant of the 2nd CCM and give mild answers. Liu himself was opposed to Christians' radical responses, such as intimidating critics, in some cases. For example, the ruling bodies of a Christian school asked a foreign consul for protection, merely because the school could not perform a religious ceremony on Christmas Day due to the ongoing CCM. Liu resolutely set himself against the school's action, pointing out that it could only intensify the conflict. He specifically said: "The whole of the Christian communities should be, peacefully, kindly and even passively, tolerant of this national campaign criticizing Christianity and in doing so the noble character of Chinese Christians will be manifest." Liu disagreed with some Christians' opinion that the 2nd CCM was nothing more than a matter of fooling around among young people full of sap. Rather, Chinese Christians, taking into account public opinion, the complexity of the participants of the movement, the wide range of topics and the worries of the Christian schools, must treat it more seriously. Therefore,

> The total Christian communities should never be conceited and self-complacent and underestimate the criticism of Christianity. It is better for Christians to be open with critics [and remain modest and respectful]. It is true that, among criticisms, there is a torrent of groundless, unfair verbal abuse. But it is also true that the vehement attack on Christian education and the defects brought to light by critics are not entirely ungrounded. Can we Christians say the Christian education does not have any defects? If not, what are the defects? Does the Christian education make a substantial contribution to China? Can people who are educated in Christian schools meet the needs of China? Is the status quo of Christian education in conformity with the original goal of education advocated by the Church? Does the Christian education manifest the spirit of Christ? Does the Christian education substantially contribute to the Chinese Christian Church? Does the Christian education cultivate the Christianized personality among students? Does the Christian education

play a role in the creation of healthy Chinese citizenship? What lies ahead of the Christian education in China?

Liu thus concluded: "The national campaign criticizing Christianity is actually the religion's true friend giving forthright admonitions. In other words, it is *this* friend's critique that gives the Church an opportunity to pocket its pride and introspect itself." Moreover, he suggested the Chinese Church should resolve to reform the Christian education. Liu said, although the Christian education in China started to grow out of a difficult situation and had made solid progress in recent years, many Christian schools did drift along. He specially mentioned the 250,000-word survey report by the Christian education committee, in which many useful suggestions were made, saying:

> How many of these suggestions have been put into effect so far? How many times have we discussed issues such as the importance of traditional Chinese scholarship, reform of curricula, Chinese management of school, dissolution or merger of less financially independent schools, and improvement of normal schools? We all have a clear idea of the truth about the existing problems, meanwhile feeling the urgency to implement reform. [However], do we really resolve to lead the reform to go into effect?

Then Liu cried out to Westerners in the Church:

> Westerners making a living from the Church should treat the national campaign condemning Christianity as a blow and a shout to waken themselves. They should no longer delay [the reform] any further! For Chinese Christians who are engaging in the Christian education, they should regard the campaign as an alarm bell, which reminds them of being well prepared and shouldering responsibility in case Westerners hesitate to move forward in reforming the Christian education on the pretext of the Chinese Christians' inability.

Liu further pointed out that Christians should intensively research several questions, that is, the components and motive power of the 2nd CCM, the movement's handling of the Christian education, the most fundamental principles of the movement, and the questions raised by the movement and relevant facts such as the Christian education's relationship with China and China's international relations, Chinese and Western churches, the religious education and the unity of Chinese education, the rights of private schools, and the relationship between nationalism and education. Finally, Liu called on Chinese Christians to give researchers more incentives to do a much more thorough study of these questions.

Inasmuch as the direct target of the campaign for taking back the right of education was Christian education, the Society for Chinese Christian

Education (SCCC) felt duty-bound to respond to the free thinkers' criticism and make a specific effort to indigenize the Christian education in China.

The SCCC's predecessor was the Educational Association of China (EAC), founded in 1890. The EAC aimed at producing proper textbooks meeting the needs of Christian schools and finding solutions to problems facing the Chinese general education by means of mutual aid. In 1893, due to the rapid increase in the number of Christian schools, the EAC became a formal organization. It was comprised only of foreigners and regularly published a special column dedicated to education in an English journal entitled *The Chinese Recorder*, through which people of Christian education could exchange ideas. In 1907, the EAC had its own journal, a monthly bulletin. Two years later, the journal was renamed *The Educational Review* and finally it became a quarterly publication. In 1912, when Christian schools were growing rapidly in China, provincial branches of the EAC were set up one after another. The EAC thus restructured itself into a national association for Christian education, connecting provincial branches. By then, the branches and headquarters had recruited a few Chinese members. In 1915, due to the influence exerted by the independence movement of the Chinese Church, the association formally renamed itself the SCCC. In 1922, the report produced by the survey committee on Chinese education suggested the SCCC should have four departments, namely, the Department of Higher Education, the Department of Primary and Secondary Education, the Department of Religious Education and the Department of Adult Education and Educational Promotion. The heads of the four departments, as suggested, constituted the National Board of Directors.

In 1924, the 2nd CCM, directly and vehemently, criticized Christian education. In the face of this, the SCCC had to respond and find a solution to the official registration of Christian schools. As a consequence, the SCCC's provincial branches all set up a Registration Council and even created a National Registration Committee (NRC). The NRC was headed by Cheng Xiangfan, who was the deputy president of the SCCC. The NRC's key members were Yu Rizhang, the leading person in the YMCA, Situ Leideng (John L. Stuart), who presided over Yanjing (Yenching) University, and Liu Tingfang, a PhD, all of whom were responsible for important issues such as the official registration of Christian schools. In order to push forward their work, Cheng Xiangfan and officials of the Ministry of Education in charge of the registration of private schools exchanged ideas in Beijing in the hope that there would be mutual understanding. The issue of whether or not Christian schools should be allowed to teach the Bible was still controversial. The Church believed:

> At present, what the Chinese society needs most is the creation of a large number of Christianized citizens, all of whom will follow the spirit of Christ and serve the country and society. For this reason, the Bible must be taught in (Christian) schools. Moreover, if the schools give up offering religious courses, they will grow finally weaker, on the grounds

that Christian schools' funding is all fully dependent on the donation of enthusiastic foreign Christians. [Contrary to the Church], the government points out that the compulsory reading of the Bible in Christian schools violates the principle of freedom of belief, inasmuch as among students studying in these schools only a very small number of them are Christian converts.[29]

Actually, there was little prospect of seeing both sides reaching a consensus.

In January 1925, Luo Bingsheng, the Secretary of the SCCC's Department of Higher Education, convened a meeting attended by leading Chinese Christians in universities affiliated to missionary societies and their governing churches. They discussed what was the future of Christian education in China. In total, a dozen renowned Chinese Christians, such as Beijing's Liu Tingfang and Hong Weilian, Guangzhou's Wei Pengdan (i.e., Wei Que), Hunan's Yan Fuqing and Wuchang's Wei Zhuomin, aired their own views at this meeting. In addition to them, the director and deputy director of the SCCC came to the meeting. For three days, these leading Christians in China thoroughly discussed important issues respecting the Christian higher education in the light of the society-wide criticism of Christianity and finally came to the conclusion that Christian schools' future contribution to China was dependent on the further indigenization, higher efficiency and more profound Christianization. To be specific, the "further indigenization" meant that Christian universities and colleges should not only be disseminators of Western civilization but also be centres of Chinese culture. By means of the Christian higher education, young Chinese people would become excellent Chinese citizens, who had a good command of Chinese culture and put into practice this culture. Christian universities were the places, where leaders of Chinese Christianity were trained. Thus, it would be better for them to train more Chinese candidates. To do that, the administrative staff of these universities should be mainly comprised of Chinese people. The directorate of the Christian universities should invite successful graduates and those who deeply sympathized with the Christian education to be members, all of whom would shoulder the proper responsibilities in implementing the universities' programmes. The "higher efficiency" required that Christian universities resolve to academically stay ahead of other Chinese universities. Therefore, they should pay attention to teaching traditional Chinese scholarship. Taking into account the fact that students' training in this aspect was very limited in their middle schools, Christian universities should formulate minimum requirements regarding the traditional Chinese scholarship, namely, that students must be able to write smoothly, compose essays in Chinese as required by higher education, and keenly appreciate the essence of Chinese culture. In helping students acquire this ability, Christian universities should set up courses focusing on Chinese language, literature, history, geography and philosophy, through which students could practise their knowledge to the full. Only Chinese scholars who attained excellent study in these fields would be eligible to teach these courses. Moreover, it must be stipulated that Chinese professors should teach these courses in Chinese and foreign-born professors should teach their subjects in English. When a Christian university was selecting professors, the Chinese candidates would be given priority if the candidates were equal in scholarship and teaching. As for the application for the position of professor of traditional Chinese scholarship, those who had a good command of English would have priority. With the help of these bilingual professors, students could simultaneously master both English and Chinese. Where the career development of the faculty was concerned, all teachers would be given equal opportunity to further their scholarship. In Christian universities, both Chinese and foreign-born professors would have a promising future and be encouraged to become top-notch scholars in their fields. The "more profound Christianization" was the hope that students studying in Christian schools would finally be entirely reformed by Christianity. Historically, religion had played a great role in the refinement of human conduct and Christianity had made a very special contribution to China. Therefore, for Christian schools, the religious ceremonies held in the campus should meet the spiritual needs of the Chinese; religious courses must be carefully selected and organized, so that students could interest themselves in Christianity; and professors should integrate themselves with students and lead students to reform themselves by acquiring the Christian spirit.[30] Among the three approaches furthering Christian education's contribution to China, the first two were obviously related to the indigenization of Christian education. Specifically, the first was about the Sinicization of administrative work of Christian schools; and the second, the Sinicization of faculty and the curricula. The third, which focused primarily on the propagation of Christianity in campuses, was actually an effort to Sinicize the Christian missionary work, on the grounds that it emphasized that religious ceremonies and subjects should be adaptable to Chinese students.

The 2nd CCM was actually an impetus to the publication of the SCCC's own journal. Originally, the SCCC, a national educational organization, had only an English quarterly. But, in reality, the majority of teachers working for Christian schools in China did not have a good command of English. It was thus a pity that most of these teachers were unable to read the English journal.[31] Meanwhile, the 2nd CCM pushed forward the indigenization of the Chinese Christian Church. As a consequence, the SCCC decided to publish a Chinese journal. As a consequence, the Chinese journal entitled *Chinese Christian Education Quarterly* (*Education Quarterly* for short) made its debut in March 1925. Cheng Xiangfan, the deputy general secretary, was the chief editor of *Education Quarterly*.

The debut edition of *Education Quarterly* stated that its goal was as follows:

> [The journal] will do its utmost to carry through the indigenization of Christian education in China, bring into full play the true spirit of Christianized education, disseminate all kinds of scientific educational

approaches, and lead Chinese and Western ideas of education to freely communicate with one another.

In order to implement the Sinicization of Christian education, the manifesto published in the debut edition of *Education Quarterly* affirmed that nationalism would be the principle of education; that state had the right to cultivate citizenship by means of education; and that such an educational endeavour was an obligation that must be undertaken by the state. Only if the state was unable to set up enough schools for all children would schools managed by individuals and corporations be allowed to operate. Meanwhile, the state must formulate standards and requirements, by which it could supervise and direct private schools. But, in reality, as confessed by the manifesto, the true situation was as follows:

> [At present, Christian schools] are set up as they please and none of them are officially registered. As a result, the implementation of nationalism, the curricula meeting the nationalist education's basic requirement to maintain national unity, the standards respecting teaching devices, and the government's rights of inspection and supervision are all not treated with respect.

In view of this, the manifesto required that the Christian primary school must respect China's education sovereignty. The manifesto mentioned the 1922 report prepared by the Chinese education inspectorate, which said Christian schools in China were not educational institutions under foreign governments' control but instead they aspired to bring happiness to China and the Chinese people. It pointed out that, contrary to the 1922 report's defence,

> Christian schools actually cannot justify themselves in terms of their forms and content. We hold that Christian schools in China should be entirely Sinicized. The management of these school should be open to the Chinese and all these schools will be managed by the Chinese, finally. Except for a few special cases, all courses should be taught in Chinese in Christian schools. Those who teach courses on the traditional Chinese scholarship and social sciences should pay particular attention to this. Christian schools at all levels must be officially registered. The financial affairs of these schools should be gradually transferred to Chinese Christians. In doing so, China's education sovereignty will not be endangered; nor will the Christian education be inadaptable to the true Chinese conditions. Thus, it can be said that, if Christian schools really want to find a place in the system of national education and enjoy full rights, they must transform themselves from missionaries' schools to the Chinese people's schools and from foreign churches' schools to the Chinese Christianity's private schools.[32]

In a word, Christian schools must be Sinicized. The manifesto, acknowledging that in fact Christian schools did attach much greater importance to the Christianization of education, emphasized that Christian schools' endeavour had a positive thrust, which was as follows:

> [Christian schools aspire to] reform young students by means of Christ's enthusiasm for saving the world and the spirit of service and sacrifice. Through this Christian education, the young Chinese gain immeasurable power of religion, so that they will not be affected by snobbishness when they do patriotic activities. Moreover, these young students, who have already been equipped with Christ's abundant love and willingness to sacrifice, will not be easily thwarted by dangerous environments but will carry through their mission serving the society to the end.

In addition, the manifesto stressed that the Christian education based on sectarianism was not at all the Christianized education advocated by Chinese Christians. This indicated that even Christian schools should abandon the Christian education that was of a sectarian nature. The Christianized education favoured by Chinese Christians was an education such that it nurtured the souls of young students with religious morality, that is, the spirit of Christ, and it convincingly harmonized with the nationalist education and facilitated the cultivation of young students' patriotic feelings and aspirations to serve society. In a word, this Christian education might clear up the 2nd CCM's misunderstanding of Christianity.

The publication of this manifesto produced an immediate response from Christians and free thinkers. Chinese and Western Christian educators repeatedly discussed it and finally formulated nine basic principles regarding Christian education, all of which were embodied in the published *Manifesto of Chinese Christian Educational Circles* (hereinafter referred to as *Education Manifesto*).[33] The main content of the *Education Manifesto* was as follows:

1. Christian schools can play special roles and assist public schools in China. On the one hand, they can provide children with a Christianized education. On the other hand, they can be the proper places, where those who prefer the Christianized education want their children to be schooled.
2. Private schools should be democratic. Apart from state-run public schools, individuals and corporations are all allowed to set up private schools in the light of the democratic spirit and democracy adopted by many countries. Both public and private schools must meet the basic requirement stipulated by the state. And private schools should never contradict the interests of state and society.
3. Private schools can contribute to the progress of education. It is generally recognized that the progress of education is dependent on the diversity of forms of schooling and the maximum freedom of management of the school. If the state puts an end to this freedom, applies restrictions to all

schools, and demands that, no matter how big or trivial, all educational affairs must be handled in accordance with the uniform standard, the development of national education will be affected. Therefore, private schools should be given maximum freedom and at the same time they should strictly abide by the essential criteria required by the state. The more freedom private schools can have, the greater progress in education will be made. The more progressive education is, the more benefit to the country will be given.

4. Private schools can be conducive to the freedom of religious belief. Teaching religion in private school is in accordance with the principle of freedom of faith, which is unambiguously stipulated by the national constitution and a general praxis of countries governed by the people. In accordance with this principle, individuals not only can, freely and conscientiously, believe in religion but also have the freedom to teach their own children the religion. This principle should be applied to all religions.

5. Christian schools should be part and parcel of the system of national education. Private schools should be, of course, administered by the national education authorities and one of parts of the system of national education. To achieve this, all private schools must be registered in the relevant departments of the government. All registered schools must abide by the educational laws and regulations, adapt themselves to the academic standards stipulated by the government, and be supervised by the education authorities. Moreover, private schools should be given freedom to operate. The Christian education does expect this and at the same time shows sincere respect for China's sovereignty in education. As far as the Christian educative association focusing on research and consultation work is concerned, it cannot be a substitute for the education authorities but an auxiliary organ aiming to increase solidarity and efficiency.

6. Christian schools should be allowed to teach religion. Although the form of education varies greatly, the basic goal of the varied forms of education without exception is the cultivation of a healthy personality and morality. Herein lies education's contribution to the future of the country, just as Christians believe firmly. But, in practice, when it comes to the registration of Christian schools, the education authorities, earnestly and tirelessly, tell applicants that the official registration is premised on the restraint on teaching religion and the abandonment of Christianized schools. However, this practice is not only against the freedoms of teaching and belief but also contradicts the basic principle of Christian education and finally hinders Christian schools from making a special contribution to Chinese education.

7. Christian schools can help in the cultivation of patriotic feelings. The Christian spirit is actually embodied in enlightened patriotic activities. For this reason, it can never be at odds with patriotism. Christian schools always aim at nurturing students' patriotic feelings. If not, they would be treated as institutes disloyal to the Christian education. The accusations

that Christian schools destroy the national character of students and act as megaphones for imperialistic propaganda are totally groundless. Both Chinese and Western Christian educators deeply reject the motive of these irresponsible accusers.
8. Christian education can be in the interests of the country. Christian schools devote themselves to benefitting the country and its people as far as possible, even though they are set up and managed by Western missionaries and their governing churches. In terms of spirit, management and maintenance, these schools are essentially Chinese. It is always what Chinese and Western Christian educators expect. Even Christian churches, which consistently support these schools financially, have similar aspirations. Fortunately, their dreams have come true in China, where the management and maintenance of Christian schools are being gradually transferred to Chinese Christians.
9. The perpetual foundation of Christian education is not the privileges given by (unequal) treaties with China but the enthusiasm of Christian communities and the healthy public opinion (about Christianity and the Church) in China.

These nine points indicated that the Christian educational circles did not want to give up teaching religion from the ethical perspective in Christian schools. But at the same time, Christian educators did carefully consider the 2nd CCM's criticism of Christian education. For example, in responding to the criticisms that Christian schools availed themselves of unequal treaties to grab privileges and that they taught students to be unpatriotic, Chinese Christian educators clearly pointed out that the Christian education was under the administration of the state, congruous with patriotism, in the interests of China, and independent of unequal treaties. Overall, the *Education Manifesto* was more progressive in comparison with previous ones, even though many Western participants of this discussion did not understand the indigenization of Christian education in China as well as the enlightened Chinese Christians did.

The vast majority of Chinese Christians agreed with the idea that Christian schools did need to set up religious courses. For them, teaching religion was part and parcel of the Christian education. Exactly because of this, the educators of the 2nd CCM and their counterparts in the Christian education could by no means reach any consensus. But, in fact, there was indeed a very small number of Chinese Christians, who actually supported the critics. Among them, some argued that religious education should not always be conducted in Christian schools, but instead it could be carried out in places other than school campuses. Take Zhao Guanhai, for example.[34] He said: "No matter how developed Christian schools will be, the religious education should never be fully dependent on them." Thus, Zhao suggested that the Church itself should organize stratified religious education classes corresponding to the general education. His proposal was as follows:

The well-developed Anglo-American churches have done what the Chinese Church should do. Even in the United States, religious ceremonies and teaching the Bible are banned in all public schools. Consequently, the religious education of the American Church has to be conducted in places outside school campuses, that is, the halls of churches. Frankly, this really efficiently works.

In addition, the family was naturally an institution to teach religion. Zhao also advised the Church to make use of existing dormitories, summer schools and mass education places to teach religion. Of course, his suggestions were criticized by many members of the Church. A more heated debate was thus launched.

In addition to criticizing Christian schools, many activists of the 2nd CCM objected to Christianity from the perspective of nationalism. Therefore, quite a few Christians responded to these critics. Among them, some positively affirmed nationalism and tried their best to prove that Christianity was congruous with nationalism and thus could be adaptable to the Chinese society. Take Wu Leichuan, for example. He, doctrinally and theologically, demonstrated that Christianity and nationalism did not necessarily contradict each other. His statement read: "In my opinion, although many threads of Christian doctrines are superior to nationalist principles, parts of them can condescend to be propitious to nationalism."

Wu, corroborating this, resorted to the personality of Jesus, the main thrust of Jesus's teaching and the national character of the Jewish people. First, the personality of Jesus. Religion was the centre of the politics, etiquette and customs of the Jewish kingdom. Thus, if the religious idea changed, all other things would change accordingly. For Jesus:

> He spent his life reforming religion. He resolved to fight for the society and died with no regrets. Jesus might be the first patriot in the history of humankind. Therefore, Jesus's purity, bravery and fortitude are exactly what the present-day Republic of China needs most.

Second, the teachings of Jesus. The two most basic Christian doctrines—to love God and to love others as oneself—were both ascribed to Jesus. If Chinese people really believed in Christianity, they would sincerely defend the truth and serve society. As the number of such Chinese Christians increases, they would definitely exert a very good influence on society. Third, the national character of the Jewish people. Those who advocated nationalism must attach the greatest importance to the national character. Jesus was born in the era when the Roman Empire oppressed the Jewish people. Although his country was too weak to make a difference, Jesus exerted all his energy to reform the country on a large scale, hoping that as soon as the Jewish people were awakened, they would lead the Roman Empire to change fundamentally. Herein the national character of the Jews was manifested. By contrast, the Chinese were sluggish, disorganized and disunited, even though they did have many good characters. Jesus's personality and teaching were precisely the best remedy for the defects of the Chinese. Finally, Wu's conclusion was that Christianity was such a religion that it taught people to love themselves, love society and love their country and thus there was no conflict between Christianity and nationalism.[35]

What Chen Baoquan opined was similar to that of Wu Leichuan. First, he expounded and verified the reconciliation of Christian doctrines and nationalism. Meanwhile, he contended that the 2nd CCM had reason to treat Christianity as something running counter to nationalism, on the grounds that Christianity had spread in China by means of unequal treaties and Christian schools availed themselves of the privileges of refusing to register officially with China's education authorities, rejecting China's requirement respecting the curricula, disobeying the principle of separation of religion from politics, and clinging on to the medieval missionary work. Among the Chinese young people, the popular idea that Christianity was against nationalism was not totally ungrounded. But, on the other hand, Chen held that this religious phenomenon was actually temporary and it was unreasonable to simplistically think Christian doctrines were essentially against nationalism.[36] All these essays recognized nationalism from the perspective of patriotism and in doing so they demonstrated that both Christians and free thinkers in China had the same patriotic feeling.

Unlike Chinese Christians such as the above-mentioned Wu, who commented favourably on nationalism, some treated nationalism with reserve. For example, Xu Baoqian said:

> On the one hand, nationalism has made a contribution to history. But on the other hand, needless to say, nationalism can lead to a war of aggression. [In view of this, the national campaign condemning Christianity may pose two hazards to the country.] First, at most, critics help the country find a solution to be powerful and prosperous, meanwhile paying no heed to what the standards of power and prosperity should be—material or spiritual? Nor do they care what the international ethical foundation of their solutions is—might or truth? Second, this national campaign is nationalist in name. In fact, it is an imported goods, or simply a duplication of European and American praxis. It can neither carry forward the essence of traditional Chinese culture nor shoulder China's global mission.

At the same time, Xu fully recognized the 2nd CCM's two well-grounded requirements, that is, taking back the right of education and abrogating unequal treaties with China. He pointed out that, inasmuch as the Christian education was based on universal fraternity, in no way could it depend on unequal treaties nor should it make use of education to propagate religion, otherwise it would do harm to China's education sovereignty. Xu went further, arguing that independence, one of the prerequisites of education, should not be equated with a coercive uniform policy such as the entirely ungrounded demand that all students in Christian schools must read the Bible; that coercive policies and free scholarship should never be placed in the same category; and that Christian schools should abandon their belittlement of the Chinese language and cultural essence, which could be found in a few public and private schools, too. His final conclusion was that the best method of counterbalancing Christian schools was by reforming schools that were not affiliated to any Christian organizations.[37]

Echoing Xu, Gao Houde argued against nationalism. In one of his articles, Gao comparatively analysed *Exhortation to Chinese Learning* by Zhang Zhidong, a renowned reform-minded governor-general of late Qing, and *The Nationalist Education* by Yu Jiaju and Li Huang from the SYC. According to Gao, Zhang Zhidong was really patriotic, because, on the one hand, he advocated the preservation of traditional Chinese culture and, on the other hand, encouraged China to assimilate cultures of other countries. By contrast, Yu Jiaju's discourse was a mass of contradictions. Nationalism in Yu's book was not the Chinese nationalism but something imported from the West. The new Chinese nationalism was not a product of the nineteenth century but a thought adaptable to the modern spirit. Gao thus warned:

> The restriction produced by nationalism in its narrow sense is as pernicious as the bad governance attributed to despotic rule. Freedoms of publication, belief and education are [indispensable] foundations perfectly in harmony with any form of modern nationalism. [Therefore,] the new Chinese nationalism should accord with the cosmopolitanism [and] be so magnanimous and so tolerant that it is open to all forces conducive to progress [and the development of Chinese education in particular]. [Moreover,] the new Chinese new nationalism should not be non-religious nor anti-religious. Rather, it should be tolerant enough to accommodate all religious beliefs and activities.

Overall, Gao affirmed Zhang Zhidong's idea, meanwhile negating viewpoints developed by Yu Jiaju and Li Huang.[38] It should be pointed out that, although the afore-mentioned Christians all criticized nationalism, they unanimously held that the Christian education must play a role in preserving traditional Chinese culture, pay attention to the national character, and call for the abrogation of unequal treaties. All these efforts helped to push forward the indigenization of Christian schools.

Before the Shanghai Massacre, it was generally held among Chinese Christians that the 2nd CCM's accusation that Christianity was the tip of a spearhead of imperialism was entirely groundless and completely untenable. As a result, only a small number of Christians responded to their critics. The few response articles penned by Zhao Guanhai[39] and Peng Jinzhang[40] all resolutely defended Christianity and refuted the criticisms. Even so, the patriotic feeling was very obvious in their writings.

In his article, Zhao Guanhai enumerated ten differences between Christianity and imperialism. Contrary to imperialism, which turned human beings into tools, practised obscurantist policy, defended class oppression and oppressed women, the Church and Christian schools did their best to advocate the idea that everyone is equal, to promote mass education, to oppose the class system, to emancipate women and to give women full rights. In imperialist countries, aristocrats bled the people to the extreme, ingratiated themselves with capitalists, worked hand in glove with warlords and treated other countries and peoples as if they were inferior. On the contrary, the Christian Church and its schools did their best to be self-supporting, to improve the status of the proletariat and the workers, and to disseminate anti-war thought and internationalism. Imperialist countries had wild ambitions and embraced jingoism. Unlike them, the Christian Church and its schools loved others as themselves and even treated enemies as friends, meanwhile earnestly promoting religious emancipation and freedom of belief. Zhao evidenced the positive roles the Christian Church played in Chinese society by citing instances, such as when the great Chinese Christians like Sun Yat-sen and others made contributions to the founding and development of the Republic of China, missionaries supported the Hundred Days' Reform and the Revolutionary Army overthrowing Qing, the Church equally provided men and women with schooling, and Christian organizations set up schools and hospitals in China. Finally, he concluded that, in comparison with those overenthusiastic Chinese nationalists, the Church and Christian schools were actually more far-sighted, because they had realized that the only way of national salvation did not lie in empty slogans but in the intensive study; more broad-minded, because they knew well that the national salvation of China and the endeavour to rehabilitate the world were inseparable; more noble-minded, because they discerned between right and wrong in strict accordance with God's law rather than with secular merits; and more open-minded, because they always made judgements through reason and should never abandon themselves to emotions.

Peng Jinzhang stressed that Christianity and imperialism were as incompatible as fire and water. The reason why some critics of Christianity regarded this religion as a running dog of imperialism was that Christianity was indeed used by imperialism and in some cases a few Christians were indeed as wildly ambitious as politicians and warlords. Peng himself did not defend Christianity in this regard. But he pointed out that this was not Christianity's fault. If, Peng contended, Christianity were a form of imperialism, it would have met two requirements: (1) that the founder of Christianity gained power by means of his religion; and (2) that the basic Christian doctrines had a tendency to reward imperialism. However, Christianity did not conform to the two requirements. Digging into the life of the founder of Christianity, we find that it was actually anti-imperialist and ardently promoted the spirit of serving others. Nor were there any Christian doctrines that were consistent with imperialism. As far as the fact that Christianity was used by imperialism was concerned, it was not Christianity but imperialism that committed this sin. In many cases, religions other than Christianity were used by imperialism, too. For countries and individuals who paraded their Christian faith meanwhile invading other peoples, what they did was personal conduct against the Christian ethics. Moreover, Peng sincerely suggested critics take into account the fact that many non-Christian countries perpetrated aggression against other countries and imperialism was not at all a specialty produced only by Christianity.

Although Chinese Christians did not think the 2nd CCM's criticism of Christianity was grounded and merely responded to critics in a lukewarm way, the debates did improve the Chinese Christians' observation of imperialism and led them to join the anti-imperialist movement in the wake of the Shanghai Massacre.

The 2nd CCM was a direct impetus to the discussion of indigenization of the Christian Church in China. Xie Fuya provides us with a good explanation. He said:

> This national campaign criticizing Christianity can be divided into three genres. The first, having itself based on nationalism, severely rebukes Christian schools and advocates the separation of religion from education. This criticism is worthy of consideration. The second criticizes Christianity from the perspective of Communism, denouncing this religion as a running dog of capitalism and imperialism. Facts and public opinions will respond to this criticism. I will not comment on this. The third, critically and academically, rethinks Christianity in the light of the Chinese national character and makes the conclusion that Christianity is too intellectually narrow-minded, Christian doctrines paying close attention to heavenly rather than human affairs are too close to superstition, and thus Christianity is not helpful but harmful to China. I personally hold that the third genre of criticism deserves most further study. In the meantime, I think the entirety of the Chinese people should candidly discuss the problems besetting the country. Frankly, Christianity is indeed well represented in present-day Chinese society, education and institutions. It is a significant truth obvious to all. Thus, no matter whether or not Christianity is helpful or harmful to China, this religion can by no means be ignored at present. If it is helpful to the country, we should study how to make full use of it. If it is harmful to the country, we should make an urgent effort to rectify it.[41]

Xie's words perfectly indicated that the 2nd CCM did push forward members of Christian Church's discussion of the relationship between Christianity and the Chinese nation and culture.

When it came to Christianity's integration with the Chinese culture, one of Xie Fuya's treatises was worth being discussed.[42] Xie analysed the reasons why Western missionary work in China could not be successful, pointing out:

> What Western missionaries propagate in China is not entirely the true way of Jesus. Few Western missionaries have a good command of the essence of Chinese culture. They do the missionary work in the light of Jesus's spirit of "fulfilling the law."

Where the reason why the Chinese generally had an aversion to Christianity was concerned, it was that missionaries' doctrines, which resolved to destroy conventional Chinese habits and beliefs, were too crude to gain even the slightest popularity among the well-educated Chinese scholar-officials and that missionaries thought too highly of themselves, looked down on others, acted like masters, and finally became much less attractive to the lower echelons of Chinese society. Because of these, Christianity had failed to take root in China. Xie contended that many Chinese people did not know that Christianity changed in pace with the development of history and mistakenly regarded modern Christianity as a duplicate of the medieval Christianity. He pointed out that the doctrines of modern Christianity had been radically reconstructed due to several factors. The first factor was science, in which the theory of evolution played the greatest role. The second factor was philosophy, in which the philosophy of life and pragmatism exerted the strongest influence. The third factor consisted of socio-political elements. According to Xie, the modern Christian doctrine was built on five intellectual threads. The first was humanism, by which Christianity shifted the centre of gravity from God to the value of humans. In other words, the Christian doctrine returned to Jesus's own thinking, which asserted that God was the father of man, man was the son of God and the entire universe was a family of love. The second was this-worldliness, through which Christianity shifted attention from the Other World to This World. Intellectually reconstructed Christianity believed that the Heavenly Kingdom in the ideal society could come true and expand in the real society and recognized the value of the human body, which might be treated as the temple wherein God resided. The third was positivism, which helped Christianity transform from the arbitrary phase of theologizing and the chaotic phase of mythologizing to the positive phase of scientific knowledge. It was in the positive phase that Christianity, science and society harmonized with one another. The fourth was socialism, which inspired Christianity to metamorphose from an individual faith to a social religion, abandoning the selfish aspiration to gain entrance into Heaven and exemption from going to hell and devoting itself to saving the entire society. The fifth was activism, which emancipated Christianity from the isolation of man and God and handed over the submission of the soul to God to the measure of serving the people. In a word, Jesus's practical spirit should be carried forward by means of activism. All five intellectual threads could be attributed to the personality of Jesus. In addition, Xie argued that modern Christian thought was at least partially influenced by the Eastern culture. For example, a number of Westerners were intellectually open to Buddhist karma. Therefore,

The state-of-the-art Christian intellectual edifice is not only sustained by the above-mentioned five pillars but it also has a Buddhist corner tower and Daoist windows. It is such a Christian Church that is built on the East, oriented to the West, and renowned for a myriad of varied scenes.

"If Christianity is open-minded enough to accept Buddhist noble ideas, what lies ahead of it must be brilliant and impressive." Xie furthered his discussion, demonstrating that it would be necessary and possible for Christianity to integrate with Confucianism. According to him, Confucius's idea that benevolence was meant to love all people was globally incomparable. Thanks to this Confucian teaching, the Chinese nation was the people who knew best the ethics in the world. Xie thus concluded:

The Chinese nation must shoulder the responsibility for intermingling Christianity and Confucianism. Originally, people regarded Christianity as one of the best seeds of ethics, taking into account the Christian teaching that God was the benevolent father, the universal fraternity prevailed in human society, and the Heavenly Kingdom was a perfect family. Unfortunately, this seed was sown in the West devoid of ethnic attainments. As a consequence, after struggling for two thousand years, it merely produced one or two flowers with dry, wrinkled petals, which were frequently used by the privileged classes. Finally, the truth about Jesus was covered just as a dust storm clouds over the sun. What a pity! It is generally held among people of insight that the true Christianity has not yet been discovered in the West. From now on, the seed of true Christianity shall be sown in the land known for its rich ethical resources. Thus, the Chinese nation should not decline to shoulder the responsibility for cultivating and watering the seed of true Christianity.

Xie said the fusion of Christianity and Confucianism not only could improve the Christian religion and Western civilization but also could contribute to the traditional Chinese thought. If a culture kept growing but was complacent, refused contact with the world, and disliked assimilating new cultural and intellectual elements, it would remain stagnant, sink into atrophy and finally head for extinction. Therefore, China should never close its door to the world. Inasmuch as Christianity had already arrived in China, the Chinese should understand and try it. At this point, he especially pointed out that what China should assimilate was not the Christian *jiao* (dogmas) but the Christian Dao (Way). To put it another way, the Christian *jiao* was not very helpful but even harmful to China; by contrast, the Dao of Jesus helped to nourish the country. Xie thus explained:

There is a huge difference between Dao and *jiao*. Dao is life. Dao is the course in which humans practise their morality to be benevolence. *Jiao* is specific teaching, or expedient explanation. The Confucian classic known as *The Doctrine of the Mean* explains the difference between Dao and *jiao* in the most subtle way, saying: "According with nature epitomizes Dao and practising Dao begets *jiao*." The Christian Dao refers to the thoughts of Jesus and the life wherein the spirit of Jesus nestles; and the Christian *jiao*, laws and regulations that evolve from explanations of the Dao through the ages and constantly change according to time and circumstances.[43]

In China, where Christianity had existed over one hundred years, what was disseminated through missionary work was unexceptionally *jiao*. Consequently, Christianity did not yet exert any significant influence on Chinese culture. If Christianity really wanted to influence China and make a contribution to China, it must carry forward the Christian Dao, in which there were three elements that could be closely combined with Chinese culture. The first was the main thrust of Jesus's thinking, that is, God was father of all humans and all humans were brothers and sisters. Jesus gave equal treatment to all people, regardless of age, sex and origin. Herein lay the highest ideal of true love. Although Jesus did not advocate the five most basic human relationships as Confucius did:

> In his mind, these relationships are self-evident and need no elaboration. Throughout his life, Jesus showed consideration for all people and never acted against these basic human relationships. It is particularly worth mentioning that Jesus used the father-son relationship to analogize the relationship between God and humans. How wise and far-sighted was his analogy!

For Xie, Jesus's unity of Heaven and man and relevant ethical thinking adequately complemented the established Chinese thought in this regard. The second was the positive spirit of Jesus. Jesus fearlessly pursued the truth. He had a strong, compassionate feeling for all humankind. His faith was profound, broad and optimistic. All these perfectly harmonized with the Confucian golden mean and rectified malpractice. Xie thus said:

> Jesus's positive spirit can only be found in the teaching of the Golden Mean. Therefore, we know how profound Jesus's positive spirit is. The teaching of the Golden Mean can only be epitomized in Jesus's positive spirit. Therefore, we know how extensive Jesus's positive spirit is. In future, the fusion of Christianity and Confucianism will be the greatest!

The third was the perfect personality of Jesus. Humanity needed a model personality, which was the motive power of the evolution of the world and the improvement of human nature. The model should be Jesus's personality, about which even enemies of Jesus were unable to carp. Compared with Jesus, Confucius was merely a paragon of a certain time in a certain place. "China might not need a living model of personality. If it needs one, Jesus can be the model that is good enough to make contribution to the country." In a word, Jesus really could contribute to China.

Why should we study the relationship between Christianity and Chinese culture and how to conduct this study? Duan Guanglu set forth the answers in one of his papers.[44] He, first of all, discussed the motive for this study. First, the new cultural movement liberated the Chinese people from the old culture by means of criticism and brought new life to the Chinese culture. As far as the nutriment of new cultural life was concerned, it consisted of brand-new ingredients and ingredients scientifically extracted from the old culture. Only when the two types of ingredients were refined, purified and syncretized would the new, good culture nutriment be created. How to select the brand-new nutriment greatly mattered to the rehabilitation of Chinese culture. The wrong selection would not create anything nutritious but produce a deadly poison instead. Christianity was perfectly the right choice. The Chinese should, fairly and scientifically, study and try Christianity. This was exactly one of the motives for the study of the relationship of Christianity and Chinese culture. Second, although Christianity had existed in China over one century, the Christian Church was still Western and rootless. As soon as the international relationship changed drastically, this Church would disappear immediately. For this reason, how to indigenize the Christian Church in China was an extremely important issue. Indigenization was the Chinese Christians' spirit of distinguishing themselves. The effort to carry forward this spirit must be based on the inherent nature and national instinct, both of which were nurtured in the Chinese culture that had lasted for thousands of years. Meanwhile, first-rate nutriment contributing to the fusion of Christianity and Chinese culture was indispensable to the indigenized Christian Church. Therefore, exploring what the ingredients of this nutriment were and how to produce them and make them suitable for China and able to meet the needs of the time constituted the second motive for the study of the relationship between Christianity and Chinese culture. There were two points respecting the interrelation of Christianity and Chinese culture. One was religion; the other was culture. The scope of culture was very extensive, including science, literature, ethics, politics, economy, art, and so on. Religion was merely one of the components of culture. But it was from religion that culture stemmed. Psychologically, religion was the orientation of emotional instincts; and culture was the result of the evolution of reason. Christianity differentiated itself from other religions in the standards of values, such as the view of God, ethics, care for believers, its ultimate goal, the personality of founder, the sources of clericalism and religious vitality. At the same time, the Chinese culture was different from other cultures. Therefore, Duan analysed the difference between the Eastern and Western cultures. The Western culture was dynamic and the Eastern culture was tranquil. Duan, citing Liang Shuming, a renowned Chinese scholar, wrote: "The Western culture has a positive spirit to move forward, so that two brilliant cultural products, namely, science and democracy, are created. The Eastern culture has an artistic spirit, loves ancient times and develops an abstract, intuitive methodology."

In the Eastern cultures, the Chinese culture and the Indian culture were different from each other. Liang Shuming pointed out that the Chinese and Indian cultures walked different paths. For China, it tended to change, accommodate, and balance its own wills and desires. By contrast, India preferred to renounce and turn back. Inspired by this, Duan contended:

> [The characteristic of Chinese culture] is such a spirit that it aspires to be impartial, reposeful, harmonious and balanced. It has the following results. In the physical world, there is a natural contentedness. In the human society, people have been accustomed to the common practice in which persons of good morality are competing for greater popularity. Moreover, people are deeply influenced by families and think highly of the big family wherein five generations are living under one roof. In the end, this spirit influences the Chinese so greatly that they are perfectly in harmony with the rest of the world, acquire an optimistic, broad vision, and aspire to even out all things. Through which, we can grasp the most distinctive character of the Chinese culture.[45]

On the basis of above analyses, Duan proposed three research methods that could be applied to the study of Chinese culture. The first was the method of comparison-elimination. To be specific, researchers should comparatively study how Christianity and the Chinese culture treated the material, spiritual and social aspects of human life and then preserve the best and eliminate the worst. The second was the method of harmonization. After criticism and elimination (of the worst), researchers should lead Christianity and Chinese culture to harmonize each other. In doing so, an indigenized Christianity would be created to advance the new Chinese culture. The third was the method of propagation. In the light of the result of harmonization, researchers should study how to more efficiently propagate this indigenized Christianity.

Duan, inquiring into the spiritual, material and social dimensions of Christianity and Chinese culture, made an analysis of their advantages and disadvantages. Then, after a comparative examination, the disadvantages would be eliminated. For example, the spiritual disadvantages of Christianity were that it failed to make due contributions to human ideals; that it had a strong bias towards inheritance, established customs and conservatism, all of which were actually obstructions to culture; and that it bred a number of superstitious followers and thus was unable to illuminate truth. As far as the spiritual disadvantages of Chinese culture were concerned, they were that superstitious belief in spirits and predestined fate and woe prevailed; that some Chinese blindly followed officials; and that some Chinese obstinately adhered to established praxes. Moreover, the material and social disadvantages attributed to Christianity and Chinese culture should be eliminated, too. On the other hand, their advantages should be harmonized with each other and carried forward. The spiritual advantages of Christianity were the moral creativity, enthusiasm for serving truth, and inclination for modernity. The spiritual advantages of Chinese culture were optimism accommodating people to any circumstances, pacifism promoting peace, and evenhandedness renowned for its magnanimity, generosity and tolerance. By blending together the spiritual advantages of Christianity and Chinese culture, the inappropriateness of doctrines of imported Christianity would be eliminated and the weakness of the Chinese cultural spirit be rectified. For example, if the Chinese (cultural) optimism assimilated Christian moral creativity, it would be the true optimism teaching people not to be content with temporary ease and comfort but to acquire proper methods by positively adapting themselves to any circumstances. Another example was the Chinese pacifism. If it assimilated the Christian spirit of serving the people and sacrificing for the people, the passive expectation of peace would be turned into the positive creation of peace. In addition, the combination of socio-material advantages of Christianity and the Chinese culture would definitely render good results. For example, if the Chinese personality of *junzi* (people of great virtues) and the noble, intelligent Christian prophets' spirit of fighting against vicious power were blended together, the Chinese *junzi* would have a strong will to combat evils. If the Chinese family spirit was combined with the socially idealistic Christian millenarianism, there would be more perfect consequences of social transformation.

In the end, Duan discussed how to propagate Christianity in China. First of all, the community of Chinese *junzi*, namely, Chinese intellectuals, should be introduced to Christianity. In the meantime, the ordinary people and rural residents in particular should be exposed to Christianity. To do this, the missionary work should promote mass education and the family-based reading group. In this regard, Duan said: "The truly Sinicized Christianity does not exist in schools nor in churches nor in tall rostrums for public speeches but in the families of all social classes." In a word, the true, ultimate foothold of Sinicization of Christianity lay in the Christianization of all Chinese families.

On 1 May 1925, Fan Bihai delivered a speech in a seminar on moral education of the youth that was held in Hangzhou.[46] In this speech, Fan stressed that the Chinese culture not only could merge into Christianity but also could make progress through this integration. He explained that there were some prerequisites for this course. First, contextually, the Chinese culture referred only to the best elements of Chinese culture. Those wrong, absurd elements handed down generation after generations and deteriorated social customs should be all discarded. Second, Christianity did not at all denote the Christian Church but the most basic doctrine of Christianity. Duan defined culture as the endeavour to teach people to be civilized, which was comprised of religion, ethics, philosophy, science and art. Different peoples were good at one aspect. For example, the Hebrews were renowned for their well-developed religion; the Greeks had advanced philosophy and art and later were known for their science in the Renaissance; the Indians prided themselves on developing religious philosophy; and the Chinese were famous for their highly refined ethical philosophy. In ancient China, ethics and philosophy were well integrated; religious faith was much less developed; and science and art had sprouted and grown very slowly. Thus, the issue of ethics was particularly indispensable to present-day discussions of China. Chinese ethics had quite a long history. Fan reconstructed this history, saying:

> When Confucius was sorting out ancient historical documents, he chose the eras of Tang and Yu [i.e., Emperors of Yao and Shun] as the starting point of the periodization of history. The two chapters entitled *Yaodian* (the Canon of Yao) and *Gaoyaomo* (the Counsel of Gaoyao) in *The Book of History* had, extensively and profoundly, set forth the essence of Chinese ethics the most. According to the two treatises, ethics originated from Heaven and are applied to the entirety of humankind. What are the ethics? They consist of the five most basic orders [respecting human relationships]. How to lead ethics to come into effect? It depends on the five ways of morally cultivating people. Sequentially, ethics proceed from oneself to others and from one's own family, to the country and, finally, to the entire world and humankind. What is Dao (the Way)? The heavenly-decreed ethics are Dao. What is *de* (the Virtue)? The implementation of ethics is *de*. For humankind, how to upwardly harmonize with the Intention of Heaven and downwardly achieve good governance on the Earth? As soon as ethics are universally implemented, the harmony between Heaven and humanity, the worldwide good governance, and the peace prevailing over the entire planet will come true immediately. [Thanks to] Confucius, who made a great effort to illuminate the doctrines of sage kings such as Yao and Shun and carry forward the great teachings of three great eras led by the Emperor Yu, King Tang and the kings Wen and Wu respectively, the Confucian ethics have grown fully-fledged.[47]

Confucianism finally became the orthodoxy of Chinese culture. Accordingly, ethics represented the orthodoxy of Chinese culture. From this point of view, Fan dissected and explained *The Confucian Analects*. He contended that Confucius's *ren* (benevolence), the key of Confucian thinking, was a combination of *zhong* (being true to principles of one's own nature) and *shu* (exercising one's doctrines on the principle of reciprocity). To put it another way, *zhong* was that what you wanted to be done to yourself, so you had to do it to others first; and *shu*, "[w]hat you do not want done to yourself, do not do to others."[48] The Confucian ethics consisting of filial piety, fraternal duties, loyalty and truthfulness could be explained in the light of *zhong* and *shu*. *Zhong* could be embodied in Confucius's sincere wishes that "[they] are, in regard to the aged, to give them rest; in regard to friends, to show them sincerity; in regard to the young, to treat them tenderly."[49] These wishes could be applied to the whole of humanity. *Zhong* and *shu* could thus be generalized as the principle that a sovereign should "[love] what the people love and [hate] what the people hate,"[50] by which personal moral cultivation could be extended to the grand mission bringing good governance to the entire country and the world. Moreover, *zhong* and *shu* could be translated into the spirit of service and sacrifice, just as [Mencius said:] "When we do not, by what we do, realize what we desire, we must turn inwards, and examine ourselves in every point."[51] Through these analyses, Fan tried to demonstrate that it was Confucian ethical principles that were firmly rooted in the Chinese national psychology and theses exerted a very positive influence on Chinese society. He pointed out:

> At present, even though bad persons usurping power run amok, there are fair criticisms [against them] in the society. Even though education is not yet made universal nationwide, many rural residents, who are very poorly educated, remain unchangeably honest, moderate and faithful. [This moral stability] should be attributed to the Chinese culture, which has nourished the spiritual world of the Chinese for thousands of years and become the second natural instinct of the Chinese nation.

The above discussion was followed by an analysis of Christianity. According to Fan, Christianity could be summarized in three sentences. First, God was the Heavenly Father. Second, all humans were brothers and sisters. Third, we should build a Heavenly Kingdom of Love in this world by means of service and sacrifice. Christianity recognized only these three points and paid no heed to other doctrines. For this reason, there was no conflict between Christianity and the above-mentioned Confucian ethics and this reconciliation could be well corroborated. Take the two greatest Christian teachings—to love God and to love one's neighbours as yourself—for example. To love God meant that even serving the youngest brother could be equated with serving God. Therefore, just as Confucianism endeavoured to preserve the original mind and cultivate nature, Christianity never taught people to follow God by abandoning all human affairs. And, to love one's neighbours in the Confucian context could be extended to a wide range of human relationships between father and son, between younger and elder brothers, between husband and wife, between friends, and so on. Fan thus concluded:

> Consequently, there are the Confucianization of Christianity or the Christianization of Confucianism. The fundamental common denominator between them is indeed discernible. For those who believe in Christianity and despise Confucianism and those who are strongly confident in Confucianism while rejecting Christianity, they are all blind and biased.

Fan held that, although the Chinese culture was broad and profound, it did need to assimilate Christianity. The reason why was twofold. On the one hand, China could more efficiently tap the inexhaustible treasure trove of Chinese culture by using the foreign method of excavation. For example, the philosophy developed by Laozi and Zhuangzi was similar to the new modern philosophy in many aspects and to some extent, Mozi's logics and the new Western science shared common ground. Under such circumstances, if we did not read thoroughly books on Western philosophy and science, we would be unable to grasp the profundities of ancient Chinese philosophy. Where the Chinese ethics were concerned, they had already been tainted by some brazen eight-legged essays. But Christianity could not only help to eliminate needless derivatives parasitic on the Chinese culture but also lead us to learn the essence of the original Chinese culture, instil a new, ardent spirit in us, and revive the ancient, atrophied Chinese ethics. On the other hand, the restoration of culture or refurbishing a culture was actually a cycle around the world. This cycle was not a simplistic repetition. Rather, it was a spiralling upward movement assimilating new elements. Take the restoration of Confucianism in the Northern Song dynasty (960–1127), for example. The restored Confucianism actually took in well-developed Buddhist and Daoist elements and thus the syncretism of Confucianism, Daoism and Buddhist engendered a brand-new intellectual system. Now, Chinese culture had the opportunity to creatively repeat what had taken place in the Northern Song. In over one hundred years, Christianity had stirred the centre of Chinese culture. For this reason, the rising tide of cultural restoration was actually preparatory work for accepting fully-fledged Christian elements. Fan believed that Chinese culture incorporating new Christian elements would definitely glow brilliantly.

At that time, there were indeed a number of similar essays affirming the fusion of Christianity and Chinese culture. Take Xu Zuhuan, for example.[52] He contended that the characteristics of Chinese culture were reverence for Heaven, peace (i.e., denouncing war and promoting universal love), valuing righteousness, condemnation of undue profits, filial piety, fraternal duties, Grand Harmony, benevolence and unity of body and spirit (or unity of life and living). All of these characteristics could be found in the Bible. Finally, Xu concluded that Christianity and Chinese culture could perfectly inspire and blend with each other.

The above-mentioned articles focused on the unity of Chinese culture and Christianity. Few of them paid attention to the unity of the Christian Church and Chinese culture. Unlike them, one of the articles authored by Wang Zhixin discussed this issue and how the Christian Church could have indigenized itself in China in this way.[53] Wang said:

> Christianity can be likened to a wheat seed, which can be sown as one please and grows appropriately regardless of place. But there are two things worthy of attention. First, the seed must take root in the soil and imbibe local nutriments. Second, it must die first and then begin to grow and finally bear fruit.

Therefore, promoting a Sinicized Christian Church should not be simplistically equated with advocating nationalism. If Christianity wanted to take root and grow in a country, it must absorb the country's culture and thoughts, on the grounds that this country's religion must have a national character. Take Buddhism, for example. Buddhism was introduced into China in the Former Han dynasty (202 BC–8 AD) and then it blended into the indigenous Chinese culture and imbibed Chinese culture nutriments. As a consequence, there was a Sinicized Buddhism, which was totally different from the original Indian Buddhism. Another example was the peanut. Peanut was an imported crop. Even so, it was planted and nurtured in the Chinese soil, so that it became a Chinese product. Few people say it was foreign peanut. But in the case of Christianity, this religion did not at all absorb any Chinese cultural and intellectual nutriments due to the ineradicably tenacious cultivation done by the hereditary Western customs, culture and thoughts, even though it had lived in China for quite a long time. As a result, so far, Christianity was still garbed in Western dress and contemptuously treated by the Chinese as a heavily foreign religion. These indicated that Christianity did not have any seeds sown in the soil of Chinese culture and thoughts. For Christianity, if it really wanted to be a Chinese product, the key was not that there should be Christianity *in* China but that there should be *Chinese* Christianity. Figuratively speaking, the seed of Christianity should be sown in the soil of Chinese culture and thought and at the same time the shrouds enwrapping Christianity, such as Western rituals, customs, habits and thoughts should be allowed to rot in the soil. Then, the seed would sprout, grow and finally bear the fruits of Sinicization. Unfortunately, even to this day, Christianity was still basically under foreign missionaries' control and afraid of being stained with even the slightest grain of Chinese dust. How could Western Christianity swallow its pride and go to the fields? This explained why, even now, there was not any seeds of Christianity in the Chinese soil. In a word, Christianity in China was completely not indigenized.

As for the indigenized Christian Church, Wang said:

> In the Chinese context, an indigenized Christian Church refers to such a Western Church that it metamorphoses into a Chinese Church, successfully adapting itself to Chinese national character by means of reform. This metamorphosis is not an act shaking the Christian truth to its foundations but an effort to help to blend together the ancient Chinese culture and the Christian truth, make Chinese Christians' religious life adaptable to the Chinese conditions, and prevent Christianity and the Chinese from misunderstanding each other.

At that time, there had been some enthusiastic Chinese Christians, who attempted to reconcile their religion and Chinese culture in Sinicizing church buildings, Christian wedding ceremonies and funerals and hymns. But their effort was merely formalistic. It was an approach helping Christianity be close to the Chinese culture but not the basic method of sowing the seed of Christianity in the Chinese soil. The reason was:

> There is none of the blood of Chinese culture in the life of Christianity in China. Therefore, there is no true syncretism of Christianity and Chinese society just as flesh and blood of human body, even though both are growing closer like a firmer handshake. Thus, the most fundamental issue was not form but spirit. If the seed of Christianity could be sown in the soil of Chinese culture and the Chinese culture be turned into the blood of Christianity, there would be no distinction made between the Christianity *in* China and the *Chinese* Christianity. If this is done, Christianity will be as stable as a huge rock in China.

Thus, what was Chinese culture? Wang held that to answer this question was not an easy job. Neither Westerners and quasi-Westerners nor the ordinary Chinese knew the answer. He tried to shed light on this from three perspectives. The first was ethical embodiments of Chinese culture. The crystallization of Confucian moral teaching was Five Relationships. Specifically, "[there] should be affection [between] father and son; righteousness, between sovereign and minister; attention to their separate functions, between husband and wife; a proper order, between old and young; and fidelity, between friends."[54] The five relations epitomizing the essence of humanity were indelible through all ages. Among them, filial piety and fraternal duties were extended to the sincere care for people's life and death and posthumous affairs dedicated to ancestors, so that the pure and sincere national character of the Chinese could incomparably last for three thousand years. Virtues such as filial piety and fraternal duty did play a pivotal role in this course. But, at present, the Western culture increasingly encroached upon China and the Westernization intrinsic to Christianity, which was embodied in the small family system, abandonment of filial piety, and so on, was completely inconsistent with the established Chinese ethico-moral codes. In Wang's opinion, this was not the true colour of Christianity but a cluster of habits shrouding Christianity, layer upon layer. He reminded his readers of the fact that Christianity did pay great attention to the affection between father and children and the distinction made between males and females. For example, Jesus was obedient to his parents. Precisely for this reason, Wang contended that the Christian culture was essentially a product of Eastern thinking and had a very close relationship to the Chinese culture. "It is the Easterner who strips off shrouds enwrapping Christianity and reveals its true colours." The second was the spiritual embodiments of the Chinese culture. Wang said:

> Gentleness is an excellent spirit of the Chinese nation. Besides, the Chinese are known to the world for their hard-working spirit, ability to withstand insult, tolerance towards faults of others, unperturbed mind in

face of unpleasant things, repeated introspection, abandonment of contention, reposeful disposition and consistent contentedness.⁵⁵

The Westerners, who boasted that their character was dynamic, alleged that the character of the Chinese was inertia. In other words, the national characters of the two peoples were opposed to each other. The spirit uttered by one of Confucius's famous sayings that "persons of great virtue are open-minded and composed" ("Shu'er" of *The Confucian Analects*) was really part and parcel of the world culture. Frankly, Christianity did sometimes recommend nonresistant endurance to people. It can thus be said that the relationship between the Christian spirit and the spirit of Eastern peoples was extraordinarily close. The true qualities that Christianity manifested were exactly the distinctive characters of Chinese culture. The third was behavioural embodiments of the Chinese culture. The Chinese people's only behavioural choice was reflected by Confucius's sayings such as "[t]he mind of the superior man is conversant with righteousness; [and by contrast] the mind of the mean man is conversant with gain"⁵⁶ and "gain is not to be considered prosperity[,] [which should] be found in righteousness."⁵⁷ But as soon as Christianity was introduced into modern China, the Western utilitarianism started to exert an influence on the Chinese youth. Christianity itself did not preach utilitarianism. But preachers of Christianity were very utilitarian, paying unduly excessive attention to the number of people joining the church. This contradicted the inherent Chinese character, which required that people should do what they should do, meanwhile caring little about what they would gain. On this point there was the fiercest disagreement between the Eastern culture and Western Christianity. If Christianity was able to absorb the Chinese cultural spirit and turn it into its own flesh and blood, there would not be any mutual misunderstandings between them.

In the end, Wang made five suggestions regarding how to found an indigenized Christian Church in China. First, there should be well-trained, truly indigenized Chinese Christian leaders. These leaders were Chinese Christians who fully respected the Chinese culture and had a very good command of the characteristics of the Chinese spiritual heritage. Unfortunately, the present-day Christian Church in China hardly ever educated such talented people. Those whom this Church trained were nothing more than quasi-foreigners. Their theology was completely Western. They only took foreign language seriously and treated the Chinese language and scholarship as something worthless. In such an atmosphere where the Chinese Church was crazy about foreign things and obsequious to foreigners, people educated by this Church could only be ill-adapted to Chinese society. Therefore, the department in charge of training leading Chinese Christians must be overhauled. Second, the true meaning of the indigenization of Christianity should be disseminated nationwide. Whether or not an indigenized church could make a success would depend on how the masses of the people perceive it. A small number of leading Christians could by no means secure its success. For this reason, the church should try every possible means, such as texts and speeches, to disseminate indigenization as extensively as possible. Third, foreign missionaries' help was indeed needed. Chinese Christians should help foreign missionaries understand such a point that Christianity in China was, in the final analysis, *Chinese* Christianity and they could only temporarily rather than perpetually put it under their control. The indigenized Christian Church in China would never escape the root of Christ. Therefore, foreign missionaries should understand this and provide help to the Chinese Church. Fourth, there should be more Sinicized materials for the dissemination of Christianity. Christianity did spend much energy and time propagating itself in China. But the Christian missionary work focused on the bottom layer of society and failed to extend to the Chinese intelligentsia. The main reasons for this failure were that missionaries knew little of the traditional Chinese scholarship; and that their materials for propagation were predominantly Western and few of them were based on Chinese history. Where the Christian propaganda work was concerned, it relied on the translation of Western works. Chinese creative works were seldom seen. By contrast, the reason why Buddhism was greatly popular among the well-educated Chinese was its highly Sinicized writing. In view of this, it would be better for Christianity to adopt more Sinicized materials. Fifth, the Chinese Church's system of etiquette and rites should be revised. The Chinese and the Chinese women in particular were originally renowned for their religious piety. It was imperative that the Church should abolish Western rites that were psychologically estranged from the Chinese and revise the existing Christian ritual system to be spiritually adaptable to the Chinese people. This was a matter of great urgency in indigenizing the Christian Church in China.

Some essays exploring the indigenization of Christian Church in China focused on a specific aspect. For example, Liu Tingfang discussed the reform of Christian etiquette and rites.[58] He, first of all, asserted that etiquette and rites should not be abolished on the grounds that they were indispensable to Christian converts' religious life. Religious etiquette and rites, which epitomized the religious spirit, were by nature progressive and always open to reform. In other words, these etiquette and rites would like to change themselves to meet the spiritual needs of Christians. The Chinese Church was the home, wherein Chinese Christians lived their spiritual life. Therefore, all etiquette and rites should adapt themselves to the life of Chinese Christians. The creation of the Chinese Church's own system of etiquette and rites was thus one of the most basic missions of the Church. But at the same time, Liu did not think the Chinese Church should isolate itself from churches of the rest of the world. In reality, the Chinese Church and churches worldwide were of the same origin. In this sense, the Chinese system of Christian etiquette and rites should be consistent with the established global praxis. Some etiquette and rites were actually accepted and shared by Christians worldwide. Thus, the Chinese Church should not abandon them on the pretext of promoting indigenization. When the Chinese Church was formulating its own etiquette and rites, it should consult all the existing etiquette and rites of churches of other countries. The Chinese Church had full freedom to decide whether or not to adopt other countries' ritual systems. Liu suggested that any foreign etiquette and rites that accorded with the Christian truth and adapted themselves with the Chinese should be incorporated into the Chinese Church's experiment.

To sum up, theoretically and practically, the 2nd CCM did, at least to a certain extent, push forward the indigenization of the Christian Church and Christian schools in China. In comparison with the past, leaders of Chinese Christian Church did improve their theoretical understanding of indigenization. But, in practice, they really did a very poor job. Take the effort to take back the right of education, for example. Christian schools did not reform themselves substantially at all, just as an old proverb goes: "The mountain that laboured and brought forth a mouse." It was due to the unprecedented criticism of the Church in the wake of the Shanghai Massacre, when there was a strong surge of nationalism, that the endeavour to indigenize Christianity in China was taken to new heights.

Notes

1 Quoted in Zhang Qinshi, *Trend of Religions in China in the Last Decade*, 271–272.
2 TSO, "The Reason Why Missionary Education Prevails in China" (教会教育盛行的原因), *The Vanguard* (前锋), No. 2 (December 1923). Quoted in Yang Tianhong, *Christianity and Modern China*, 225.
3 Yang Xiaochun 杨效春, "The Christian Propaganda and Campaign Taking Back Right of Education" (基督教之宣传与收回教育权运动), *The Educational World of China* (中华教育界), Vol. 14, No. 8 (February 1925), 4. Quoted in Wang Chengmian 王成勉, *The Rise and Fall of Christian Literary Society* [文社的兴衰] (Taibei, Taiwan: Christian Cosmic Light Holistic Care Organization, 1990), 15.
4 For Yu's detailed discussion, see: Yu Jiaju 余家菊, "The Problem of Christian Education" (教会教育问题), *The Nationalist Education* (国家主义教育), October, 1923. Quoted in Zhang Qinshi, *Trend of Religions in China in the Last Decade*, 332–336.
5 "The Student Manifesto of the Holy Trinity School of Guangzhou" (广州圣三一学生宣言), *The Young Chinese* (中国青年), Vol. 2, No. 32. Quoted in Yang Tianhong, *Christianity and Modern China*, 245.
6 Quoted in Yang Tianhong, *Christianity and Modern China*, 255.
7 Quoted in Zhang Qinshi, *Trend of Religions in China in Last Decade*, 338–339.
8 Quoted in ibid., 339–342.
9 Chen Qitian 陈启天, "Proposed Reasons and Methods Respecting Taking Back the Right of Education" (我们主张收回教育权的理由与办法). Quoted in Zhang Qinshi, *Trend of Religions in China in the Last Decade*, 343–344.
10 Ibid., 342–365.
11 Hu Shi 胡适, "Barriers Impeding Christian Education in Present-Day China" (今日教会教育的难关), *Chinese Christian Education Quarterly* (中华基督教教育季刊), Vol. 1, No. 1 (March 1925), 7–13.

12. For the full text of the *1924 Manifesto*, see: *Awakening* (觉悟) [a supplement to *The Republican Daily* (民国日报)], 19 August 1924. Quoted in Zhang Qinshi, *Trend of Religions in China in the Last Decade*, 376–379.
13. "The Truth about Mister Sun Yat-sen's Christian Belief" (孙中山先生是否基督徒真相之宣布), *The Christian Occupation of China*, No. 51 (10 April 1925), 3.
14. For detailed discussions, see: Li Chunfan 李春蕃, "The Christian Missionary Work and Imperialism" (传教与帝国主义), *Awakening*, 19 August 1924. Quoted in Zhang Qinshi, *Trend of Religions in China in the Last Decade*, 381–386.
15. For detailed discussions, see: Mei Yunlong 梅云龙, "Christianity and China" (基督教与中国), *The Condemning Christianity Movement* (反对基督教运动), October 1924. Quoted in Zhang Qinshi, *Trend of Religions in China in the Last Decade*, 381–386, 387–395.
16. Quoted in Xie Fuya, "A Survey of Religions and Anti-Religious Movements in Recent Years" (近年来宗教及非基督教运动概况), *Annals of Chinese Christian Church*, No. 8 (1925), 21.
17. Ibid.
18. "The NCCC's Response to the Ongoing Condemning Christianity Movement" (本会应付非基督教运动之进行), *The Christian Occupation of China*, No. 51 (10 April 1925), 3.
19. Wang Wenxin 王文馨, "A Method of Eliminating Society-wide Criticism against Christianity" (一个消弭非基督教运动的方法), *The True Light* (真光), Vol. 24, No. 5 (May 1925), 15–18.
20. Wu Zhenchun 吴震春, "A Furthered Discussion of 'Setting Doubts about Religion'" ("宗教辨惑说"疏辨), *The Episcopal Church News*, Vol. 17, No. 23 (February 1924), 10.
21. Tu Zheyin 屠哲隐, "An Honest Discussion of Christianity and Criticism of Christianity" (基督教与非基督教平议), *The Life Monthly*, Vol. 5, No. 7 (April 1925), 53–57.
22. Li Denghui 李登辉, "The National Education and Christianity" (国家教育与基督教), *Chinese Christian Education Quarterly*, Vol. 1, No. 1 (March 1925), 25.
23. Ibid., 26.
24. Ibid., 25.
25. Wang Biting 汪弼廷, "Is it Time to Take Back China's Right of Education?" (中国收回教育权的日子到吗), *The True Light*. Reprinted in *The Episcopal Church News*, Vol. 18, No. 5 (March 1925), 10–14.
26. Wei Que 韦悫, "The Christian Education and National Education" (基督教教育和政府教育), *Chinese Christian Education Quarterly*, Vol. 1, No. 1 (March 1925), 32–35.
27. Jianwu 健吾, "Sincere Advice for Christian Schools" (对于教会学校的忠告), *The Episcopal Church News*, Vol. 18, No. 5 (March 1925), 3.
28. Liu Tingfang, "Study of Criticism of Christian Education: The General Attitude of Entirety of Christian Community" (反对基督教教育运动问题的研究——基督教全体的态度), *The Life Monthly*, Vol. 5, No. 5 (February 1925), 1–5.
29. Anon, "Movements and Important Files in Relation to Christian Circle of Education" (基督教教育界运动与重要文件), *Chinese Christian Education Quarterly*, Vol. 1, No. 1 (March 1925), 43.
30. Anon, "Results of Conference of Chinese Administration Staff in Christian Universities" (基督教大学中国行政人员会议的结果), *Chinese Christian Education Quarterly*, Vol. 1, No. 1 (March 1925), 49–50.

31. Liu Tingfang, "Doctrines I Proposed for Christian Education in China" (我对于基督教在中国教育事业的信条), *Chinese Christian Education Quarterly*, Vol. 1, No. 1 (March 1925), 14.
32. Comrades (同人), "The Manifesto" (本刊宣言), *Chinese Christian Education Quarterly*, Vol. 1, No. 1 (March 1925), 1–5.
33. Anon, "Manifesto of Chinese Christian Educational Circles" (中华基督教教育界宣言), *Chinese Christian Education Quarterly*, Vol. 1, No. 2 (June 1925), 1–4.
34. Zhao Guanhai, "What Lies Ahead of Christian Education in China?" (我国宗教教育之将来), *To Speak Without Reserve* (尽言). Quoted in *The Episcopal Church News*, Vol. 18, No. 10 (June 1925), 3–5.
35. Wu Leichuan, "Is There Conflict between Nationalism and Christianity?" (国家主义与基督教是否冲突), *The Life Monthly*, Vol. 5, No. 4 (January 1925), 4–5.
36. For Chen Baoqan's detailed discussion, see: "Are Christian Doctrines against Nationalism?" (基督教教义是违反国家主义的吗？), *Chinese Christian Education Quarterly*, Vol. 1, No. 1 (March 1925), 18–19.
37. Xu Baoqian 徐宝谦, "A Notice to Those Who Are Exclusively in Favour of Nationalism" (敬告今只提倡国家主义者), *The Life Monthly*, Vol. 5, No. 4 (1925), 1–3.
38. For his detailed discussion, see: Gao Houde 高厚德, "The Nationalism Meeting Needs of Present-Day China" (今日中国需要之国家主义), *Chinese Christian Education Quarterly*, Vol. 1, No. 1 (March 1925), 22.
39. Zhao Guanhai 招观海, "Imperialism and the Christian Church" (帝国主义和基督教会), *The Episcopal Church News*, Vol. 17, No. 24 (December 1924), 24–26.
40. Peng Jinzhang, "Christianity and Imperialism" (基督教与帝国主义), *The True Light*. Quoted in *The Episcopal Church News*, Vol. 18, No. 9 (May 1925), 5–6.
41. Xie Fuya, "New Christian Thoughts and Basic Chinese National Thinking" (基督教新思潮与中国民族根本思想), *Progress of the Youth*, No. 82 (April 1925), 1.
42. Ibid., 1–15.
43. Ibid., 11.
44. Duan Guanglu 段光路, "Christianity and the Chinese Culture" (基督教与中国文化), *Progress of the Youth*, No. 82 (April 1925), 16–29.
45. Ibid., 19.
46. Fan Bihai, "The Chinese Ethical Culture and Christianity" (中国伦理的文化与基督教), *Progress of the Youth*, No. 84 (June 1925), 1–10.
47. Ibid., 3.
48. *Lunyu*, or *The Confucian Analects*, trans. James Legge. Available at: https://ctext.org/analects/wei-ling-gong/ens.
49. Ibid. Available at: https://ctext.org/analects/gong-ye-chang/ens.
50. *Liji*, or *The Book of Rites*, trans. James Legge. Available at: https://ctext.org/liji/da-xue/ens.
51. *Mengzi*, or *Mencius*, trans. James Legge. Available at: https://ctext.org/mengzi/li-lou-i/ens.
52. Xu Zuhuan, "The Relationship between Christianity and Chinese Culture" (中国文化与基督教的关系), *Progress of the Youth*, No. 80 (April 1925).
53. Wang Zhixin, "Exploring Indigenization of the Christian Church in China" (中国本色教会的讨论), *Progress of the Youth*, No. 79 (January 1925), 11–16.
54. *Mengzi*, or *Mencius*, trans. James Legge. Available at: https://ctext.org/mengzi/teng-wen-gong-i/ens.
55. Ibid., 14.

56 *Lunyu*, or *The Confucian Analects*, op. cit.
57 *Liji*, or *The Book of Rites*, op. cit.
58 Liu Tingfang, "The Issue of the Chinese Church's System of Etiquettes and Rites" (中国教会礼节仪式的问题), *The Life Monthly*, Vol. 5, No. 3 (December 1924), 2–4.

Bibliography

Anon. "Manifesto of Chinese Christian Educational Circles" (中华基督教教育界宣言). *Chinese Christian Education Quarterly* (中华基督教教育季刊). Vol. 1, No. 2 (June 1925).

Anon. "Movements and Important Files in Relation to Christian Circle of Education" (基督教教育界运动与重要文件). *Chinese Christian Education Quarterly* (中华基督教教育季刊). Vol. 1, No. 1 (March 1925).

Anon. "NCCC's Response to the Ongoing Condemning Christianity Movement" (本会应付非基督教运动之进行). *The Christian Occupation of China* (中华归主). No. 51 (10 April 1925).

Anon. "Results of the Conference of Chinese Administration Staff in Christian Universities" (基督教大学中国行政人员会议的结果). *Chinese Christian Education Quarterly* (中华基督教教育季刊). Vol. 1, No. 1 (March 1925).

Anon. "The Truth about Mister Sun Yat-sen's Christian Belief" (孙中山先生是否基督徒真相之宣布). *The Christian Occupation of China* (中华归主). No. 51 (10 April 1925).

Chen, Baoqan. "Are Christian Doctrines against Nationalism?" (基督教教义是违反国家主义的吗？). *Chinese Christian Education Quarterly* (中华基督教教育季刊). Vol. 1, No. 1 (March 1925).

Comrades (同人). "The Manifesto" (本刊宣言). *Chinese Christian Education Quarterly* (中华基督教教育季刊). Vol. 1, No. 1 (March 1925).

Duan, Guanglu 段光路. "Christianity and the Chinese Culture" (基督教与中国文化). *Progress of the Youth* (青年进步). No. 82 (April 1925).

Fan, Bihai 范皕海. "The Chinese Ethical Culture and Christianity" (中国伦理的文化与基督教). *Progress of the Youth* (青年进步). No. 84 (June 1925).

Gao, Houde 高厚德. "The Nationalism Meeting Needs of Present-Day China" (今日中国需要之国家主义). *Chinese Christian Education Quarterly* (中华基督教教育季刊). Vol. 1, No. 1 (March 1925).

Hu, Shi 胡适. "Barriers Impeding Christian Education in Present-Day China" (今日教会教育的难关). *Chinese Christian Education Quarterly* (中华基督教教育季刊). Vol. 1, No. 1 (March 1925).

Jianwu 健吾. "Sincere Advice for Christian Schools" (对于教会学校的忠告). *The Episcopal Church News* (圣公会报). Vol. 18, No. 5 (March 1925).

Li, Denghui 李登辉. "The National Education and Christianity" (国家教育与基督教). *Chinese Christian Education Quarterly* (中华基督教教育季刊). Vol. 1, No. 1 (March 1925).

Liu, Tingfang 刘廷芳. "The Issue of the Chinese Church's System of Etiquettes and Rites" (中国教会礼节仪式的问题). *The Life Monthly* (生命月刊). Vol. 5, No. 3 (December 1924).

Liu, Tingfang 刘廷芳. "Study of Criticism of Christian Education: The General Attitude of Entirety of Christian Community" (反对基督教教育运动问题的研究——基督教全体的态度), *The Life Monthly* (生命月刊). Vol. 5, No. 5 (February 1925).

Liu, Tingfang 刘廷芳. "Doctrines I Proposed for Christian Education in China" (我对于基督教在中国教育事业的信条). *Chinese Christian Education Quarterly* (中华基督教教育季刊). Vol. 1, No. 1 (March 1925).Peng, Jinzhang 彭锦章. "Christianity and Imperialism" (基督教与帝国主义). *The True Light*. Quoted in *The Episcopal Church News* (圣公会报). Vol. 18, No. 9 (May 1925).

Tu, Zheyin 屠哲隐, "An Honest Discussion of Christianity and Criticism of Christianity" (基督教与非基督教平议). *The Life Monthly* (生命月刊). Vol. 5, No. 7 (April 1925).

Wang, Biting 汪弼廷. "Is it Time to Take Back China's Right of Education?" (中国收回教育权的日子到吗). *The True Light*. Reprinted in *The Episcopal Church News*, Vol. 18, No. 5 (March 1925).

Wang, Chengmian 王成勉. *The Rise and Fall of the Christian Literary Society* [文社的兴衰] (Taibei, Taiwan: Christian Cosmic Light Holistic Care Organization, 1990).

Wang, Wenxin 王文馨. "A Method of Eliminating Society-wide Criticism of Christianity" (一个消弭非基督教运动的方法). *The True Light* (真光). Vol. 24, No. 5 (May 1925).

Wang, Zhixin 王治心. "Exploring Indigenization of the Christian Church in China" (中国本色教会的讨论). *Progress of the Youth* (青年进步). No. 79 (January 1925).

Wei, Que 韦悫. "The Christian Education and National Education" (基督教教育和政府教育). *Chinese Christian Education Quarterly* (中华基督教教育季刊). Vol. 1, No. 1 (March 1925).

Wu, Leichuan 吴雷川. "Is There Conflict between Nationalism and Christianity?" (国家主义与基督教是否冲突). *The Life Monthly* (生命月刊). Vol. 5, No. 4 (January 1925).

Wu, Zhenchun 吴震春. "A Furthered Discussion of 'Setting Doubts about Religion'" ("宗教辨惑说"疏辨). *The Episcopal Church News* (圣公会报). Vol. 17, No. 23 (February 1924), 10.

Xie, Fuya 谢扶雅. "A Survey of Religions and Anti-Religious Movements in Recent Years" (近年来宗教及非基督教运动概况). *Annals of Chinese Christian Church* (中华基督教会年鉴). No. 8 (1925).

Xie, Fuya 谢扶雅. "New Christian Thoughts and Basic Chinese National Thinking" (基督教新思潮与中国民族根本思想). *Progress of the Youth* (青年进步). No. 82 (April 1925).

Xu, Baoqian 徐宝谦. "A Notice to Those Who Are Exclusively in Favour of Nationalism" (敬告今只提倡国家主义者). *The Life Monthly* (生命月刊). Vol. 5, No. 4 (1925).

Xu, Zuhuan 许祖焕. "The Relationship between Christianity and Chinese Culture" (中国文化与基督教的关系), *Progress of the Youth* (青年进步). No. 80 (April 1925).

Zhang, Qinshi 张钦士. *Trend of Religions in China in the Last Decade* [国内近十年来之宗教思潮] (Beijing: Jinghua yinshuju, 1927).

Zhao, Guanhai 招观海. "Imperialism and Christian Church" (帝国主义和基督教会). *The Episcopal Church News* (圣公会报). Vol. 17, No. 24 (December 1924).

Zhao, Guanhai 招观海. "What Lies Ahead of Christian Education in China?" (我国宗教教育之将来). *To Speak Without Reserve* (尽言). Quoted in *The Episcopal Church News* (圣公会报). Vol. 18, No. 10 (June 1925).

Internet Resources

Mencius. Trans. James Legge. Available at: https://ctext.org/mengzi/.
The Book of Rites. Trans. James Legge. Available at: https://ctext.org/liji/. *The Confucian Analects*. Trans. James Legge. Available at: https://ctext.org/analects/.

4 Chinese Christianity in the Shanghai Massacre and the Northern Expedition Periods, 1925–1927

The Shanghai Massacre and the Chinese Christians' response

On 15 May 1925, the capitalists of a Japanese cotton mill murdered over a dozen workers. On 30 May 1925, Shanghai workers and students, protesting at the atrocity perpetrated by imperialist Japan, gathered together in Nanjing Road and staged a mass demonstration. They were shot by the police of a British concession of Shanghai. This massacre left 13 workers dead and several dozen injured. It was historically known as the May 30th Massacre (hereinafter referred to as the Shanghai Massacre). The Shanghai Massacre ignited the anger of all the Chinese people. Many Chinese cities, driven by the nationalist feeling, launched a general strike of workers, students and merchants. When the strike was still going on, the imperialists in China cracked down bloodily on protesters and committed greater sins against the Chinese people. Take the brutal British army, for example. On 11 June, they massacred the Chinese in Hankou, Hubei. Twelve days later, in Shamiandao Island of Guangzhou, the British army machine-gunned protesters, when they were holding a huge demonstration attended by over one hundred thousand residents. The massacre left 52 dead, over 170 seriously wounded and incalculable many slightly wounded. On 2 July, British warships fired on protesters in Chongqing, perpetrating the Chongqing Massacre. The savage acts of foreign troops made the Chinese people angrier. According to incomplete statistics, in the period of the Shanghai Massacre, over six hundred Chinese cities witnessed anti-imperialist patriotic movements and more than 1,7000,000 patriots participated in these movements. This was unprecedented in the history of modern China.[1] Some researchers held that the patriotic movement triggered by the Shanghai Massacre marked the national awakening of the Chinese people and the surge of Chinese nationalism.

In the second round of the national campaign condemning Christianity, quite a few critics contended that Christianity and imperialism were inseparable, in which imperialism used Christianity as a weapon of invasion and Christianity was the tip of the spear of a cultural invasion. This criticism was actually not very popular among critics of Christianity, among whom some even said such an accusation was too radical or too communist. The

DOI: 10.4324/9781003345169-4

Shanghai Massacres and the atrocities against the Chinese that ensued taught the masses of the people, including Chinese Christians, that they should gain a clearer understanding of imperialism. Massacres and atrocities perpetrated by the British army in the name of Christian values completely unmasked the inherent evilness of imperialist Britain. Consequently, not only an increasing number of free thinkers but also many Chinese Christians agreed with the criticism that Christianity was the spearhead of imperialism. At the critical time when the national dignity had to be safeguarded, ardently patriotic Chinese Christians devoted themselves to the anti-imperialist movement just as all Chinese free thinkers did.

Immediately after the Shanghai Massacre, Christian organizations nationwide set up corps in support of the protesters. Take Jiangsu, for example. There were special corps, through which Christians gave support to anti-imperialists, in Shanghai, Nanjing, Zhenjiang, Suzhou, Changshu, Xuzhou, Jinshan, Yangzhou and towns, such as Lulangqiao and Banqiao (in Jiangning). Christians published manifestos and open telegrams, strongly and angrily denouncing the imperialist powers perpetrating the heinous crimes against innocent and totally unarmed Chinese people in China. At the same time, they raised a huge amount of money, which was used to support students, workers and merchants in Shanghai's general strike. For example, on 2 June, patriotic Christians in Shanghai convened a meeting:

> in which they suggest the Shanghai Council of Chinese Christians (SCCC) take action. [According to their suggestions], apart from sending a telegram to the central authorities in Beijing and Nanjing and asking them to seriously deal with relevant matters and demand the Shanghai Municipal Council (SMC) [the alleged highest ruling body of concessions in Shanghai] to publish the truth about the Shanghai Massacre, (1) perpetrators of the Massacre must be tried and punished; (2) victims and their families must be compensated; (3) the governing regimes and related authorities standing behind the perpetrators must apologize for their offences; (4) there must be Chinese representatives in the SMC; and (5) the unequal treatment given to the Chinese in concessions ruled by foreigners must be abolished.[2]

On 4 June, the SCCC sent an open telegram regarding the Shanghai Massacre to Christian churches in Beijing, Tianjin, Jinan, Taiyuan, Xi'an, Chengdu, Chongqing, Fengtian (present-day Shenyang), Andong, Harbin, Kaifeng, Changsha, Hankou, Nanchang, Anqing, Nanjing, Suzhou, Hangzhou, Ningbo, Fuzhou, Shantou, Xiamen, Hong Kong, Guangzhou, Yunnan, and so on. Many Christians refuted the imperialists' vicious slander that the massacre was caused by students' radicalism, communist tendencies and breach of the peace. In their manifesto, Chinese Christians in Nanjing angrily pointed out:

In Shanghai, the Japanese cotton mill owners and the police of the British concession arrested and murdered Chinese students and citizens on successive days. So far, dozens of Chinese residents have been brutally killed. It has already turned into a bloody massacre shocking the world. Among the Chinese people, who are being horribly humiliated and persecuted, a wave of fierce wrath has rolled up in them. Even foreigners believing in truth and humanity are so enraged that they sharply denounce the cruelty and ferociousness [of Japan and Britain]. As far as the Shanghai Municipal Council (SMC) is concerned, it frames protesters as being radical and disturbing the peace and pastes public notices to shamelessly justify themselves. But these notices are actually confessions admitting their brutality and ruthlessness. How could totally unarmed students and innocent, curious onlookers disturb the peace? [The police of the British concession said] they were forced to shoot at the crowds. But in fact, they fired their guns merely ten seconds after sending out a warning and the victims were shot in the back by the police. So obviously this should be classified as voluntary manslaughter. It is more loathsome to see the authorities of the concession, falsely and maliciously, accusing students and citizens of being communist. Such an accusation is really ruthless and inhumane. Those who were murdered and injured by the police are diligent and prudent students and good citizens having decent jobs. A few students, driven by the ardent patriotism, lectured to the audience along the road. The listeners were primarily passer-by coming and going. When they were being arrested, they did not even know what was really taking place. Suddenly and unexpectedly, the police of the British concession shot them, who did not know what was going on till they died. How could these victims be so falsely accused of being radical? [Thus, we], being filled with a common hatred for our enemies, resolve to be united and make a concerted effort with people from all walks of life to seriously negotiate with the authorities of the concession. We demand that those who are unfairly arrested must be released, the curfew imposed by the authorities of the concession must be cancelled immediately, victims and their families must be compensated, the murderers and assailants must be punished, [the authorities of the concession] must apologize for its offences and promise that similar incidents will never happen again, and finally all unequal treaties with China must be abrogated and all concessions and ceded territories be returned to China. In order to achieve these demands, we must struggle against foreign forces in a united, concerted way.[3]

A manifesto by Christians of the Baptist Church in Guangdong and Guangxi was published in the wake of the Shaji (Shakee) Massacre in June 1925. In this manifesto, Christians expressed the strongest condemnation for the British army's savage act against the Chinese and extended the deepest condolences to their compatriots murdered by the British imperialists. Their manifesto said:

> [These massacres committed by the British army] are unprecedented in the history of the world. Little did we foresee that Britain, which always boastfully says it is a civilized country, would perpetrate such inhuman, heinous crimes against humanity in broad daylight! [The] imperialist Britain, which wilfully murdered our compatriots, must be entirely responsible for the atrocities. [Britain's] savage acts completely run counter to the Christian universal love and spirit of service.[4]

Many Christians made clear their attitude towards the Shanghai Massacre. Cheng Xiangfan expressed great indignation over the massacre, saying:

> Fortunately, at present, the Chinese people have awoken from their dream and acquired a deep national consciousness. The movements that fight against imperialism and strive to abolish unequal treaties have been launched. We Christians all along love the country and remain loyal to the country. We never fall behind in serving the society. The ideas that all humans are compatriots and all peoples are created equal are indispensable constituents of the Christian spirit. For this reason, we Christians will carry through this [anti-imperialist] movement to the end.

Cheng deeply believed that China needed Christianity. But he suggested:

> The propagation of Christianity must be conducted in a frank and forthright way. However, in reality, the Christian missionary work is carried out under the escort of gunboats and greatly benefits from [unequal] treaties that weak countries have to sign under coercion [imposed by foreign powers]. Not only is this against the basic diplomatic morality but it also disgraces Christianity and agonizes Chinese Christians. How can the Christian way of saving the world be disseminated by means of [the colonial] power?[5]

Even Feng Yuxiang, a famous general who believed in Christianity, published an open letter criticizing Britain, a boastful Christian state, for perpetrating such an inhuman massacre against young Chinese students that was an unpardonable disgrace not only to Christianity but also to entire humanity. General Feng fulminated against Christian churches worldwide on the grounds that none of them cleared their position on the massacre. He felt deeply sorry for this. Feng sharply pointed out: "Christian churches are so cowardly that they are afraid of displeasing powerful foreign regimes [in London and elsewhere] and falling from grace from the capitalist class." Seemingly, Feng held, these churches thought their regimes' heinous crimes might be passed over in silence. In view of this, the general appealed: "The more oppressed [by foreign powers] we feel, the harder we should fight against them. We Chinese Christians should always make a greater effort to purify the personality of Christian followers and defend the reputation of the Christian Church.."[6] These essays all demonstrated that Chinese Christians as a whole were as patriotic as the free thinkers.

Contrary to ordinary Chinese Christians, who were extremely angry at imperialist Britain, the vast majority of foreign missionaries in China took a very different position on the massacres against the Chinese. It was said that a few foreign missionaries from the United States and those who worked for Yanjing (Yenching) University in particular showed profound sympathy for China and wanted to urge the foreign powers to revise the existing unequal treaties. But apart from a few foreigners, the overwhelming majority of foreign missionaries merely paid lip service to the Chinese victims of the massacres and at the same time refused to comment on the atrocities perpetrated by their governing regimes on the pretext that these incidents should be fairly investigated. Quite a few missionaries, and British ones in particular, were die-hard apologists for imperialism, viciously spreading the slander that the massacre was caused by the students who intentionally were breaking the law. These imperialist Christian defenders, brainwashed by the one-sided story fabricated by the SMC, which dictated the administrative affairs of concessions in Shanghai, chose to believe that the police of the British concession were forced to massacre students because the policemen had to defend themselves by shooting.[7] A number of foreign missionaries were deluded by reports invented by English newspapers such as the *North China Daily News* into believing that there would be a repeat of the Boxer Uprising, which dealt a heavy blow to foreign Christian forces in China at the dawn of the twentieth century. These missionaries even fanatically asked their governing regimes in London and elsewhere to crack down on the Chinese with much harsher approaches. Some even went to extremes, whitewashing and supporting the massacre perpetrated by the police of the British concession. A few missionaries brazenly said, taking into account the tens of thousands of people who died in warlord conflicts and banditry, people should not make a fuss about several dozen deaths in the Shanghai Massacre. Corresponding to these imperially minded missionaries, most missionary schools did not support students' patriotic acts. Usually, they disbanded the schools by terminating the semester early or declaring a holiday in advance. Jinling Women College, Fujian Union School, Dongwu (Soochow) University, Hujiang University (University of Shanghai), South China Women College and Huazhong (Huachung) University were examples. Bai Shide (Alexander Baxter), who put Lingnan University (also known as Canton Christian College) under his control, refused to state clearly his stand on the Shaji Massacre perpetrated by British troops in Guangzhou. In like manner, Bu Fangji (Francis Pott), who ruled over one of Shanghai's missionary schools known as Saint John's University, unjustly forbade students to fly a flag at half-mast in honour of the workers murdered by the British police in the Shanghai Massacre and even threatened students with closing the school.

The foreign missionaries' attitude was a brutal insult to the national feeling of Chinese Christians. The patriotic enthusiasm was thus aroused among them. The students of missionary schools broke through the impediments imposed by the school authorities and threw themselves into the anti-imperialist patriotic movement. According to incomplete statistics, in merely six months after the Shanghai Massacre, there were over 40 student strikes in missionary schools. In several missionary universities, students and Chinese faculties required that their schools should be taken back by the Chinese. For example, patriotic students and teachers forced Bai Shide to resign from the school's leading position; and all patriotic students of Saint John's University dropped out of this school and set up a new university known as Guanghua (Kwang Hua).

On the other hand, foreign missionaries' appalling attitude towards the victims of massacres of the Chinese helped Chinese Christians get a clearer, deeper understanding of imperialism. For example, immediately after the Shanghai Massacre, many Chinese Christians wrote to British missionaries in China, criticizing that they were actually against the Christian justice and fairness. Some of them, hearing gory detail of the massacres, realized that some missionaries did play a vanguard role in the imperialist invasion of China. Chinese Christians of Fenzhou, Shanxi, sincerely pointed out:

> When the First World War was still going on, the wild arrogance and rabid nature of missionaries from the United Kingdom had already created a very bad impression among the Chinese. Even to this day, these British missionaries are a disgrace to Christ. The United Kingdom prides itself on destroying countries on the planet, occupying the land of other peoples, invading nations by means of commerce, and conquering the globe with its navy. But however proud, these are precisely the crimes and sins, to which Britain must repent of. British missionaries walk on air under the aegis of special articles of unequal treaties and are obsessed with self-aggrandizement. They think only by doing so will the civilization and extraordinariness of Britain be manifest. It is thus no wonder that, when Europe was being gnawed by the World War, a famous Shanghai-based Christian institution had the impudence to publish an illustrated magazine bearing the name of *Sincerity* and sold it nationwide. This magazine was nothing more than a megaphone for the British Empire's military force. The United Kingdom is notoriously known for its trade with China by smuggling opium. It has committed its full share of crimes in history and in the world. Recently, the British Empire incessantly instigates riots in Tibet, invades Pianma (a town of Yunnan), and grabs Hong Kong ... All the week British missionaries loudly prattle about empty Christian doctrines. Whenever it comes to reality, they immediately abandon Christ and worship the mighty force of their master empire

... All these abominable facts demonstrate that you British missionaries come here neither for the love for Christ nor for the love for the Chinese. Imperialism is your highest ideology, so that your missionary work and schools founded by you are none other than spearheads of imperialism.[8]

Therefore, some Chinese Christians asked foreign missionaries to go beyond nationality, sectarianism and power and suggested that it would be better for them to be mediators, advisors, friends of China and agents of Christ. In other words, foreign missionaries should not stand with imperialism but instead adhere to justice, disseminate Jesus's gospel of peace, understand the Chinese culture and conditions, and make friends with the Chinese. Otherwise, they would be declared *personae non grata*.[9]

The notorious record of foreign missionaries' acts in China did help Chinese Christians gain a much clearer understanding of imperialism. Take the SCCC's patriotic speech on Sunday, for example. The audience of the speech was comprised of members of all Shanghai-based churches. This speech commented on the Shanghai Massacre, pointing out that the police of the British concession had conducted a wholesale slaughter of innocent Chinese and at the same time hypocritically kept on saying they respected the law. In order to cover up the crime, the police of the British concession refused to tell the truth and the Western media, colluding with the colonial authorities, spread rumours such as the Chinese students were radically influenced by the Soviet Russia and blindly against foreigners and there would be a new anti-foreign revolt similar to the Boxer Uprising. As we know, the true essence of Christianity should lie in fraternity, equality and freedom. But foreign preachers of Christianity, who philosophized about Christ in normal times, immediately discarded their Christ in the wake of the Shanghai Massacre and abided by the law of the British concession instead. The law of the British concession, which was made by Westerners to rule over the Chinese, actually emphasized the police rather than Christ. Christianity in China was really a shame. Chinese Christians must rethink this even though it could recall a painful experience. This retrospection includes two points. First, in no way did Christianity arrive in China with pure virtues such as love, benevolence and peace. Rather, it came here under the escort of armed forces. Second, the Christian truth was beautiful empty talk and hardly ever was put into practice by foreign missionaries. Whenever it met a mighty power, it would readily kowtow to the power and give up its freedom. Those self-styled preachers of Christian truth were actually megaphones for powers. The survival or death of Christian truth was fully dependent on whether or not Chinese Christians were ready to die in pursuit of it. How to respond to the Shanghai Massacre would be a touchstone for Chinese Christians' courage and wisdom. The final conclusions were as follows:

> First, Chinese Christians should affirm that preachers are only preachers and Christianity is only Christianity. Christianity can by no means be

equated with Christ; nor can preachers symbolize Christianity. In doing so, the conscience of we Chinese Christians will be fully independent of Western Christian preachers. Second, we Chinese Christians should state clearly that we admire Christ and do our utmost to carry forward his thoughts. We will not flinch from the faith due to the massacre. Rather, we will nerve ourselves to move forward. Third, Chinese Christians should make a concerted effort to mobilize Christians nationwide and people all over the world to support [China's anti-imperialist movement]. Fourth, Chinese Christians should expose all the oppressions imposed by foreign imperialist powers on China. In the meantime, foreign missionaries' malpractice in administering the Chinese Church must be corrected as soon as possible. Fifth, Chinese Christians should urge people from all walks of life to strictly observe the order and not to partake in any meaningless riots, which may be used [by the police of the British concession or British troops] as an excuse for a crackdown. If necessary, Christians should stand up and stop people. Sixth, Chinese Christians should try every peaceful means to positively support workers on strike. Seventh, if Westerners and Chinese of justice set up a special group investigating the truth about the massacre and finding solutions, Chinese Christians should wait patiently and respect their effort.[10]

The above speech convincingly indicated that Chinese Christians did have a strong patriotic feeling and at the same time they were really disappointed in the foreign missionaries in China and the status quo of the Chinese Christian Church. Therefore, they held up the spirit of Christ, making a clear distinction between Christianity and Christ and between missionaries and Christianity. The distinction they made laid the theoretical foundation of the Chinese Christians' fight against the Christian Church under imperialist rule. It was the new height of Chinese Christians' understanding of imperialism in the wake of the Shanghai Massacre.

The patriotic movement after the Shanghai Massacre was the impetus to the indigenization of the Chinese Christian Church. According to Wu Leichuan, although Chinese Christians unanimously participated in the patriotic anti-imperialist movement in the wake of the Shanghai Massacre, many foreign missionary societies, and British ones in particular, imposed restrictions on their Chinese followers' effort to raise funds for workers and students. The conflicts between Chinese Christians and foreign missionaries were inevitable. Whenever Chinese Christians thought even their participation in the patriotic movement was limited by foreign missionaries,

> They feel so grieved for the truth that they actually do not have true, full freedom at all. Some of them are greatly hurt and thus filled with righteous indignation and ungovernable rage. They have realized that, under the circumstance that foreigners are foreigners and Church is Church, the simplistic opposition to foreign missionaries does not help the situation, so

long as there is no truly independent Chinese Church. [Therefore,] in this sense, it is the best time for Chinese Christians to set up a self-governing, self-supporting and self-propagating Chinese Christian Church.[11]

Many Chinese Christians, who were agonized by foreign missionaries' and their governing churches' oppression, drew inspiration from patriotism and sought to be fully independent of foreign missionary societies. Followers of British missionary societies in China set an example in this endeavour. Take the Kaifeng branch of the China Inland Mission (CIM), for example. Members of CIM Kaifeng published an open letter renouncing their relations with Britain. After breaking with the CIM, these patriotic Christians founded the Kaifeng Chinese Christian Church (KCCC), which would be in accord with Christ's spirit of upholding truth and standing against power and striving to develop the personalities of the nation, the Church and Christians. The KCCC was a Christian institution achieving full economic independence, self-government and self-support. It stressed:

> Christianity cannot speak on behalf of the entirety of Christ. Nor does a missionary symbolize Christianity. [Therefore, members of the KCCC prefer to completely cut off relations with the British CIM and sincerely] hope that all Chinese Christians of British missionary societies would like to set up similar independent Chinese churches. [Finally, the KCCC concludes that] imperialism must be overthrown and all unequal treaties with China be abrogated. The KCCC does expect the material and spiritual help from people in all walks of life. With your help, we do believe that we will make a success in creating an indigenized and powerful Christian Church in conformity with Christ's spirit of upholding truth and standing against power. This Church can play a role in saving the barbaric, hegemonic Britain and Japan under the rule of regimes in London and Tokyo respectively.[12]

In this situation, Chinese Christians in Shanghai tried their best to overcome difficulties such as financial inadequacy and finally founded the independent SCCC. In its announcement, the SCCC said:

> The suggestion that there should be a self-governing, self-supporting and self-propagating Chinese Christian Church has been made for quite a long time. All Chinese Christians should shoulder their responsibility in building such a Church. Originally, we belonged to the Shanghai branch of the China Inland Mission and spend years achieving independence. Inasmuch as Shanghai is a treaty port, we do need more funds for our cause. As a consequence, independence is delayed to this day. Now, the urgency of the situation demands we set up an independent Chinese Church immediately. Thus, on 5 July 1925, our brothers and sisters work hand in hand and formally found the Shanghai Chinese Christian Church.[13]

In Wenzhou, some Chinese Christians formally put an end to their relationship with the United Methodist Church Mission (UMC), on the grounds that the UMC's British preachers, rudely and unreasonably, prevented them from expressing the patriotic feeling in the wake of the Shanghai Massacre. These Chinese Christians, hearing the news of the Shanghai Massacre, asked the UMC to negotiate with the London regime by sending a telegram. A British preacher of the UMC churlishly refused their request. Not only did this preacher act against justice and fairness but he also adhered to the parochial British nationalism and aggressively, arrogantly and unjustly slandered patriotic Chinese Christians. His rudeness infuriated Chinese Christians. In order to safeguard the Christian justice, express their love for their country, extend condolences to victims of the Shanghai Massacre, and work in concert with their compatriots, Chinese Christians decided to become independent from the UMC and founded a self-governing Church.[14] Their manifesto of independence was as follows:

> Dear brothers and sisters, do you love the country? China was originally a great country. Unfortunately, China is now bullied by the United Kingdom at will. In recent years, the British Empire has been attacking our country, disrespecting China's national dignity and grabbing Chinese land. If things go on like this, our country will perish. If we Christians are true patriots, we should be independent from foreign missionaries and their governing churches. If we are not independent and rely on foreigners instead, we will be treated as slaves or servants and be bullied forever. Brothers and sisters, do you love the Church? Yes, we love it. The Church was originally an institution of morality. But now it is used by foreign regimes as a weapon of invasion. The universal fraternity advocated by Jesus has been totally ruined by the Church. At present, free thinkers are strongly opposed to the Christian Church, criticizing that the Church is nothing more than a slave or a running dog serving foreigners. The foreigners can be best described by an old saying that goes "all saint without, all devil within." The good reputation of Christianity has been entirely damaged by them. If we Chinese Christians want to protect the reputation of Christianity, we must avoid traps set by these foreigners. That is to say, we Chinese Christians must extricate ourselves from imperialism.[15]

In the meantime, in their manifesto denouncing foreign brutality, Chinese Christians in Wenzhou pointed out:

> The original Christianity is based on the universal fraternity ... But the atrocities perpetrated by the British regime and Britain's aggressive wars against other peoples and unequal treaties with other countries go against the most basic Christian doctrine and the religious spirit. As a result, the honour of the Christian Church is completely discredited and even Christ

is stigmatized. [In view of this, we strongly suggest] all fellow Christians in China found an independent Chinese Christian Church and at the same time renounce the ties to foreign missionary societies. By doing so, we can extend condolences to the Chinese victims of the massacre and fulfil our obligations as Chinese citizens.[16]

Although the vast majority of foreign missionaries acted very badly when the Shanghai Massacre was going on, it should be pointed out that a few missionaries and especially those who worked with Chinese Christians in some institutions of the Church did show deep sympathy for the Chinese people. The few foreign missionaries, cooperating with Chinese Christians, published joint manifestos regarding the Shanghai Massacre and tried their best to mediate in these incidents. For example, on the day after the Shanghai Massacre, the National Christian Council of China (NCCC) convened an unscheduled meeting attended by members of the executive committee's Shanghai office. These members discussed an emergency plan and visited Chinese and English newspapers' editorial offices, where they sincerely suggested chief commentators take heed in reporting the massacre and suspend their conclusion until the truth had been brought to light. On 8 June, the executive office wrote to the SMC, requiring that there should be enough Chinese directors in the SMC on the grounds that the majority of the population of the International Settlement of Shanghai were Chinese, who paid 80 per cent of the collected taxes. It suggested the SMC set up a committee of investigation, in which:

> The number of Chinese members must be adequate. All these Chinese members will partake in a rapid, fair and thorough investigation. Results of this investigation will be published as exact as they are. So that the truth about the Shanghai Massacre will be made public and there will be objective, just conclusion in the public opinion.[17]

Soon, the NCCC's open letter to the entirety of Chinese Christians was published.[18] The letter made six suggestions regarding the massacre. First, both foreign and Chinese Christians should remain calm and lend an ear to God. In other words, they should suspend their judgement until the truth was revealed. Second, there were external and internal reasons why the massacre took place. The internal reasons were the rampant conflicts between warlords, tangled warfare, political corruption, mass impoverishment, the uncontrollable opium trade, underdeveloped education, drastic changes in the thoughts of students, and a popular strong aversion to unequal treaties. The external reasons were the imperialist powers' incessant invasions and oppression, increased coercive unequal treaties with China, white supremacy and foreign powers' smuggling drugs and arms into China. Third, Christianity and patriotism were not incompatible like fire and water. Ideally, Christians should be the noblest patriots and citizens having the best personality. Christians should always adhere to the truth, meanwhile abstaining from doing harm to their own countries. Christians should be resolutely opposed to the selfish, blind and arbitrary patriotism disregarding the basic interests of other countries. In other words, Chinese Christians' observation of the Shanghai Massacre should go beyond the parochial understanding of state and race. Fourth, when the situation was still very grim, Chinese Christians should be very cautious and try their best not to be misled by materialism, excessive anger or disappointment, scepticism about God, selfishness, resentment and a revengeful heart. Chinese Christians should adhere to the Christian spirit that truth outweighs power and do their utmost to help Christian teachings about modesty, principles, justice, tolerance and fraternity come into effect and lead God's blessings to spread all over the world. Fifth, some Christians who intentionally ignored the society on the pretext of the separation of religion from politics should be criticized. The letter held instead:

> Thoughts, words and deeds of Chinese Christians should always accord with the basic Christian principles. No matter when individuals, groups or the country are in danger, Chinese Christians should be unswervingly faithful to these principles. If Christians can always act like this, the people's politico-socio-economic life will be improved fundamentally and the Way of Christ will forever be the leading authority reigning over the relations involving countries and peoples in entire world.

Sixth, the status quo of the Chinese Church should be carefully studied and improved. To be specific,

> The Chinese Church and foreign missionary societies in China should try their utmost to catch up. The Christian organizations of present-day China should be examined through constructive criticisms and then be improved by various methods, in the hope that by doing so, the Christian way of life could be made more practical, more completed, and more accordant with the thoughts, acts and life of the Chinese people.

In addition, some huge groups, such as the whole of the Chinese and foreign faculties teaching at Yanjing University, the Chinese and foreign staff of the YMCA and the YWCA in Beijing, the Chinese foreign clergy of the Beijing Congregational Church, the secretariat of the National Council of Young Christians, and the senate of faculty and staff of 14 missionary schools in Beijing, published their announcements about the Shanghai Massacre. In spite of being politely lukewarm, these announcements unanimously said: "The Shanghai Massacre is a naked violation of the Christian doctrine and the root cause of this massacre lies in unequal treaties with China and hostility between Chinese and foreigners." According to Liu Tingfang,

The wording of this announcement is very cautious and stable. Exactly because of its prudence, reading the announcement is like appreciating Lord Yan's [i.e., Yan Zhenqing] calligraphy, which is very penetrating. This indicates that the announcement is jointly finished by the Chinese and Westerners (including some Britons), who work for the Church. These authors discuss the incident thoroughly, give their comments, and finally reach a consensus. In view of this, we should not be pessimistic about the possibility of cooperation between the Chinese and Westerners within the Church.[19]

Some thought-provoking Christians realized very quickly that there was a close relationship between the anti-imperialist patriotic movement triggered by the Shanghai Massacre and the future of Chinese Christianity. Wu Leichuan discussed this relationship in detail and contended that it should be attributed to four reasons. First, all significant events, no matter where they happened in a certain country or in multiple countries, unexceptionally affected religion. For example, the First World War changed people's view of Christianity. Similarly, the Shanghai Massacre was no exception. Second, inasmuch as Christianity was introduced into China from Europe and America and missionaries always preached how beneficial Christianity was to China, people usually thought what European countries and the United States did was the Christian endeavour. Third, the main reason why the Shanghai Massacre took place was that foreign powers grabbed concessions and had extraterritoriality, both of which, plus special articles regarding the Christian missionary work, were brought about by unequal treaties. For this reason, whenever the Chinese were humiliated by foreign powers, they would immediately connect their sufferings with Christianity. Fourth, in recent years, the banner of national campaigns criticizing Christianity was nationalism. Critics argued that, as soon as the Chinese believed in Christianity, they would forget their country. As far as church-run schools nationwide were concerned, they played a pivotal role in making young students less patriotic. Therefore, critics suggested students discontinue their schooling in missionary schools. Those who were brutally murdered by the police of the British concession were students. Those who bravely protested against the perpetrators of the massacres were students, too. Moreover, missionary schools were under foreigners' despotic rule. Recently, in some missionary schools, students collectively left school due to school authorities' prohibiting students from participating in patriotic movements. Saint John's University, for instance, fanatically imposed restriction on patriotic students, creating a very bad impression on the Chinese. Wu concluded that the Shanghai Massacre would seriously affect the future of Chinese Christianity. If foreign Christians could demonstrate justice in calling for the revision of existing unequal treaties, the Christian spirit would manifest itself. But if Christian churches paid no attention to justice and humanity and bent their knees to foreign powers, or if the United Kingdom remained arrogantly haughty and other countries chose not to defend justice, China would be bullied by foreign powers as they pleased. But foreign powers could by no means win the popular support in China. Thus, one could imagine what really lay ahead of Christianity in China. In view of this, Wu suggested the Chinese Christianity positively make two preparations. First, the mentality of Christianity should be rectified. In the past, Christianity spent too much time prattling on about God's kindness and the principle of universal love, all of which led people to ignore their own country. But in fact, Jesus himself was an ardent patriot and his teaching about the Heavenly Kingdom was filled with the justice of God. Thus, from this time onward, the propagation of Christianity in China should be based on Jesus's teaching about the Heavenly Kingdom and lay stress on strict rules, by which the Chinese would realize that they should make unremitting efforts to improve themselves and polish their personality through various undertakings. If this was done, China would be well governed, grow increasingly strong and prosperous, and protect itself from being bullied. Second, China must have its own Christian Church, that is, a truly indigenized Church that was fully independent of foreign missionary societies and achieve self-government, be self-supporting and self-propagating.

The second round of the campaign for taking back the right of education and the educational world's response

According to Liu Tingfang's study, among students who supported the general strike after the Shanghai Massacre, most were Christians. Moreover, many delegates of students and members of the executive committee of the patriotic movement were enthusiastic Christians and some were even students at theological seminaries. In addition to them, a number of participants were students who were financially supported by the Christian Church. All of these student Christians threw themselves into the patriotic movement. Therefore, Liu disagreed with such accusations that the Christian education destroyed the national character, taught people to be less patriotic, led students to be Westernized and slavish, and trained the youth to be slaves of foreign masters.[20]

Liu's defence was widely recognized by Chinese Christians. For example, Liu Zhan'en wrote an article, saying:

> [The Shanghai Massacre] is almost a touchstone for schools run by Christian churches [on the grounds that it has the popular, conventional understanding of Christian schools as broken]. [In reality,] how enthusiastic are those students who are from Christian schools and participate in the movement! Many of them are leaders of this movement. Are they servile servants of foreigners? Do they lack patriotism? I do believe that, in comparison with students from non-Christian schools, students of Christian schools are more patriotic.

Moreover, Liu held that the anti-imperialist patriotic movement helped to increase the status of Chinese teachers and staff in Christian schools. Originally, Western missionaries were sceptical about the (administrative) ability of Chinese employees. A researcher pointed out that, originally, Western missionaries thought the Chinese administered Christian schools through patriotic feeling rather than by following Christian doctrines at the time when nationalism was surging and the Chinese were unable to maintain school discipline and teaching excellence because they were easily influenced by students and political pressures.[21] Contrary to this, it had been factually proven that schools ruled by foreign missionaries turning a deaf ear to Chinese teachers' opinions and acting arbitrarily experienced large-scale student strikes and schools respecting what Chinese teachers suggested kept running smoothly. Liu did mention that some foreign missionaries were notoriously known for their despicable performance in the Shanghai Massacre. These missionaries, according to Liu's observation, talked glibly about the emulation of Jesus in normal times, but meanwhile showing no interest in justice. Chinese Christians were badly disappointed at their attitude towards the massacre. What's worse, it was in the light of these missionaries' poor performance that some free thinkers concluded that Christian schools were tools used by imperialist powers to culturally invade China.[22]

Exactly because of these missionaries and the unfair restrictions imposed by the Christian schools, the national feeling and patriotic enthusiasm of a large number of students were frequently oppressed. Consequently, people had a stronger aversion to Christian schools. Most importantly, several months after the Shanghai Massacre, the national campaign criticizing Christianity shifted the centre of gravity from anti-imperialism to the effort to take back the right of education.

In July 1925, the national campaign criticizing Christianity was directed at Christian schools again. Then the seventh conference of the National Student Union (NSU) was convened in Shanghai. At this meeting, student delegates intensely discussed the problems caused by Christian schools and how to solve these problems and passed a general resolution, finally.[23] The resolution pointed out:

> Christianity is the weapon whereby the ruling class oppresses the ruled class, [as well as being] a hired thug of imperialism. [In Christian schools], students are not allowed to act and think freely, meanwhile being forced to believe in Christianity. [Nor] are students permitted to participate in the patriotic movement. [But instead, they are required to read the Bible.] [Christian schools hope, by doing so], the Chinese youth, who will be the true heroes of the country in future, can be, spiritually and intellectually, fooled and brainwashed to be falcons and hounds of imperialists and servilely serve the imperialist exploitation of China and her people. Precisely for this reason, the national campaign criticizing Christianity is ever increasing. In the meantime, the demand to take back the right

of education and abolish Christian schools becomes increasingly strong and can be heard nationwide. In many schools run by Christian churches, student strikes and dropouts are actually unstoppable. A series of massacres against innocent Chinese, where the SMC, the United States, the Marine Corps, the Shanghai Volunteer Corps and the British navy, all of which are boastfully comprised of Christians, are murderers and responsible for killing dozens of Chinese residents in Shanghai, Hankou and Shamiandao Island, along with a Christian priest who testifies in a Christian mixed court that the British police had the right to shoot the totally unarmed Chinese people, teach the ordinary Chinese that Christianity is no other than the tool of imperialist invasion. Even very senior Chinese Christians, who witness the massacres and foreign clergy slandering innocent Chinese people, see clearly the truth that the Christian religion is an accomplice of the imperialist invasion of China. By now, the national campaign criticizing Christianity has developed into an open anti-imperialist movement.

The NSU went further, proposing several approaches to push forward the movement. One of them was the Condemning Christianity Week around Christmas, by which regional campaigns criticizing Christianity could be oriented towards the positive anti-imperialism. The NSU suggested:

> Each summer and winter vacation, the student association and council should urge students to go to the countryside and industrial areas, where they reveal crimes and sins perpetrated by Christianity for the public. [In doing so], workers and peasants will be mobilized to join the campaign criticizing Christianity and take concerted action.

The methods adopted by the campaign criticizing Christianity included leaflets, pamphlets, magazines, lectures. and costume parades. In order that two hundred thousand young students in missionary schools could be liberated, the NSU made three specific suggestions. First, the Ministry of Education of China should work out special programmes, by which Christian schools could be abolished or taken back by the Chinese. Second, student unions nationwide cooperatively should set up a committee of taking back the right of education and push forward the fulfilment of educational sovereignty. Before the recovery of the education right, this committee should not only persuade the young Chinese not to study in Christian schools but also suggest those who had studied in Christian schools discontinue their schooling. Third, for students who studied in Christian schools and were financially funded by Christian churches, they could receive economic aid and transfer to schools for free thinkers. Last but not least, the NSU's resolution encouraged regional student associations and unions to partake in activities organized by the YMCA and the YWCA and in doing so, they could expose conspiracies of such Christian organizations for the Chinese youth and lead these organizations to reconstruct themselves.

In August, the executive body of the national campaign criticizing Christianity rallied the people nationwide to stand against Christianity and Christian schools. Its Beijing branch condemned Christian schools for their crackdown on students participating in the patriotic movement after the Shanghai Massacre and called for the closure or recovery of schools run by foreigners. Under the circumstance that the campaign taking back the right of education became increasingly strong, many Chinese Christians enthusiastically supported this endeavour. In many Christian schools, all Chinese students or a number of Chinese students chose to drop out. In the aforementioned Saint John's University, almost the whole of the teaching faculties and students left and founded a new university. In like manner,

> Students in Fuzhou-based Christians schools such as the Anglo-Chinese Institution, the Union School and the Trinity School, Guangzhou's Sacred Heart School and the Sino-French School, Kaifeng's Saint Andrew's School, the Jibian School and the Sino-American School, and Christian educational institutions in Beijing, Wuchang, Nanchang and Jiujiang drop out collectively or partially.[24]

As a consequence, in 1925, the number of students of Christian schools sharply decreased and many had to shut down.

In face of this worsening situation, Chinese educators suggested Christian schools should improve themselves. Some, inspired by criticisms against Christianity, advised Christians schools to register with the regional education authorities; to increase the number of Chinese headmasters, teachers, staff and directors; to pay greater attention to the Chinese culture; to restrain themselves from overemphasizing English; and to abolish coercive religious education, such as the forced Bible-reading session and Christian service and replace it with the cultivation of a Christianized personality.[25] Some, who disagreed with the cancellation of religious education in Christian schools, approved the nationalist education's significance to Christian schools.[26] They held that the Christian education should not be against the patriotic feeling; that education should help to preserve the national and cultural character of China; that the curricula of Christian schools should be adaptable to the Chinese conditions; that the majority of administrative staff of Christian schools should be Chinese; and Christian schools should be officially registered with the education authorities and open to the supervision of the government. They were opposed to Christian schools' conventional praxis, in which the teaching of Chinese language and scholarship was overlooked, and the teaching of foreign education was over-emphasized, and the Christian education on the whole was overwhelmingly Westernized. These observers pointed out that, if Christian schools could not reform themselves, they would increasingly be out of sync with the spirit of the times and be unable to win sympathy from the Chinese. In addition, some observed that, if foreigners attempted to make use of Christian schools to preach Christianity, they must seriously treat the Chinese habits and psychology, sincerely respect the Chinese culture, and teach the Western culture in a subtle, subliminal way. Foreign missionaries should allow students themselves to comparatively study the advantages and disadvantages of Western and Chinese cultures, meanwhile abandoning their ungrounded cultural superiority. If they could not do this, they should return the management right of the school to Chinese Christians.[27] In order that the Christian education could be Sinicized, Chinese Christians repeatedly persuaded foreign missionaries to register Christian schools with the education authorities as soon as possible. Only when Christian schools were officially registered would they be recognized by the government and able to keep running. Similarly, only when Christian schools were registered and accredited would their graduates be socially recognized. Otherwise, it would be very hard for graduates of Christian schools to find a job. Moreover, the goal of foreigners, who came here and ran schools, should be to make the country and its people happy. They should never run counter to the programmes and the new school system formulated by the Ministry of Education of China, let alone damage Chinese education. The reason why Christian schools must increase the number of Chinese Christians in charge of the management of school was that these schools must be adaptable to Chinese conditions. For foreigners, who did not know much about the true situation of China, they were heavily dependent on the foreign experience and perspective. Consequently, they made the Christian education too Westernized to be acceptable to the Chinese. What the Chinese needed was an indigenized Christian education adaptable to the Chinese conditions. The fulfilment of such education should not depend on foreign missionaries.[28]

On 16 November 1925, China's Ministry of Education (MOE), influenced by the national campaign criticizing Christianity, promulgated a six-article law regarding the recognition of schools that were financially dependent on foreign donations. The six articles were as follows:

1. Any foreigners, who wanted to donate money to set up schools complying with laws and regulations promulgated by MOE, must apply for permission from the regional or national education authorities just as required by MOE's relevant stipulation.
2. The school name must be marked as 'Private'.
3. The leaders of school must be Chinese. In some cases, wherein heads of school were originally foreigners, the deputy head must be Chinese, who would apply for the education authorities' approval and recognition on behalf of his or her school.
4. If a school had the directorate, over half of the directors must be Chinese.
5. The goal of these schools could by no means be the propagation of Christianity.

6. The curricula of these schools must meet the MOE's requirements and the religious course could not be compulsory in these schools.

These above-mentioned six stipulations posed a great challenge to Christian schools. Especially two—leaders of Christian schools must be Chinese and the religious course could not be compulsory—were really challenging. In reality, by 1925, only a very small number of headmasters of primary and secondary Christian schools were Chinese. All the positions of president and vice-president of missionary universities and colleges were monopolized by foreign missionaries. Where the directorate of a missionary university or college was concerned, it had very few Chinese directors. A national league of Christian universities and colleges, driven by the patriotic movement after the Shanghai Massacre, promised that, after 1925, over half of the directors would be Chinese. For example, by the end of 1925, there were eight Chinese directors in the directorate of Jinling University (aka the University of Nanking). But, overall, the reform of Christian schools was unsatisfactory. Although Chinese Christians agreed with the official registration of Christian schools with the education authorities, foreign missionaries were still worried, because they held that they should follow the instructions of missionary societies financing their schools. The most stubborn problem was that most missionaries did not want to give up the religious religion in Christian schools. Even a few Chinese educators disagreed with the full annihilation of religious education in Christian schools. By the second half of 1926, when the Nationalist Revolution was sweeping across the whole country, Christian educators, forced by the drastically changing situation, found a solution, finally. Take Wu Leichun, for example. After reading the MOE's six stipulations, he pointed out that the appointment of Chinese headmasters or presidents and the abolishment of religious education in Christian schools were the two most critical issues. Wu personally suggested Christian schools, which were externally rebuked by critical free thinkers and internally faced with students' demands, reform themselves according to the needs of the time and relevant laws. In his eyes, the key did not lie in whether or not foreign operators of Christian schools would like to apply for official registration but whether or not the Chinese were able to keep these schools running smoothly. Thus, the proposed three basic requirements regarding the qualifications of principals/presidents and deputy principals/presidents of Christian schools in China, all of whom should be carefully hand-picked, were indispensable. First, the candidates must be Chinese Christians. Second, the candidates must work for or had worked for the schools. Third, the candidates must be morally good, academically excellent and administratively strong. But in reality, although in economically advanced metropolises and provincial cities, the number of candidates meeting the three requirements was not small, only a few of them wanted to play a leading role in Christian schools. What's worse, the financial resources of Christian schools were a huge problem. An overwhelming majority of Christian schools were financially dependent on foreign donors, who stubbornly insisted that the courses on the Bible could not be cancelled. This meant that, once the religious course was kicked out of these schools, Christian schools' funds would be cut off.[29]

Even so, some enlightened missionary universities flexibly treated the religious course and education after the autumn of 1925. There were three types of flexible handling of religious education in Christian colleges or universities. First, some, such as Lingnan University, Yanjing University and William Nast College (a middle school, in fact), adopted a laissez-faire policy on religious activities on campus. To be specific, students in these schools had the full freedom to decide whether or not they would partake in religious activities, such as morning and evening prayers, Sunday School, Christian service in church and Bible-reading class. The school authorities would always keep their hands off all these affairs. Consequently, these Christian schools would fully meet the MOE's requirement that there should never be any compulsory religious courses in schools. Second, some granted students partial freedom. That is to say, except for the compulsory Sunday course on the Bible, religious activities in school were conducted on a voluntary basis and at the same time the number of religious courses was significantly reduced. For example, in Fujian (Fukien) Christian University, the compulsory religious course that originally lasted for four years was shortened to a two-year course. Qilu (Cheeloo) University went further, finishing this course in one year. Third, some applied a binary mode to the religious education. Take the Sunday meeting, for example. This meeting was divided into two groups. One was the Christian service. The other was the general lecture on ethics. Students had the freedom to decide to take both or either of them. It was said that these free approaches had good results, one of which was that students were neither suspicious nor antagonistic to their (Christian) teachers.[30]

In this phase, Christian educators in China discussed whether or not Christian schools should conduct the religious education on campus and how to Sinicize the Christian education and take back the right of education. There was a heated debate on whether or not Christian schools should make the Bible-reading class compulsory. Xu Songshi made a good observation about this.[31]

There were six reasons why the abolition of religious education in Christian schools should be put into effect. Frist, the MOE had promulgated relevant laws and regulations, by which Christian schools should abide. Otherwise, Christian schools would be closed down. Second, the abolition could moderate the criticism of Christianity. The coercive Bible-reading session was one of main reasons causing the attack on Christian schools. Exactly because of the compulsory Bible-reading course, many students decided to discontinue their education in Christian schools. If Christian churches made concession, the number of students would increase. In the long run, it would benefit Christian schools. Third, the Bible-reading course should be cancelled on the grounds that (1) students could by no means be moved by the mechanical, formalistic Bible-reading; (2) students were sick of and averse to reading the

Bible; and (3) compulsory Bible reading was not the only approach to cultivate the spirit of students. Fourth, the abolition would create a good impression among the students. Once the compulsory religious religion was made voluntarily selective, students would have a good opinion of (Christian) teachers. Fifth, the compulsory religious course should be replaced with important subjects such as the course on Chinese scholarship. This was an attempt to gain a double advantage. Sixth, the abolition helped to prepare a good future for students of Christian schools. If the government prohibited local public authorities from employing graduates of Christian students, that would be a huge problem. As soon as the compulsory Bible-reading course was cancelled, Christian schools would be the same as schools for free thinkers. If this was done successfully, Christian schools would become more stable and students would have a brighter future.

The reasons why Christian schools should reject the MOE's regulation were as follows:

1. The MOE's regulation was inconsistent with the national constitution. Christian schools had their own regulations. Therefore, the Bible-reading course could be held by Christian schools in the light of the freedom of religious belief.
2. Bible reading was one of the key tasks of Christian schools.
3. Bible reading would not upset the education system. The purpose of an educational system lay in keeping students' general ability to study, so that it did not contradict reading the Bible.
4. The aim of the Bible-reading course in Christian schools was that students could be taught how to be good citizens. In other words, it was conducted for the interests of the students.
5. The propagation of the gospel should be based on the teachings of the Bible. Otherwise, Christians would have a guilty conscience.
6. The Christian Church should not always yield to the national campaign criticizing Christianity.

The national association for Christian education carefully considered and weighed up pros and cons. It spent much time discussing this issue and finally concluded: "Christian schools can decide spontaneously how to respond [to the MOE's regulations] in a longer time limit in the hope that they can find the best and widely recognized solution."

Xu Songshi contended that the cancellation of the Bible-reading course was a very complicated issue. According to him, this issue was related to anti-imperialism and the abrogation of unequal treaties, as well as revealing the truth that students felt a strong aversion towards Bible-reading teachers who had their own problems. Xu stressed that the purpose of guiding students to read the Bible was not to force them to believe in Christianity but to cultivate their spirit. This issue should be tackled at the roots. That is to say, Christian schools must transform into China's own Christian schools and in doing so they could repair their bad reputation as running dogs of imperialism. The most fundamental reason why people abhorred Christianity was that Christianity acted as the imperialism's pet poodle. In other words, the Bible-reading course was not the root cause but something skin-deep.

Finally, the national association for Christian education formulated a specific programme. Politically, Christian schools should observe the MOE's special regulations promulgated on 16 November 1925 as far as possible and indicate that they would never intentionally violate these regulations. Moreover, within a certain time limit, the Christian Church's general agency regulating all Christian schools should, lawfully and appropriately, make an explanation to MOE and require the cancellation of statutes to which Christian schools would find it difficult to follow. Administratively, (1) the Chinese would be appointed principal/president or deputy principal/president; (2) the Chinese would be in the majority in the directorate of Christian schools; (3) the voice of Chinese teachers and staff would be significantly increased in the faculty meeting; (4) if possible, Christian schools should be returned to Chinese Christians as soon as possible; (5) free thinkers and parents of students should be informed that there were compulsory courses on the Bible and what the purpose of these course really was; and (6) students were required to fill in the form declaring unambiguously whether or not they would take the compulsory Bible-reading course, when they chose to attend Christian schools. Pedagogically, (1) members of the national association for Christian education and the teaching staff of Christian schools should work together and try their best to find the best methods of teaching the Bible; (2) the time of Bible-reading course should be reduced to the most appropriate length; and (3) the course on the Bible could never be even the least coercive.

As indicated by above specific approaches, in many main aspects, the national association for Christian education had already accepted the MOE's regulations and pushed forward the Sinicization of Christian education in China. But, on the other hand, it was still far from meeting the MOE's requirement regarding the teaching of the Bible in Christian schools. Even so, Chinese Christian educators emphasized that the course on the Bible was conducted on a voluntary basis. However, there was an inextricable contradiction, namely, that if students did not prefer the course on the Bible, could they abandon it freely? If they could, would the course on the Bible be compulsory? The true result of the reform allowing religious course to be conducted on a voluntary basis was that the Bible-themed courses could only be optional. The sweeping Nationalist Revolution dealt a blow to religious education in Christian schools. As a consequence, in most cases, religious courses in the campus existed in name only.

In order that the religious subject could be preserved in the school campus, some suggested Christian schools reform existing religious course to meet the needs of Chinese students. For example, Shi Yufang, who had done fieldwork in over ten secondary schools run by Christian churches in Jiangyin, Nanjing,

Wuhu and Ningbo, concluded that religious courses conducted there were all unsatisfactory. The main reasons were as follows:

1. The aim of religious education was misconceived. Specifically, the aim of this religion was not to lead students to have a correct view of life but to pass examination through studying the Bible.
2. There were not any specially trained teachers who could teach religious courses well and be of benefit to students.
3. Textbooks of religious education were not only outdated but also not adaptable to the psychology of Chinese students.
4. The pedagogy was really inflexible and unattractive.

In view of this, Shi proposed an improvement programme, by which the religious education would have an unequivocal goal of cultivating the personality of students, Christian schools could employ more qualified and more professional staff to teach religion and benefit students, and appropriate textbooks and vivid pedagogy suitable for the psychology and needs of young students would be applied to the religious education.[32]

Some extended the discussion on the aim of religious subject in Christian schools to the exploration of the basic aim of Christian education. Lin Buji, for instance, argued that the Christian education had direct and indirect aims. The direct aim was applicable to students; and the indirect aim, to the Church, society and the state. Both were worthy of attention. The general aim of Christian education was quadripartite. The first was the cultivation of personality. It consisted of the moral, intellectual, physical and social education. The intellectual education focused on knowledge, emotion and will. The Christian education aspired to apply the spirit of Christ to the training of morality, intelligence, the body, and sociality and to the refinement of human knowledge, emotion and will. The second was the propagation of Christianity. The third was the improvement of society, which meant that the Christian education would be used to dispel blindness, make people happy, develop economy, and maintain social customs. The fourth was to serve the country. It was stressed that the Christian education was not against nationalism but helpful to the pure, true nationalism.[33] In addition, some directly analysed how to Sinicize Christian schools in China. Wei Fulan (Francis John White) suggested that Christian schools be returned to the Chinese as soon as possible, fully administered by the Chinese and operated in accordance with the Chinese strategy.[34]

Among the observers who discussed the campaign for taking back the right of education, Zhang Shizhang did a comprehensive, deep study.[35] First, he divided the history of the campaign into five phases.

> Phase I: Beginnings, which started from March 1922, when Cai Yuanpei published "On Dependence of Education" and ended in the publication of "The Problem of Christian Education" authored by Yu Jiaju in February 1923.

Phase II: Preparation, which extended from February 1923 to April 1924, when protesting students of Guangzhou-based Trinity School published a manifesto, which was followed by the attempt to take back the right of education in June.

Phase III: Establishment, which began in June 1924 and culminated in the publication of a special supplement entitled "The Endeavour to Take Back the Right of Education" compiled by *The Chinese Education*.

Phase IV: Accommodation, which commenced in December 1925 and completed with the promulgation of MOE's special regulations regarding the official registration of schools financially depending on foreign donations.

Phase V: Amelioration, which dawned in the early winter of 1925.

Then, Zhang did a psychological study of the campaign, arguing that it could be divided into four groups, that is, the nationalist group, the communist group, the Christian group, and the money-oriented group. The common ground of these groups lay in their love for the country and will for competition. But at the same time, they each had their own distinct psychology. The nationalist group disliked and envied foreigners; the communist group had a strong sense of gratitude and the courage to destroy [anything established]; the Christian group had a sense of shame and was always possessed by fear; and the money-oriented group was obsessed with fame and gain. Finally, Zhang comparatively analysed several main ideas such as the suggestions made by Yu Jiaju and Chen Qitian, the manifesto by the Chinese Christian educators, what Li Huang of the SYC and Wu Zhefu, a religious educator, had said, and the opinions of famous foreigners such as George Bernard Shaw and H. G. Wells. His conclusion was that education was not sovereignty but one of the people's rights; that education was children's right, parents' responsibility and the state's duty; that China had not yet lost its education sovereignty nor did it fulfil its obligation to popularize education; that China should stand against foreign powers' educational invasion, meanwhile tolerating Christian education; that the nationalist education was worth being praised but the highly politicized nationalist education be opposed; that, formally and methodologically, education should separate itself from religion, but spiritually and teleologically, it should neither be politicized nor be money-oriented; that (the Christian) education should be carried out in accordance with the religious spirit and state laws and regulations; that the assertion that Christian schools were built on unequal treaties was groundless; and that there were two possibilities for the survival of Christian schools. Zhang's analysis ended in the programme of improvement, which suggested Christian schools in China be financially independent, officially registered, and stop sending students to study abroad.

It was after the Shanghai Massacre that Christian schools intensively discussed the problems plaguing them and how to reform themselves. But it was in the period of the Northern Expedition that the official registration of Christian schools in China was greatly pushed forward.

Direct responses to the Condemning Christianity Movement and the campaign against unequal treaties

While the campaign for taking back the right of education was being conducted, the national movement criticizing Christianity developed in depth and breadth. After the NSU's seventh national congress held in July 1925, many regional student unions, responding to the NSU's spirit and call, set up an alliance condemning Christianity in schools. For example, the Shanghai Student Union (SSU) told all Shanghai-based schools that such an alliance should be founded as soon as possible. According to the SSU, the key points respecting such an alliance were as follows:

> First, each school should set up its own alliance condemning Christianity. Then these alliances form the Shanghai Condemning Christianity Alliance (SCCA), which will play a leading role in the regional movement criticizing Christianity. Second, the alliance should expose the dark side of Christianity. To do this, there should be a special journal. Third, the alliance should make efforts to develop the criticism of Christianity among the young people and especially those who are from the countryside and Christian schools. Fourth, the alliance should give support to students who launch strikes in Christian schools. Fifth, the alliance should persuade students to discontinue their schooling in Christian schools. Sixth, the alliance should dissuade young people from attending Christian schools. Seventh, the alliance should tell the public that what it stands against is not students of Christian schools but the Christian education itself. So far, the alliance has published a ten-day periodical devoting itself to the criticism of Christianity. Moreover, it should urge all regional student unions to make a concerted effort to launch a large-scale project of criticism of Christianity around Christmas. Therefore, a special issue is indeed needed.[36]

Thanks to the effort made by student unions, a huge number of schools set up the alliance criticizing Christianity and published their manifestos, most of which pointed out that Christianity was the running dog of the capitalist class and imperialism, the accomplice of the capitalist exploitation of labouring people, a tool for oppressing the people and the peasants in particular, the tip of the spearhead of cultural invasion by foreign powers, and an institution training slaves of foreign masters, arguing against science, and banning patriotism. The Guangzhou-based alliance condemning Christianity distributed citywide a pamphlet entitled "To All Compatriots for Condemnation Against Christianity," which vehemently railed:

In the twentieth century, when science has greatly developed, all forms of religion should cease to exist. Christianity is one of these religions. Therefore, it is not at all an exception and should be eliminated. This is the historical reason why we are against Christianity. At present, China is almost at the gates of death due to the oppression imposed by international imperialism. In such circumstances, there is no way to save the country except by overthrowing international imperialism by uniting all the social classes of China. Christianity is a tool used by international imperialism to invade weak and small countries globally. It is a knife killing people without spilling blood. If we aspire to put an end to international imperialism, we must have all its tools, including Christianity, broken. This is the political reason why we are opposed to Christianity. [Christianity prattles on about freedom, equality and fraternity in normal times. But in reality, crimes, such as the murder of innocent Chinese protesters in the Shanghai Massacre, intervention in lawsuits in the interior of China, and oppression against students of Christian schools, are all perpetrated by imperialism and its Christian agents in the country. In view of this, we earnestly suggest] the Chinese Christian Church and Christian schools positively participate in the anti-imperialist movement. Only by doing this will the revolutionary Chinese people think you are different from imperialist Christian agencies and may not be the running dog of imperialism.[37]

Many alliances mobilized students to publicly criticize Christianity exactly on Christmas Day 1925. Moreover, they printed out a huge number of pamphlets against Christianity. For example, the executive committee of the NSU distributed "Condemning Christianity" nationwide as a Christmas present. In Shanghai, on 25 December 1925, the SCCA organized large-scale public lectures and passed out flyers to local residents. In addition, some free thinkers' journals, such as *Awakening*, published critical articles, among which were Li Shuzhen's "Against Religions" and "Reasons Why We are Against Religions," Xiao Chunü's "What Causes the Condemning Christianity Movement," and Juru's "Condemning Christian Schools."

In face of the new round of the national campaign criticizing Christianity, some conservative and close-minded Christians either turned a deaf ear to criticisms or chose to be staunch apologists, blindly defending Christianity. Contrary to them, some Chinese Christians and young Christian students in particular enthusiastically participated in the movement. The burst of their enthusiasm can be mainly attributed to the fact that the patriotic feeling of young students was oppressed by the authorities of Christian schools and young Christians' strong discontent. Of course, the strategy of the alliance criticizing Christianity did contribute to this. Digging into manifestos published by the NSU and the Shanghai Student Union (SSU), readers can find that they all stressed that the national campaign was not against students of Christian schools but the Christian education itself. Rather, the alliance and national campaign supported students and aspired to intellectually emancipate them, on the grounds that these students were actually being oppressed by Christian schools.

At the same time, some intellectually enlightened Chinese Christians assumed an open-minded attitude towards various criticisms against Christianity, holding that many reasons why free thinkers were averse to the Christian religion were correct and constructive to the Chinese Church. For example, Zhao Zichen said the national campaign criticizing Christianity awakened the Chinese Church's self-consciousness. Moreover, due to this campaign, Chinese Christians became deeply suspicious of religion, meanwhile experiencing rapidly growing self-consciousness. Zhao pointed out that Chinese Christians were actually very unhappy with the old, conservative Christianity and started to act against it. They particularly attacked the coercive religious education in Christian schools. Some Chinese Christians had discarded Christianity and returned to Confucianism or converted to Buddhism. Criticisms of Christianity reexamined the conduct and personality of Jesus, who was the founding patriarch of Christianity. Most importantly, critics investigated Christianity from political and intellectual perspectives. They treated Christianity as the running dog of foreign capitalism and one of reasons for the imperialist invasions inflicted upon China. They regarded Christianity as the spearhead of foreign powers' commercial and cultural invasion of China, on the grounds that Christian schools, on the one hand, applied coercive religious education to students and thus deprived them of the freedom of belief and, on the other hand, it encroached upon China's educational sovereignty and attempted to lead the Church to play a decisive role in the national education of China. In addition to these, some critics pointed out that religion such as Christianity was contrary to science. By now, criticism had been translated into action. That is to say, free thinkers who were critical of Christianity had successfully instilled their criticisms into Christian schools. As a result, a number of Chinese Christians became resentful of the Christian life and method. Then Zhao presented how to reform and improve Christianity. He suggested that the Christian religious life must assimilate ethical elements; that Christianity must pay attention to growing itself internally and making itself adaptable to the socio-scientific environment; that Christians should interpret their own religious experience in the light of rationalism; and that Chinese Christians should create a new society by means of Christianization.[38]

Xu Baoqian said the national campaign criticizing Christianity was, by and large, conducive to helping Christianity. The reason was twofold. On the one hand, the campaign caused the Chinese to attach importance to Christianity and study it intensively. On the other hand, precisely by means of this campaign, Christianity could purify itself by abandoning those followers who were less confident in Christianity and encouraging faithful, enlightened Christians to seriously rethink significant questions such as whether or not China needed Christianity.[39]

Ying Yuandao provided a clearer analysis. He said:

> Due to the campaign criticizing Christianity, enlightened members of the Church profoundly reconsidered the criticism. They have realized that Chinese Christians should make a much more positive effort to promote the indigenization of Chinese Church, eliminate the excessive Westernization of the Church, lead the Church to blend with the Chinese culture, and finally create the Chinese nation's own Christian Church that is not only adaptable to the needs of Chinese religious life and thought but also closely relevant to the Christian intellectual movement.[40]

When it came to how to respond to the campaign criticizing Christianity, some Christians suggested that the religion itself stop criticisms by performing a self-examination and rectifying itself. For example, Liu Ganzhi contended that many criticisms of Christianity were worthy of recognition on the grounds that the critics were actually, to some extent, friends of the Church. He particularly pointed out that, for followers of the Christian Church, the best way of responding to criticism of the Church was retrospection and self-cultivation.

Some argued that criticisms of Christianity must be analysed concretely, just as the saying went: "Right is right and wrong is wrong." The catch-all attitude, which suggested Christians treat the criticism as it was, was inadvisable. In this regard, Liu Tingfang said:

> Personally, I think, for the self-rectification of the Chinese Christian Church, what the critics say should be used as the mirror, through which we Christians can reexamine ourselves and make an item-by-item analysis of their criticisms. [For example, some rebuked that the Christian Church was] the running dog of imperialism. Hearing this, we Christians should examine our own conscience and ask ourselves: "Is it the truth existing in the Church? Are the idea of the Church and imperialism compatible with each other? Does the organization of the Church conform to imperialism? Is the Church's attitude truly suspiciously imperialistic? What are the Church's behaviours that are synonymous with imperialist invasions?"

After studying and analysing the above-mentioned questions, Christians should do their utmost to assume an objective attitude towards the truth in accordance with the scientific spirit. If there were indeed mistakes, the Church should not conceal but acknowledge them. Of course, it was absolutely unnecessary for the Church to over-act in admitting mistakes that were not of its doing. Liu thus said:

> Those who are truly able to stop slandering the Church by means of self-rectification and self-cultivation are the Christians who bear

responsibility without grudge. They paid the greatest attention to all criticisms of the Church and at the same time, they investigate the truth about the Church in the most meticulous, most detailed and most precise way. They objectively judge all facts they have obtained. Their aim is the discovery of truth. If the truth is not yet discovered, they should never make any comments. When the truth that the Church did make mistakes as its critics said is discovered, they will not treat them as taboos but instead candidly acknowledge the faults. In like manner, if the Church did not make such mistakes and was treated unjustly, they will immediately defend the Church and resolutely deny any groundless accusations.[41]

In order that he could do a comprehensive study of the campaign criticizing Christianity, Liu further analysed the reasons and speeches condemning this religion in another paper. Why was the Christian Church opposed in China? Liu explained: "The Christian Church is well-organized, tightly-knit, and substantially down-to-earth. For this reason, the Church cannot be ignored by the Chinese. Likewise, the campaign criticizing Christianity casts the first stone at the Christian Church."

Where the attack on the Christian Church was concerned, it was divided into three groups. The first was the criticism of the Church:

1. Key points of criticism against Western missionaries were: missionaries' acts belied their words; missionaries showed contempt for the personality of the Chinese on the strength of their governing regimes; missionaries were the spearhead of imperialism; missionaries were one of the key players of unequal treaties; missionaries were running dogs of the capitalist class; and missionaries were cultural aggressors.
2. Chinese Christians should be criticized, too, on the grounds that they were unpatriotic, that they were lackeys of foreign missionaries, that they believed in Christianity merely for survival, and that they were hypocritically kind.
3. The missionary work in China had defects in the goal of charity work, Christian education, and issues of labour and economy.
4. The Church's history was notorious for its misdeeds.

The second was the criticism of Christian doctrines:

1. Christian doctrines were superstitious.
2. Christian doctrines could be likened to narcotics.
3. Christian doctrines made people spiritually dependent on religion.
4. Christian doctrines preached passive pacifism putting the Chinese at the mercy of foreign powers.
5. Christian doctrines attached importance to spirit rather than to body and thus destroyed human life.
6. Christian doctrines impeded the fulfilment of intellectual freedom.

7. Christian doctrines were completely scientifically unacceptable.
8. Christian doctrines were impracticable empty theories.
9. Christian doctrines were useless to human thoughts and culture.

The third was the criticism of Jesus Christ.

1. The historicalness of Jesus was denied.
2. The (moral) character of Jesus Christ was denounced (but in fact, few critics did this).

After a careful study of the afore-mentioned criticisms, Liu concluded that the criticism of Christianity focused on the Church and the relationship between the Church and foreign missionaries in particular. He held that the criticism of the Church would disappear automatically, as China steadily improved itself in leading politics back on the right track, taking back the extraterritoriality grabbed by foreign powers, and revising or even abrogating all the unequal treaties. As long as the Chinese Church could achieve self-government and be self-supporting, the reason for the criticism of Christianity would become ungrounded. For example, if Chinese Christians strived for an indigenized Church, made the Church financially independent of foreign money, trained talented people for the Church, and led the Church to govern itself, criticisms of Christianity would be seriously weakened. So long as Chinese Christians could improve their own moral characters by discarding the dependent mentality and meanness and being truly patriotic citizens, criticisms of Christianity would be further weakened. Moreover, Liu suggested that, in face of the criticism of Christian doctrines, Chinese Christians should conduct true studies of Christian doctrines, reappraise the value of Christian doctrines in accordance with scientific principles, re-illuminate the profundity of Christian doctrines in the light of experience and the environment, and reinterpret the essence of Christian doctrines by means of the Chinese spiritual culture. In the meantime, Chinese Christians aspiring for science should work hard on the development of science in China. Liu did believe that, by doing so, Christians themselves would not only understand science and Christian doctrines but also carry forward existing doctrines. This progress would, according to Liu, benefit even those who criticized Christianity.[42] Liu's thorough study of the campaign criticizing Christianity indicated that the basis of his endeavour was the improvement of Chinese Christian Church, that is, the indigenization of the church in China. In fact, other similar papers all finally focused on the indigenization of the church.

Within the Church, many agreed with what Liu Tingfang advocated, namely, that Christianity and the Church should re-examine themselves by means of a thorough study of the campaign criticizing them. It was in the course of retrospection that the indigenization of Chinese Christian Church would be pushed forward. Take Zhao Guanhai's analysis, for example.[43] According to Zhao, there were six types of criticism of Christianity, that is, political (i.e., nationalist), social (i.e., Communist), scientific, educational (i.e., in relation to educational sovereignty), historical and cultural (i.e., in relation to the traditional Chinese cultural essence). One by one, Zhao defended Christianity. For example, he contended that Christianity was originally uncompromisingly against imperialism; that Christianity was originally socially oriented and made great efforts to help oppressed people; and that Christianity was originally obedient to truth, including scientific truth; and that Christianity was originally antagonistic towards turning Christian schools into tools of cultural invasion. But at the same time, Zhao critically reexamined the problems of the Chinese Christian Church. For example, politically, with the exception of very few missionaries, who uttered their disapproval of existing unequal treaties with China, the overwhelming majority of foreign missionaries were as silent as cicadas in late autumn and did not have the guts to say no to inequality and injustice. When it came to labour relations, it was an indisputable truth that European and American churches were raised, controlled and used by capitalists, even though in China industry was still underdeveloped and capitalism still in its incipient stage. Scientifically, the Church was neither fully tolerant of the modern scientific spirit nor adopted modern scientific methods as much as possible. As regards the official registration of Christian schools with the educational authorities, Zhao suggested the Church should respect Chinese law and finish the registration as soon as possible. He finally concluded:

> It is true that the Chinese Christian Church does not play any roles in the failure of Chinese diplomacy in modern times. It is also true that the Church obstinately adheres to the established conservative attitude towards international relations and diplomacy and never makes any attempts to change it. Consequently, the Church cannot get rid of the bad reputation of being in collusion with imperialism.

Like Zhao, Xu Baoqian suggested Christians, first of all, should make an analysis of the content and faction of criticisms and then adopt appropriate attitudes and policies.[44] Xu said criticisms of Christianity could be divided into three groups, namely, the rationalist, the nationalist, and the Communist. The rationalist criticism was based on humanism and was strongly against theology; the nationalist criticism was premised on the love for the country; and the Communist criticism tried to interpret human life from the economic perspective. Then he proposed a ten-item policy responding to the national campaign criticizing Christianity. For example, the Church could cultivate followers' spiritual life in the light of the noble personality of Jesus Christ, rehabilitate the Christian faith by scientific methods, participate in patriotic campaigns aspiring for the abrogation of unequal treaties and recovery of the right of education, lead itself to be truly self-governing, self-supporting and self-propagating, try its best to make Christian thoughts, institutions and organizations and the inherent Chinese cultural spirit compatible with each other, and spiritually fight against unjust social organizations and institutions.

Some Chinese Christians, among them Zhang Yijing, Liu Weihan, Lu Guanwei and Tan Jiansun, strongly disagreed with the criticisms that Christianity was the running dog of imperialism and capitalism and the antithesis of modern science, and acknowledged that the Church did need to pay attention to reform, independence and indigenization. Tan Jiansun said:

> The Chinese Church's dependence on foreigners is not perpetual but temporary. We actually realize this inappropriateness very early. Precisely for this reason, there are various movements promoting indigenization, self-government, self-support and self-propagation. It is no news that the management right of Christian schools in China should be returned to the Chinese. Therefore, there are pre-arranged plans regarding the restoration of Chinese administration of Christian schools. Of course, we have already known that the politics must be separated from religion, foreign missionary work in China should never be conducted under the escort of (unequal) treaties, and the movement abrogating these treaties was inevitable. Unfortunately, critics of Christianity neither know nor care about the fact that we Christians have already realized all these issues. But instead, they keep gabbling on about these. So boring are their incongruous comments, which can be described as an old saying that goes "the mouth of a horse is on the head of an axe." Contrary to these irresponsible critics, the true patriotic young Chinese would like to joyfully shake hands with Chinese Christians, show their support and sympathy for the Church and Christian schools' reforms, and sincerely hope that the Chinese Christian Church can be indigenized, self-governed, self-supported, self-propagated and united and Christian schools be returned to the Chinese as early as possible. These things are what we are earnestly desiring.[45]

Liu Weihan disliked very much the accusation that Christianity was the talisman defending imperialism and capitalism, countering that it was a slur confusing right and wrong and calling white black.[46] But at the same time, he candidly pointed out that, in the present circumstances, the Church did face three matters of the utmost urgency, that is, the fulfilment of indigenization, reform of existing Christian schools, and the development of the textual work of propagation.[47] All these indicated that Christians should attempt to push forward the indigenization of Christian Church in responding to the campaign criticizing Christianity.

It should be particularly pointed out that the national campaign criticizing Christianity was a direct impetus to the Church's endeavour to abrogate all unequal treaties with China. A Christian magazine, which was ironically entitled *The Christian Occupation of China*, had observed:

In recent years, undue prerogatives, such as the extraterritorial jurisdiction, which is grabbed by foreigners through unequal treaties, have already been notoriously known to the Chinese and the world. The outbreak of the Shanghai Massacre against the innocent Chinese made the Chinese people extremely angry at foreigners and unequal treaties. The Chinese unanimously hold that the abrogation of unequal treaties is a matter of the utmost urgency. Under such circumstance, those, who originally merely study this issue, have to change their attitudes drastically.[48]

The imperialist Shanghai Massacre against the Chinese thoroughly activated the patriotic feelings of Chinese Christians. Wang Zhixin, a Chinese Christian living in Nanjing, was a pioneer in the Chinese Christians' endeavour to abrogate unequal treaties. Not only did Wang organize a council promoting the abrogation of unequal treaties but he also published a journal entitled *Voice*. Working in concert with Wang, Chinese Christians set up similar council nationwide. A number of councils, such as those in Nanchang, Guangzhou, Danyang (in Jiangsu), Chuxian County (in Anhui), Wuxing (in Zhejiang) and Hengshan (in Hunan), published manifestos appealing for the abrogation of all unequal treaties. Guangzhou council's announcement, entitled *The Manifesto of Chinese Christians' National Movement Abrogating Unequal Treaties*, was the most famous. According to this manifesto, the Chinese Christian Church should, first, be independent from all unequal treaties imposed on China by foreign powers, and then mobilize people from all walks of life to appeal for the abrogation of unequal treaties. Authors of this manifesto briefly reconstructed the history of Christianity in China and analysed why the signing of unequal treaties impeded the development of Christianity in China. Then they concluded that there were three reasons regarding the national movement against unequal treaties. First, originally, the Christian Church did not make any distinctions between races and nations. Exactly for this reason, in any countries, the Church should not have any prerogatives but be protected by the country's laws only. The Church was a spiritual organization, so that its development was solely dependent on the moral accomplishment and popular support from local residents. At present, the national liberation of China had been perfectly justified and China's demand for the abrogation of all unequal treaties had been approved by all humanists on the planet. The Chinese Christian Church was an organization built on Christian doctrines. Therefore, it was totally intolerant of any unequal treaties imposed on China by foreign powers. It should never resort to unequal treaties, which were embodiments of the unjust foreign power, for help in the name of a worsening environment, on the grounds that the protection from these unequal treaties was obtained at the cost of the most precious support and sympathy of the Chinese people. In a word, the Church should agree with the abrogation of unequal treaties for its own sake. Second, Christianity held that all countries and all peoples be treated equally and the praxis in which the strong and the big bullied the weak and the small was totally unacceptable. Under no circumstances should one country invade another country. All unequal treaties imposed by foreign powers on China were completely against Christian doctrines and international laws and rules. As soon as the special article regarding the Christian missionary work in China was incorporated into unequal treaties, foreign missionaries grabbed the prerogatives overriding Chinese laws. As a consequence, not only did China lose face but many corrupt practices were created. In view of this, the Church should suggest that all unequal treaties must be abolished in accordance with international law. Third, the life of Christianity was fully dependent on Christians' trust in God rather than on any unjust power and its embodiments, such as unequal treaties. The status of the Christian Church in the present-day world is based on martyrs who died for the cause of (Christian) justice, which could have moved compatriots. Without this spirit, the religious life of Christianity would die or disappear, even though the Church could develop in form. If the Church's survival is premised on protection by foreign powers, the Church is a castle built on quicksand rather than on massive rocks. Therefore, all unequal treaties must be abrogated in order that the Christian truth could manifest itself. The conclusion of this manifesto was as follows:

> Those, who truly believe in Christ, treasure the truth, and remain loyal to the country, will definitely unanimously agree with above-mentioned three reasons. In a year, Chinese and foreign Christians from all over China have spent much time and energy lecturing on this issue, namely, the abrogation of unequal treaties. We Christians have reached a consensus that the abrogation of unequal treaties is the matter of the greatest urgency in present-day China. Specifically, on the one hand, all Chinese Christian churches should immediately declare that they will be entirely independent from all unequal treaties and especially special articles regarding the missionary work. On the other hand, all Chinese Christian churches will earnestly mobilize people from all walks of life to launch a national movement striving for the abrogation of unequal treaties. We Chinese Christians are not that strong and powerful. But we sincerely love the country, truth and Christ just as all candid people have done. We honestly support all comrades and try our utmost to awaken the public. We are doing our best to arouse all our brothers and sisters to join the movement and make concerted effort to finish this good work that is the most vitally important for the future of the Church. Therein actually lies the glory of the Chinese Christianity.[49]

In the meantime, many church-run newspapers and journals published essays discussing the abrogation of unequal treaties. for example, *The Christian Occupation of China* published "To What Extent Does the Missionary Work Need the Protection of Treaties?"; *Brethren*, a semi-monthly, "Special Issue on the Abrogation of Unequal Treaties"; *Voice*, "Chinese Christians Should

Play a Leading Role in Movement Abrogating Unequal Treaties" by Wang Zhixin; and *The Life*, Hong Weilian's "The Revision of Treaties and Protection of Missionary Work." Some Christian media outlets, such as *Rejuvenating China*, printed *Full Text of Treaties Involving Christianity* and *The Christian Church and Unequal Treaties*. The authors of these articles all pointed out that the issue of unequal treaty demanded a prompt solution and could no longer be delayed. For example, Hong Weilian said:

> In the conditions that China is still politically instable, there are inevitably many unfair, unjust things. Even so, the revision of [unequal] treaties cannot be delayed any more in the name of the unstable situation. [We must always bear in mind that] those who are agonized and mistreated are not foreign missionaries but Chinese Christians. As a rule, the people should show devotion to the country. For the betterment of the country, the people can advocate either the incremental reform or the dynamic revolution. Anyways, Chinese Christians should never abandon their identity as the citizen of the Republic of China in the name of Christianity and acquire the weird name "jiaomin" (literally, people of the Christian religion). "Jiaomin," which denotes neither the true Chinese people nor pure Christians, is really an unbearable shame.[50]

Of course, members of the Chinese Church had a different understanding of the abrogation of unequal treaties. Some suggested that all unequal treaties must be entirely abolished or discarded; some said, treaties should be revised or turned into reciprocal ones; and some wanted all existing treaties to be left untouched. The headquarters of European and American missionary societies treated special articles regarding the missionary work in China in different ways, even though they generally held that treaties with China did need to be revised. So did the missionary societies in China. Some agreed with the overhaul of existing (unequal) treaties and special articles; and some objected to making any changes to them. Missionaries in favour of unequal treaties argued that the existing treaties should be kept intact, on the grounds that the Church as a religious group should not set foot in politics, that treaties and their special articles in particular were so helpful to the missionary work that they should not be abandoned, that the Chinese politics had not yet improved enough to be fully independent from these treaties, that so far the Church could not reach a consensus on the abrogation of treaties, that the revision of treaties would make non-religious people such as merchants feel uncomfortable; that the latest experience indicated that the abandonment of special articles favouring the missionary work would bring many difficulties, and that it was historically proven that Saint Paul had made use of his Roman identity to gain protection. Those who agreed with the abrogation of unequal treaties articulated the reasons as follows: the dependence on external forces' protection ran counter to the doctrines of Christianity, a spiritual religion; unequal treaties and their special articles regarding the missionary work in

China were the main reasons why the Chinese generally had a strong aversion to Christianity; pro-missionary articles stipulated by unequal treaties should cease to exist because of the popularity of the freedom of religious belief in China; the abandonment of prerogatives granted by unequal treaties would help Chinese Christians live a more conscientious life; unequal treaties and the Chinese Church's indigenization, which was then the matter of utmost urgency, were totally incompatible with each other; the Church should weigh up carefully the dead missionary prerogatives and the dynamic Chinese people's favourable impression of Christianity and make its final choice in the hope that its own cause could keep growing; the role that foreign missionaries had played in the formulation of pro-missionary unequal treaties should come to an end; the Church would be misperceived if it remained silent on unequal treaties; and that by now unequal treaties had been completely discredited, were weak, and much less dependable.[51]

Contrary to foreign missionary societies and their governing churches, the Chinese Church was really anxious for the abrogation or overhaul of the entirety of unequal treaties. In order to achieve this, the NCCC gathered together a number of Chinese Christians in Shanghai and convened a meeting in December 1925. The attendees' suggestions were as follows: Chinese Christians should not be intentionally different from the ordinary Chinese; the Chinese Christian Church should be treated the same way as Buddhism and Confucianism; the Church should agree with the abrogation of unequal treaties and at the same time demand legal protection in the light of recognized principles; the central government should promulgate laws regarding the propagation of Christianity because the national constitution had given all Chinese citizens the freedom of religious belief; the foreign missionary work in China should be protected according to the law; the Chinese government should protect religious groups and corporations as it did for other groups and corporations; the Church's properties created by foreign donations should be managed by a directorate in which the Chinese would be in the majority; and the Church and any institutions affiliated to the Church, such as schools, hospitals and charity agencies, must be officially registered in accordance with the law.[52]

In January 1926, John R. Mott convened a meeting in Shanghai, at which dozens of Chinese and Western leading Christians discussed the issue of unequal treaties again. They unanimously held that, inasmuch as extraterritoriality and special articles giving foreign missionaries privileges did impede the development of the Christian Church in China, both should be abrogated immediately. Moreover, they encouraged the followers of the Chinese Church to have the spirit of self-sacrifice.

Soon, the NCCC prepared 14 questions about the abrogation of unequal treaties and distributed them nationwide among clergy, preachers and Christians working for different departments, all of whom were required to express their views on this issue. The 14 questions were as follows:

1. Should the Church respond to political issues and whether or not the unequal treaty-ensued protection of Christian missionary work was consistent with the Christian doctrine?
2. Was the protection based on unequal treaties necessary under the circumstance that the freedom of religious belief had already been stipulated by the national constitution?
3. If it was unnecessary, how to eliminate these unequal treaties?
4. Would there be new articles protecting the foreign missionary work when China and foreign countries signed new treaties?
5. If there were to be such new articles, how to apply the reciprocal principle to them?
6. If relevant articles were annulled, how should the missionary societies respond to the difficulties they might face?
7. Whether or not the public properties of the Church should apply for tax-exempt status.
8. Should these properties be owned by the Chinese Church or by Chinese Christians and what would be the advantages and disadvantages that ensued?
9. Should the Church's schools, hospitals and other organizations be officially registered with the relevant departments of government?
10. Would MOE's recently promulgated six regulations regarding schools founded by foreigners affect the future of Christian education?
11. Should Christian schools be given the freedom to teach religions within the campus?
12. Whether or not free thinkers should join the directorates of Church-run schools, hospitals, youth organizations and charity agencies.
13. What would be the advantages and disadvantages of free thinkers' participation in these undertakings?
14. Was the common appeal for equal treatment of all religions including Christianity, which was proposed in concert by different religious organizations, necessary at present?[53]

In May 1926, the executive committee of the NCCC suggested that the annual conference be convened in October. Therefore, these leading Christians in China drafted a plan regarding (unequal) treaties in relation to the Christian missionary work in China. This draft plan said:

> First of all, again, the NCCC specially affirms its Christian conviction. Then, we suggest the Chinese Church, in strict accordance with the freedom of religious belief that is sincerely given to the entirety of Chinese citizens, propagate the gospels and carry out all Christian undertakings of service. In view of this, we strongly require that all types of extra-territoriality and treaties regarding the missionary work be abrogated immediately.[54]

In the course of the discussion, some local churches and Christian groups, one after another, showed their support for the abrogation of unequal treaties. For example, the manifesto by the Jiangxi branch of the Methodist Episcopal Church in its annual conference, the resolution passed by the fortieth annual conference of the Chinese branch of the American Southern Methodist Episcopal Mission, the proposal of the North China branch of the Congregational Church, the announcements made by Chinese Christian churches in Wenzhou and Kaifeng, the public notice issued by the executive office of the general assembly of missionary work in Guangxi, and the report of the Hunan Christian audit meeting all publicly supported the abrogation of unequal treaties. Some of them even directly connected the abrogation of unequal treaties with the indigenization and independence of the Chinese Church. Take the announcement of the Wenzhou Chinese Christian Church, for example. It said:

> If the Chinese Christian Church can be truly indigenized to such an extent that it blends into the Chinese culture and adopts itself to the Chinese psychology, it will be freed not only from the lack of harmony between Chinese free thinkers and Christians but also from the undue protection provided by foreigners. Such a Chinese Church will play a great role in saving the country spiritually and materially. [We Chinese] Christians should be bound by a common feeling, as well as joining the patriotic movement and striving for independence. We do worry that those who lack knowledge and experience will act so recklessly that they cause diplomatic rows and do harm to the country. Thus, the independence of the Chinese Church is a matter of great urgency. We are now trying to prevent anything unpleasant from taking place and extending the principle of benevolence to all others. In doing so, foreigners will be awakened and our compatriots be made spiritually stronger.[55]

In fact, the overwhelming majority of Chinese Christians preferred to abrogate all unequal treaties as soon as possible. The results of the NCCC's 14-point questionnaire convincingly corroborated this. Take the replies to the question "whether or not the treaties regarding the missionary work are consistent with the Christian doctrine," for example. Some 181 respondents said "No"; by contrast, only 46 "Yes" replies were received. Similarly, 190 negative answers and 65 "Yes" replies were found to "whether or not the treaties regarding the missionary work are still necessary."[56]

Even so, quite a large number of Western missionaries and priests obstructed Chinese Christians in the course of abrogating unequal treaties. For example, in 1926, Chinese Christians and Western clergy in Wuzhou, Guangxi, were in a row with each other over the issue of the abrogation of unequal treaties. Chinese Christians deeply realized how harmful unequal treaties were to the country and the people. Thus, they demanded a joint decision, in which Western missionaries should clearly state that they would be automatically independent from unequal treaties regarding the missionary work. Unsurprisingly, foreign missionaries rejected their demand. Then, Chinese Christians requested that the Church be led by Chinese leaders and its finance be open and independent. Again, foreign missionaries turned down their request. Finally, Chinese Christians reached the end of their forbearance and asked foreign missionaries to leave immediately. Foreign missionaries threatened to close the hospital affiliated to the Church. The negotiation between the two sides ended in a deadlock. The local church was thus divided. Chines Christians concluded this event, saying:

> The fulfilment of the goal of abrogating all unequal treaties regarding missionary work in China is dependent on the actual effort we make. Are we determined to abandon the so-called protection based on unequal treaties? If we really do not ask foreign missionaries to intervene in lawsuits and other matters, foreign missionaries will not have any reasons to bully the Chinese. [In view of this], we should make a concerted effort to increase our strength bit by bit and found a truly indigenized Chinese Church. We do believe Chinese Christians can endure hardship and shoulder responsibility. Although at present we merely have three poorly thatched cottages and a really small building, we do have an unswerving conviction that God is among us and running in the blood of spirit and intelligence. We earnestly welcome foreign missionaries to sincerely cooperate with Chinese Christiana [in abrogating unequal treaties]. At the same time, we absolutely say no to their habitual intimidation and temptation. Even in the Church, Chinese Christians will never abandon their own national character.[57]

This indicated that a number of Chinese Christians had already grasped the close relationship between the abrogation of unequal treaties and the indigenization of the Chinese Church.

Interaction of the Northern Expedition and Christianity in the Condemning Christianity Movement

In autumn of 1926, the Guangzhou-based Nationalist Government (hereinafter referred to as Guangzhou Government) launched the great Northern Expedition. One of the most important tasks of the Guangzhou Government was the accomplishment of a nationalist revolution. In order to achieve this goal, the revolutionary government had to stand up against the imperialist invasion of China. Undoubtedly, this would be a great impetus to the upsurge in nationalist feeling aroused by foreign powers' bloody massacres against the Chinese. In addition, due to the influence of the national campaign criticizing Christianity, and particularly because of the post-Shanghai Massacre, a popular idea was that Christianity was nothing more than a running dog of imperialism, so the Northern Expedition Army (NEA) generally treated

Christianity as something hostile towards the Chinese nation. Cheng Jingyi recorded this:

> Whenever the NEA arrives in a region, it requisitions houses of the Christian Church, Christian schools and missionary hospitals to lodge soldiers and members of political departments and the Nationalist Party Office. [Even] after the NEA has left, the expanding Party Office, which sometimes are not purely Nationalist, and relevant labour unions, peasant associations, student unions and women's associations, all of which mushroom in the revolution, [will keep using these houses].[58]

Worst of all, some ruffians availed themselves of the revolution to rob Christian churches. Consequently, the Christian Church suffered heavy losses. In some places, the properties of Christian Church were destroyed or confiscated. Specifically, "Houses of the Church were toppled down and implements and belongings robbed; what's worse, some priests were paraded through the streets, some clergy were imprisoned, and some Christians were forced to turn against Christianity."[59] Even in a few areas, some priests were mistreated very badly. For example, a Christian record alleged in Xiangtan, two Anglican preachers were bound, paraded and imprisoned; in Yaojiang of Hengzhou, a Christian preacher named Wang's hands were tied behind his back, he was paraded through the streets, and forced to denounce Christianity; and in Hajiafan of Yuezhou, a preacher named Chen Zhuqing was killed by a stone in a fight with a rural thug.[60] Some Christians claimed that, wherever the NEA passed, soldiers pasted slogans against Christianity, lectured at the door of Christian families, shouted curses at Christianity and persuaded Christians to abandon and renounce their religion.[61] At that time, the most popular slogans were as follows: "Down with imperialist Christianity!"; "Down with capitalist Christianity!"; "Down with Christianity perpetrating the cultural invasion!"; "Down with the running dog of imperialism!"; "Down with the running dog of the capitalists!"; and "Down with the running dog of Westerners!."[62] All these obstructed the propagation of Christianity and even made the missionary work very difficult. In some areas, the masses, influenced by these slogans, almost rebelled against Christianity. Rural churches felt the most pain.[63] In some places, where Christian churches had been confiscated or requisitioned, the open Christian service was not available and even other religious services were entirely banned.[64] Under such circumstances, many Christians had to live their religious life in secret. According to a Christian, in a few areas, Christians were not allowed to join any revolutionary organizations, such as labour, peasant and merchant unions and consequently they could not even buy daily necessities freely.[65] Where Christian churches in the year of Nationalist Revolution were concerned, some were economically hit hard, some lost their talented people, and some had no alternative but to slow down or even stop the propagation of Christianity. In a word,

Christian churches suffered from varying degrees of loss and pain.[66] In this revolution, the hardest-hit place was Hunan, which was followed by Anhui, Hubei, Jiangxi and Fujian. By contrast, Jiangsu and Zhejiang suffered the least. As far as the region north of the Yellow River was concerned, it was not directly impacted by the Northern Expedition. Even so, the revolutionary trend still exerted an influence on this region. The Nanjing Incident was the best-known event at that time.

In March 1927, a few armed men wearing military uniform forced an entrance into the settlement reserved for foreigners in Nanjing, where they plundered dwelling houses, diplomatic missions and chambers of commerce. These armed men beat anyone who resisted them. Some victims even died. For example, one of vice presidents of Jinling University was shot, merely because he refused to surrender his watch when he was caught. Moreover, oil companies run by foreigners were attacked. Finally, the British and American occupation troops started to shell this region and the chaos ended very soon.[67] Then, many foreigners including missionaries left China or moved to the big cities on the coast. According to one record, by July 1927, of more than 8,000 foreign missionaries, only five hundred were still living in the interior of China. Take Hunan, for example. Originally, there were approximately four hundred foreign missionaries. By now, only 30 or 40 Western Christian preachers lived scattered in Changsha, Xiangtan, Hengzhou and Yuezhou. All the Christian schools, regardless of their size, closed down in Hunan.[68] This situation did not change until the outbreak of the April 12 Anti-Communist Massacre in 1927, when Jiang Jieshi, the leader of the ruling Nationalist Party, started to brutally murder the Communists and other progressives, implement rabid anti-Communist policies, and give up the anti-imperialist stand.

Even though the Northern Expedition propelled the national campaign criticizing Christianity to new heights and dealt a heavy blow to the Christian missionary work in China, the Christian religion and its basic work were, altogether, conducted in an orderly manner. According to a researcher,

> In the course of the Northern Expedition, the movement against Christianity had been popular. But on the other hand, there were only very few cases in which clergy of the Christian Church were violently treated in a similar way to what happened in the Boxer Uprising. As for the economic losses that Christian churches suffered, we actually cannot make any sweeping generalizations. [It must be pointed out that], whether or not the revolutionary army was radically against Christianity was generally dependent on the local Christian churches' attitude towards the nationalist revolution.[69]

As a matter of fact, a large number of Chinese Christians enthusiastically welcomed the Nationalist Revolution, even though the Christian Church was indeed hit hard in the Northern Expedition. In this regard, Cheng Jingyi candidly said:

> At first glance, the Nationalist Revolution is a sharp warning to Christianity. But in fact, many Christians show sincere sympathy for the revolutionary movement. Within the Christian Church, there are indeed a number of Christians, who are really eager to make progress. When these forward-looking Chinese Christians are witnessing the lethargy of the Church and being constantly stimulated by ongoing events, they become increasing discontented with the status quo of the Church, meanwhile more enthusiastically welcoming the Nationalist Revolution.[70]

Many Christians explicitly expressed their support for the revolution. Take Zhao Guanhai, for example. Zhao, analysing the Guomindang's policies on Christianity, concluded:

> First, the nationalist government all along respects religious freedom. Precisely because of this, Christianity and other religions all have their own status and opportunity to develop in Chinese society. Second, although key members of the nationalist government have very different understandings of Christianity, they unanimously respect all religious beliefs. Third, inasmuch as there is an inextricable historical interconnection between Christianity and imperialism, anti-imperialists always stand against Christianity from the political perspective. Fourth, the nationalist government never abandons its duty to protect Christian churches, schools and hospitals from being damaged. Fifth, but, on the other hand, the nationalist government do attempt to restrict Christian schools so that China's [educational] sovereignty can be protected and the nationalist education be popularized. Sixth, the few cases, in which some Christian schools or hospitals are forced to close down or returned to local governments, are actually caused by despicable, trouble-making persons. Therefore, the nationalist government need not be responsible for this.[71]

Wang Zhixin applauded the Nationalist Revolution in one of his articles, saying:

> The people, who have long been oppressed and trampled underfoot by warlords, are now liberated! [Moreover], the will of the people has won! The end of the warlords' rule is nigh! The success of the Nationalist Revolution is in sight!

Unlike some Christians, who blamed fate and other people when Christianity was being seriously affected by the Northern Expedition, Wang suggested the Church and its followers should seriously rethink the question why Christianity suffered the most. He said:

> Among a kaleidoscopic array of religions in China, why is Christianity the hardest hit? As we know, Christianity is merely one of the religions in China. There must be reasons shedding light on the truth that Christianity is hand-picked to be the target of attack.

Wang held that the reason was threefold. First, some who were strongly against Christianity took advantage of the situation. They (mis)led the troops to set up stations in the Church, attack some priests, and paste slogans condemning Christianity. Second, the Church itself sowed the seed of its own destruction. Wang explained:

> As you sow, so do you reap. It is an iron law. Under the escort of Western powers' gunboats, Christianity grabs the privilege to propagate itself in China. Moreover, unequal treaties grant Christianity the prerogative to travel freely in the interior of China. In over one century-long diplomatic history of China, there are so many cases, in which the missionary work throws China into conflict with foreign powers and seriously damages China's sovereignty. Where foreign missionaries living in the interior of China are concerned, many of them are known to the Chinese people for their brutality and ruthlessness. [In addition], many bad Chinese Christians and clergy do evil things, such as intervening in lawsuits. [In view of this, we can thus conclude that] the Church is actually reaping as it has sown for years.

Third, imperialism reacted against the revolution. The Nationalist Revolution was a movement of national self-determination. Year after year, the Chinese nation had been invaded and oppressed by imperialist countries and it was at the end of its patience, finally. Where there was cruel oppression, there was strong resistance. Therefore, everything in collusion with imperialism should be hit. Christianity and the Church were no exceptions. To some extent, the Church was treated unjustly. But it should not pin it on the Chinese nation but on imperialism instead. Wang went further, analysing the nationalist government's attitude towards Christianity. He pointed out:

> [The nationalist government] is never anti-Christian. Everywhere the revolutionary army went, it harmonizes with local churches. [Unpleasant things taking place between the army and the Church] are not caused by the true revolutionary army but by some factions, which intentionally create disturbances on the pretext of criticizing Christianity and then shifting the blame on the army.

In the end, Wang mentioned that Christianity should be awakened in the nationalist revolution. Specifically, Christianity should be penitent about its past. That is to say, this religion did need to repent of sins it had committed against China, such as the role it had played in the imperialist invasion of China. Second, Christianity should sympathize with the nationalist revolution, join the anti-imperialist camp, and make efforts to build a new China. In doing so, this religion might truly reach the realm of freedom, equality and fraternity and be fully accorded with the spirit of Jesus. Third, Christianity should reform itself to adapt to the Chinese conditions, cut off the close relationship with imperialism, and support the endeavour to take back China's right of education. Moreover, Wang contended that, in the Chinese Church, the Chinese must be in the majority and play the leading role in the management of ecclesiastic affairs. Wang himself supported the Nationalist Revolution, calling out:

> Chinese Christians must be responsible for the country and her people, as well as showing solicitude for the world and entire humanity. Now that Christians are responsible for the Chinese people, they cannot abandon their duty to promote the revolution of civil rights [nor] should they refrain themselves from pursuing the thorough emancipation by means of truths, such as freedom and equality granted by Christ and the spirit of struggle and sacrifice.

Wang finally mobilized Chinese Christians

> [in the light of the spirit of Jesus. to] shoulder the responsibilities for annihilating all devils oppressing the people and eliminating all pains plaguing the people. In other words, Christians should not only engage in the spiritual life and spiritual revolution but also participate in the social life and politico-economic revolution. Here, I, sincerely and solemnly, tell my four hundred thousand Chinese Christian comrades that we should, resolutely and determinedly, join the revolution, through which we make concerted effort to eradicate all evils, manifest the true Christian spirit, and finally realize God's wish of creating a paradise on earth.[72]

In fact, the pressure resulting from the Northern Expedition was not entirely bad for the Chinese Christian Church. To put it another way, it was a great impetus to the reform, independence and indigenization of Chinese Church. In one year (1926–1927), Christian churches throughout the country published various announcements advocating (the Chinese Church's) independence, reform, rehabilitation and unity. According to a 1928 yearbook of Chinese Christianity, there were at least 25 pro-revolutionary manifestos or announcements published nationwide. All these written materials unambiguously indicated that the Christian reform and independence movements were all closely connected with the changing political situation at that time.

Take Hangzhou Chinese Christian Church (HCCC), which was created in the independence movement launched by Chinese Christians in Hangzhou, for example. Some observed:

> In fact, several Hangzhou-based churches had been relatively independent from a very early time. Therefore, local Christians developed a strong desire for an independent Chinese Christian Church. In recent years, they, exposing themselves to the zeitgeist, think more and more about the reform of the existing Church. At that point, the Nationalist Revolutionary Army marches into Zhejiang. As a consequence, there is an upsurge in the sharp criticism of Christianity. Christianity and the Church are thus vehemently attacked. In the meantime, Chinese Christians in Hangzhou is suddenly awakened and realize that only when Christians are truly united and become internally unbeatable will they be able to launch a counterattack. HCCC is thus set up.[73]

In Wuhan, the driving force of Christian reform was the Nationalist Revolutionary Army (NRA), too. Some observers said:

> In the fall of 1926, the NRA and other revolutionary armed forces were reunited in Wuhan. Then, the allied forces, which are as powerful as a thunderbolt, continue to advance northward. In this course, the revolutionary army takes a very hard line on the Christian Church. Its revolutionary slogans condemn Christianity as the tool of imperialism, a running dog of capitalism and the perpetrator of cultural invasion. These criticisms deeply influence the Chinese youth. The Nationalist Revolution is politically far superior to the Christian Church, which is still not yet rooted in the Chinese culture, so that it is very easy for the revolutionary force to crush the Church. As a consequence, the Christian Church has already been placed in jeopardy. At such a critical moment, Christians in Wuhan are determined to overhaul the existing Church.[74]

All the above-mentioned announcements clearly indicated that Chinese Christians had resolved to love their country, support the revolutionary army, and separate themselves from imperialism. Take the *Wuhan Christian Reform Manifesto*, for example. It resolutely stated:

> We Chinese Christians constitute one part of the Chinese citizens. The reason why we choose to believe in Christianity lies in our discontent with the old, feudal ethics and rites. We know very well that there are many misunderstandings attributed to the truths that Christ was born in a foreign land and historically interconnected with imperialism. But by now, we Chinese Christians, standing under the national flag, have already been free citizens completely independent from any political oppressions. Driven by the duty to save the country, we make clear

our attitude [towards the nationalist revolution]. We, fully and unanimously, endorse the Nationalist Government, support the Nationalist Revolutionary Army, and believe that the only way of saving the nation and the country lies in the State-Building Programme and national and foreign policies formulated in accordance with *sanmin zhuyi* (the Three People's Principles), on the grounds that we admit that the Nationalist Revolution led by the Nationalist Party (the Guomindang) is an invincible force implementing the national salvation. We are willing to join the nationalist revolution and serve this grand cause to the best of our abilities. Externally, we devote ourselves to overthrowing imperialism and reconstructing China into an independent country that can be treated equally in the world. Internally, we strive to put an end to the evil system of warlords, improving the standard of living of workers and peasants, and turning China into a society in which all people have adequate food and clothes and live a happy life. In order to achieve these aims, we know that the revolution should succeed in the world, all peoples should be treated equally, and all of humanity be ultimately united into one. [Moreover], we have profoundly realized that imperialism is not only the most ferocious enemy of the Chinese nation but also the worst foe of Christianity. [Therefore], we Christians must rise to fight against imperialism. In doing so, we not only contribute to the national liberation but also lead Christianity to emancipate itself.[75]

Some Chinese Christians went further, bravely pointing out:

We formally declare that the Christianity that was sent to China under the escort of gunboats is completely unworthy of even the slightest trust. How despicable it is! The history of Christianity in China is nothing more than a history of imperialist plunder and exploitation.[76]

Driven by the sweeping Nationalist Revolution, a large number of Christian groups and organizations published announcements appealing for the abrogation of all unequal treaties. In October 1926, the NCCC convened a conference in Shanghai. All attendees unanimously agreed with the proposal of abrogating unequal treaties. A public announcement was issued accordingly. Soon, Christian churches nationwide enthusiastically responded to the NCCC's announcement. For example, Christians in Wuhan published a similar manifesto, saying:

We Christians in Wuhan unanimously endorse the NCCC's resolution [of abrogating unequal treaties with China]. Neither do we want a Christianity that is dependent on the military prowess of foreign powers; nor would we like to see the gospels being backed up by the military force of foreign powers. The reason is that both the aggressive policy [of foreign powers] and the armed might are essentially against the Christian doctrine. [In some cases], wherein foreign missionaries love their own countries rather than Christ and are unwilling to support the Nationalist Revolution, they should better leave China. We Chinese Christians are on our own, doing our utmost to lead the Chinese Church to be fully independent from foreigners and completely cut off the relationship with imperialism forever.[77]

A similar announcement could be found from Changsha's Chinese Christians, who said openly:

> We are fundamentally against all unequal treaties, as well as being opposed to concessions, extraterritoriality, (foreign powers') usurping power controlling Chinese customs, the postal service, salt production, railways and mining, and (foreign powers') prerogatives humiliating China and forfeiting its sovereignty such as foreign battleships' right of freedom of navigation in China's inland waters. We do approve of the Chinese people's right to take back all these rights even by force.[78]

In like manner, Christians in Chengdu penned a manifesto, which was mainly directed at foreign missionaries, demanding:

> Western missionaries should write a letter in their joint names to their governing regimes, requiring that unequal treaties with China be abrogated as soon as possible. Before the abrogation of unequal treaties, Western missionaries should openly declare that they will give up the protection based on unequal treaties and seriously protest against all unjust actions (of foreign powers).[79]

The NCCC's fourth annual conference was held in October 1926. While the Nationalist Revolution was still going on, Chinese and foreign attendees intensively discussed issues such as unequal treaties and the so-called protection of Christians in accordance with these treaties.[80] Opinions differed greatly. "The majority of Western preachers contend that, inasmuch as the war is still going on, treaties can play a great role in protecting Christian churches and Christian followers. This is especially true in the interior of China."[81] Contrary to these foreigners, Chinese Christians almost unanimously approved of the abrogation of all unequal treaties. Both sides fiercely argued against each other and finally, made concessions to each other. The compromise gave birth to a manifesto, f which the key points were as follows:

> The NCCC is comprised of a large number of Christian churches and departments. Although the NCCC cannot speak on behalf of all these relevant churches and departments, it has already done a thorough,

careful study of their resolutions and proposals. This annual conference, in the name of the entirety of the NCCC and individual members, cautiously makes resolutions as follows:

First, we suggest Christian churches and missionary societies should spread the gospels and promote Christianization in the light of the religious freedom handsomely granted by the Republic of China (ROC). Accordingly, the prerogatives that churches and missionary societies have obtained through foreign treaties with China should be abrogated. Second, we suggest China and foreign countries revise the existing treaties in accordance with the two major principles of freedom and equality. Third, we appreciate very much the effort made by foreign governments to make revisions to existing treaties with China and sincerely hope that all foreign governments would like to carry through this endeavour till there are perfected results. Fourth, we hold that it is needless to blame others for things that are past and at the same time both the Chinese and Westerners should make a concerted effort to shoulder responsibility and prevent the situation from worsening further. We do believe without a shadow of a doubt that, in order to achieve our common goals, both China and the West must be perpetually patient, thoroughly tolerable and truly benevolent.

Obviously, there was considerable discrepancy between this manifesto and other Chinese Christian churches' announcement calling for the abrogation of unequal treaties. Even so, it, at least, clearly suggested Christian churches and foreign missionary societies abandon their undue prerogatives and privileges and advise their governing regimes to make revisions to coercive treaties against freedom and equality. This was actually a good result brought about by the struggle of the Chinese Christians in the NCCC.

In the meantime, the independence and indigenization of Chinese Christian Church reached new heights in the course of the Nationalist Revolution. Revolution was a great impetus to the self-government of the Chinese Church. In face of the ongoing revolution, Church members realized that the Church itself was actually in imminent danger of falling down, just like a desperate general who was besieged on all sides, a fish that was swimming at the bottom of pan, and a swallow that lived in a threadbare and tottering nest. Only when the Church became truly independent would it be able to cope with this crisis.[82] Take Christians in Hangzhou, for example. In February 1927, the revolutionary army captured Hangzhou. Three months later, five Hangzhou-based Christian churches openly declared that they were formally independent from their original missionary societies and at the same time set up the united HCCC. To be specific,

The new Chinese Church aspires to fulfil five goals, namely, the full independence from Western missionary societies, the independent management of ecclesiastic affairs, administrative independence, economic independence and the abandonment of sectarianism. [As far as] the basic attitude towards the friendly Western missionary societies is concerned, it should follow four principles, viz., that the original friendship should be maintained, that these foreign missionary societies' work of propagation should not be obstructed and these societies should give up founding churches, performing baptism, and converting the Chinese in case they damage the sovereignty of the Chinese Church, that the Chinese Church should not interfere in foreign missionary societies' schools and hospitals, all of which should be handled by the government, and that donations from Western missionary societies must be administered by the Chinese Church.[83]

Chinese Christians in Xiangtan of Hunan published a manifesto regarding the Church's independence movement. The author(s) of this manifesto held that it was the time for the Chinese Church to be independent. Thus, they said:

> Simply speaking, the independence of the Chinese Church requires that all rights of the existing Church be returned to Chinese Christians. In other words, only when the Chinese Church is self-governing, self-supporting and self-propagating will the dream of the Chinese Church come true. We would like to include those genuine foreign missionaries into our Church, meanwhile telling them that they must abandon all prerogatives based on unequal treaties.[84]

A similar announcement was prepared by Shanghai's Chinese Christians, who formally stated:

> It is much better for Chinese Christians to urge the Church to be self-governing, self-supporting and self-propagating and make efforts to take back the right of managing its ecclesiastic, educational and medical affairs. In the meantime, the Chinese Church should ask European and American churches to immediately send senior delegates to China, where they will discuss how to transfer the relevant rights to the Chinese and conduct cooperation with the Chinese Church in future.[85]

Guangdong, which was most deeply influenced by political trends, witnessed the founding of a united, independent interdenominational Chinese church in 1926. This new church publicly declared:

> All undertakings of foreign missionary societies in China should be transferred to the Chinese Church as soon as possible. From now on, foreign missionary societies must stop exercising power to interfere in any affairs in relation to the Chinese Church. The management of financial and human resources must be supervised by the special organs of the Chinese Church.[86]

In August 1926, an independent Chinese Christian church was founded in Guilin. The inaugural announcement said:

> Guilin is not a wealthy place, where the ordinary people live a poor life. [For this reason], few people think Chinese Christians are able to found an independent Church there. Despite this, we Guilin Christians, driven by our consciousness, stimulated by sharp-minded critics, and moved and required by the Holy Father, Holy Son and Holy Spirit, are determined to set up a truly independent Church, regardless of the difficulties lying ahead of us.[87]

In addition to the region south of the Yellow River, where the revolutionary army had arrived and Christian reforms were conducted region-wide, the region north of the Yellow River, which did not have contact directly with the revolutionary army, witnessed the effort to reform the Christian Church, too. Take Lanzhou, for example. The Christian Church in Lanzhou published a manifesto of independence at the end of 1926, announcing:

> The Chinese Christian Church consisting of Chinese Christians is formally founded now. It is fully independent from Western missionaries and their governing churches. The new Church resolved to achieve self-government, be self-supporting and self-propagating. [Moreover], all members of this new Church know very well that, only when the Chinese Church becomes truly independent and self-governing will it be able to make Christianity more illustrious and lead Christians to have greater self-confidence.[88]

An observer pointed out:

> Some Christian churches are really far-sighted. They know very well that the trend of revolution is so irresistible and so inevitable that it, sooner or later, will directly work on the Church. Therefore, they make early preparations by reforming themselves in case something unexpected will take place. Among these churches, the Chinese Christian Church in Harbin, the Christian Council of Guangdong (the region east of Shanhaiguan Pass) in Fengtian [present-day Shenyang], the Congregational Church of North China and the Chinese Christian Church in Beijing and Tianjin are worthy of mention. For them, the management right has been or is being returned to Chinese Christians; their schools have already been officially registered with China's education authorities; their finances have been open; and none of them pride themselves on being protected by [unequal] treaties but instead of being ashamed of this protection. They all have realized that the survival and future of Christian Church in China depend on whether or not the Church can harmonize with the Chinese national character.[89]

Zhao Zichen had commented on the Church's independence movement in this period, saying:

> Where Chinese Christians' independence movement is concerned, it is an endeavour in which all churches reach the same goal by different means. Specifically, although there is a diversity of reasons, which might be the conflict between the Chinese and Westerners within a church or the church is being plagued by endless disagreements, all churches have the same aspiration for independence. As we know, churches in the north such as Lanzhou, in the south such as Guangzhou, in the east such as Wenzhou and in the West such as Guizhou differ greatly one another in terms of environment, denomination and organization. Even so, the independent Christian churches founded in these places are all unexceptionally named after "Chinese Christian Church/Council." They differentiate each other merely by having "Chinese Christian Church" prefixed with place names. This demonstrates that these churches are psychologically consistent with one another. In China, every church is tormented by the insufficiency of financial resources and the depleted pool of talented people. Pain is inevitable. But endeavour should never be abandoned. Churches are always struggling for independence. Such an endeavour makes Chinese Christians really happy and is really attractive to enthusiastic, active participants.[90]

At that time, a huge number of articles promoting the independence of Chinese Church were published. The *Holy News* and *The Chinese Christian Literature Society Monthly* were especially known to readers. Some articles were directed at a number of clergy, who intentionally neglected Chinese Christians' general, growing demand for independence from foreign missionary societies and their governing churches. Sun Juewu, for instance, complained:

> [Christians themselves should be responsible for the rise and fall of the Church. A truly independent Chinese Church has a great mission and responsibility. In China, there are, in total, over two thousand clergy, among whom people who emulate enlightened priests such as Yu Zongzhou and Cheng Jingyi are few and far between. Most of the clergy would like to find shelter under another's roof and are unwilling to abandon the rice bowl given by foreign missionary societies. As a result, even though Western missionaries are essentially despotic and act arbitrarily, these (Chinese) clergy still resign themselves to humiliation and oppression. It is thus no wonder that critics have a full excuse for denouncing Christianity, the (reputation of) the Church itself is seriously damaged, and the moral quality (of Christians) deteriorates.] Precisely because of these, Xu Qian refuses to be baptized by any missionary societies, Feng Yuxiang chooses to believe in Christianity rather than in Westerners, and Zhang Chunyi suggests that Christianity should adopt

Buddhist traits. At present, the ruling persons of the Christian Church, who loudly prattle on about the indigenization of the Chinese Church, complacently think they themselves are perfectly in harmony with the trend of the time. But in fact, the indigenization of Christianity and the Christian Church in China has not been realized at all. The reason is not that indigenization is too difficult to be realized but that the Chinese Church itself cannot be independent from foreign missionary societies. Rather, the Church is still financially dependent on foreign missionary societies. An old Chinese saying goes: "Even a clever housewife cannot cook a meal without rice." Just like this, how can the Chinese Church be truly independent without adequate financial support? The Confucian *Doctrine of the Mean* teaches us that only when a person is truly in possession of a sense of shame will she or he have the courage to do something. We, applying this Confucian teaching to Chinese clergy, hold that, if these clergy would like to sacrifice their own interests and alleged power and emulate Saint Paul, who supported himself by making tents, they will still be able to overcome economic hardship and propagate the Christian religion. In comparison with the past, in which they were funded by foreign missionary societies and thus were despised as slaves and spies of foreign masters and as people of *chijiao* (i.e., people who are slavishly dependent on and submissive to foreign missionaries), present-day Chinese clergy, who are striving to be self-supporting, will convince people of their innocence.[91]

Wang Yuting mentioned disadvantages caused by the Chinese Church's dependence on foreign missionary societies.[92] Moreover, many articles shed light on reasons why the Chinese Church must be independent from foreign missionary societies and their governing churches.[93] They unanimously thought both the present situation and the development of the Church itself demonstrated that hope lay in the Church's independence.

Many articles discussed how to achieve the independence of Chinese Christian Church. Zhu Jingyi proposed several points regarding Christian churches in the countryside being self-supporting.[94] First, there was a misunderstanding of the Church's responsibility. Specifically, in the past, both Western and Chinese priests did not pay enough attention to the independence of the Chinese Church and consequently ordinary Chinese Christians had a very weak sense of responsibility and were unwilling to donate money to God or subsidize priests. Therefore, in order that the ambition of rural churches of being self-supporting and self-governing could be realized, the general misunderstanding must be abandoned and ordinary Christians must develop a strong sense of responsibility. Second, rural churches needed to train volunteers for the propagation of Christianity. In the countryside, the number of Christians was very small. In order to achieve a state of being self-supporting as soon as possible, the number of professional Christian preachers must be reduced and it would be better for the church to have them replaced with unpaid volunteers. Take a priest in Wenzhou, for example. He set up 47 chapels there. How he was able to accomplish this was that he spent years training local followers and finally set up a team consisting of 40 or 50 Christian volunteers, who decisively helped the local church to realize being self-supporting and self-governing. Third, rural churches should raise funds among free thinkers. Members of the church should be responsible for the money that was invested in the church's buildings and daily affairs. When it came to the Church's various undertakings, such as education and medical services, donations from society were acceptable. Fourth, in order to be self-supporting, rural churches could learn from Buddhist organizations, which usually invested in real estate. Fifth, rural churches should help to improve the life of peasants, who were generally poor and hardly able to support themselves. Specifically,

1. the Church could improve agriculture by teaching farmers how to select seeds, check the quality of the soil, remove destructive insects, and use new farm implements;
2. the Church could help to increase peasants' income by introducing them to new agricultural products and sidelines;
3. the Church could promote the rural economic cooperation, such as setting up an agricultural bank providing farmers with low-interest loans and cooperatives for agricultural products;
4. the Church could improve rural education, through which the majority of peasants could be basically educated.

Notes

1 Ren Jianlin 任建林 and Zhang Quan 张铨, *A Short History of the Patriotic Movement Triggered by the May 30th Massacre* [五卅运动简史] (Shanghai: Shanghai renmin chubanshe, 1985), 125. Quoted in Yang Tianhong, *Christianity and Modern China*, 337.
2 Anon, "Shanghai Council of Chinese Christians' Open Telegram Regarding the Shanghai Massacre" (上海中华基督徒联合会为沪案通电), *The Life Monthly*, Vol. 5, no. 9 (June 1925), 36.
3 Anon, "Nanjing Chinese Christians' Response to the Shanghai Massacre: An Angry Manifesto" (南京中华基督徒对沪案之愤恨宣言), *The Life Monthly*, Vol. 5, no. 9 (June 1925), 36.
4 Anon, "A Manifesto of Christians of Baptist Church in Guangdong and Guangxi" (两广浸会基督徒救国联合会宣言), *The True Light*, Vol. 24, no. 7 (July 1925), 79.
5 Cheng Xiangfan 程湘帆, "Christians' Statements Against Imperialism and Unequal Treaties" (基督教人士之反对帝国主义及不平等条约宣言), *The Life Monthly*, Vol. 5, no. 9 (June 1925), 45–46.
6 Anon, "Feng Yuxiang's Open Letter to All Oppressed Christians Worldwide" (冯玉祥告世界被压迫之基督徒书), *The Life Monthly*, Vol. 5, No. 9 (June 1925), 58.
7 For a detailed report, see: Liu Tingfang, "Christianity and the Chinese National Character" (基督教与中国国民性), *The Life Monthly*, Vol. 5, No. 9 (June 1925), 9.

8. Anon, "To British Missionaries: An Open Letter Penned by the Supporting Corps of Chinese Christians in Fenzhou of Shanxi" (山西汾州基督徒沪案后援会特告英传教士的忠言), *The Life Monthly*, Vol. 5, No. 9 (June 1925), 39.
9. Li Rongfang 李荣芳, "The Awareness that Foreign Missionaries Should Have at Present" (现时西教士在中国应有的觉悟), *The Life Monthly*, Vol. 5, No. 9 (June 1925), 21–23.
10. Zhong Ketuo 钟可托 and Li Zeling 李则灵, "Part One of Lecture on the Shanghai Massacre" (演讲（五卅惨案）之一), *Holy News* (圣报), Vol. 15, No. 7 (July 1925), 23–24.
11. Wu Leichuan, "The Shanghai Massacre and the Future of Chinese Christianity" (沪案与中国基督教的前途), *The Life Monthly*, Vol. 5, No. 9 (June 1925), 20.
12. Anon, "The Manifesto of the Kaifeng Chinese Christian Church Founded by Kaifeng Members of China Inland Mission Who Choose to Break with British CIM Due to the Shanghai Massacre" (开封内地会全体教友因沪案与英人完全绝交新组成开封中华基督教会之宣言), *The Life Monthly*, Vol. 5, No. 9 (June 1925), 41–42.
13. Anon, "Announcement of the Shanghai Chinese Christian Church" (上海中华基督教会通启), *The True Light*, Vol. 24, No. 7 (July 1925), 84.
14. Anon, "A Manifesto Announcing Independence from the United Methodist Church Mission" (脱离圣道会宣言), *Holy News*, Vol. 15, No. 7 (July 1925), 3.
15. Anon, "Wenzhou Chinese Christians' Response to the Shanghai Massacre: An Announcement of Independence" (温州圣道会自理宣言), *The Life Monthly*, Vol. 5, No. 9 (June 1925), 42–43.
16. Anon, "Wenzhou Chinese Christians' Annunciation Against Foreign Brutality" (温州基督徒反对强暴宣言), *The Life Monthly*, Vol. 5, No. 9 (June 1925), 43.
17. Anon, "The Executive Office's Letter to Shanghai Municipal Council on June 8, 1925" (本会致工部局函（6月8日）), *The Christian Occupation of China*, No. 54 (10 July 1925), 3.
18. Anon, "The National Christian Council of China's Open Letter to All Chinese Christians" (中华全国基督教协进会致全国基督徒书), *The Christian Occupation of China*, No. 54 (10 July 1925), 1–2.
19. Liu Tingfang, "Christianity and the Chinese National Character," *The Life Monthly*, Vol. 5, No. 9 (June 1925), 6–7.
20. Ibid., 9.
21. Jessie G. Lutz (鲁珍晞), *China and the Christian Colleges, 1850–1950* (中国教会大学史), trans. Zeng Jusheng 曾钜生 (Hangzhou: Zhejiang Education Press, 1988), 234.
22. Liu Zhan'en 刘湛恩, "The Shanghai Massacre and Christian Schools" (五卅惨案与教会学校), *Chinese Christian Education Quarterly*, Vol. 1, No. 3 (October 1925), 15.
23. "The General Resolution of the National Student Union of China" (全国学生总会议决议). Quoted in Zhang Qinshi, *Trend of Religions in China in the Last Decade*, 397–400.
24. Wang Zhongxin 王忠欣, *Modern Chinese Education and Christianity* [中国近代教育与基督教] (Wuhan: Hubei Education Press, 2000), 119.
25. Liu Zhan'en, "The Shanghai Massacre and Christian Schools," op. cit., 16–17.
26. See: Cheng Xiangfan's notes to "Manifesto of Chinese Christian Educational Circles" (中华基督教教育界宣言), *The True Light*, Vol. 24, Nos. 7, 8–10 (1925),

1–4; Lin Buji 林步基, "Christian Education and Nationalism" (基督教教育与国家主义), *Chinese Christian Education Quarterly*, Vol. 1, No. 4 (December 1925), 16–21.

27 Liu Ganzhi 刘淦芝, "Christian Schools in China Should Be Awakened at Present" (现在中国教会学校应有的觉悟), *The Life Monthly*, Vol. 6, No. 1 (October 1925), 21.

28 Zhan Wei 詹渭, "The Nationalist Christian Education" (国家主义的教会教育), *Progress of the Youth*, No. 90 (February 1926), 32.

29 Wu Leichuan, "Results of the Official Registration of Christian Schools in China" (教会学校立案以后), *The Life Monthly*, Vol. 6, No. 2 (November 1925), 2–3.

30 Miao Qiusheng 缪秋笙, "New Experiments in the Reform of Religious Education" (宗教教育的几个新实验), *Chinese Christian Education Quarterly*, Vol. 2, No. 1 (March 1926), 53–54.

31 Xu Songshi 徐松石, "Whether or Not Christian Schools Should Make Reading the Bible Compulsory?" (教会学校是否应以读经为必修课), *The True Light*, Vol. 25, Nos. 4–6 (July 1926), 49–57.

32 Shi Yufang 施煜方, "My Opinions Regarding the Improvement of Religious Subject in Church-Run Secondary Schools" (改进教会中学宗教教育科的我见), *Theological Review*, Vol. 12, No. 1 (Spring, 1926), 103–107.

33 Lin Buji, "The Basic Goal of Christian Education" (基督教之教育宗旨), *The Episcopal Church News*, Vol. 19, No. 10 (May 1926), 1–6.

34 Wei Fulan 魏馥兰 (Francis John White), "How to Carry through the Sinicization of Christian Universities and Colleges" (怎样贯彻基督教大学之中国化), *Chinese Christian Education Quarterly*, Vol. 2, No. 2 (June 1926), 22.

35 Zhang Shizhang 张仕章, "A Study of the Campaign for Taking Back the Right of Education" (收回教育权运动的研究), *Progress of the Youth*, No. 92 (April 1926), 1–15.

36 Anon, "A Recent Investigation of Campaigns Criticizing Christianity" (最近非基督教运动种种活动调查记), *The Christian Occupation of China*, No. 58 (10 January 1926), 7.

37 Quoted in Nianwu 稔五, "The State of the Condemning Christianity Movement in Guangzhou" (广州市反基督教运动的近况及批评), *The True Light*, Vol. 25, No. 1 (February 1926), 60–61.

38 Zhao Zichen, "Religious Thoughts and Life in Present-Day China" (今日中国的宗教思想和生活), *Progress of the Youth*, No. 91 (March 1926), 11–23.

39 Xu Baoqian, "The Condemning Christian Movement and How We Christians Should Respond to It" (反基督教运动与吾人今后应采之方针), *The Life Monthly*, Vol. 6, No. 5 (February 1926), 1.

40 Ying Yuandao 应元道, "The Background and Main Content of Chinese Christian Thoughts in the Recent Five Years" (近五年来中国基督教思想之时代背景及其内容之大概), *The Chinese Christian Literature Society Monthly* (文社月刊), Vol. 1, Nos 9–10 (1926), 2–3.

41 For the full discussion, see: Liu Tingfang, "How Does Christianity Stop Slandering by Self-Rectification?" (基督教在中国今日当如何自修以止谤), *The Life Monthly*, Vol. 6, No. 2 (November 1925), 5–9.

42 Liu Tingfang, "What Do You Think I Am?" (你们说我是谁), *The Life Monthly*, Vol. 6, No. 3 (December 1925), 1–14.

43. Zhao Guanhai, "The Church Should Reexamine Itself in the Condemning Christianity Movement" (反教风潮中教会应有的自省), *The Chinese Christian Literature Society Monthly*, Vol. 1, Nos. 9–10 (1926), 33–34.
44. Xu Baoqian, "The Condemning Christian Movement and How We Christians should Respond to It," op. cit., 2–6.
45. Tan Jiansun 谭健荪, "Reaction to the 1st and 2nd Volumes of *Semiweekly Criticizing Christianity*" (反基督教半周刊第一第二期), *The True Light*, Vol. 25, Nos. 7–8 (September 1926), 17.
46. Liu Weihan 刘维汉, "Unexpectedly Some Say Christianity Is a Talisman Defending Imperialism and Capitalism!" (竟还有人说基督教是帝国主义及资本主义的护符), *The True Light*, Vol. 25, Nos. 7–8 (September 1926), 1
47. Liu Weihan, "Christians Should Pay Attention to Three Matters of Great Urgency in the Condemning Christian Movement" (非基督教声中基督教人应当注意的三个问题), *The True Light*, Vol. 25, No. 1 (January 1926), 42–45.
48. Anon, "Western Missionary Societies' Opinion about the Relationship between Missionary Work and Treaties with China" (西国宣教会对于传教条约问题之意见), *The Christian Occupation of China*, Vols. 63–64 [a combined issue] (10 September 1926), 2.
49. Anon, "The Chinese Christian Church's Opinion about the Relationship between Missionary Work and Treaties with China" (中国教会对于传教条约问题之意见), *The Christian Occupation of China*, Vols. 63–64 [a combined issue] (10 September 1926), 9.
50. Quoted in ibid.," 11.
51. Ibid., 2.
52. Ibid., 8–9.
53. Ibid., 2.
54. Ibid., 8.
55. Ibid.
56. Ibid., 10.
57. Biaofeng 表峰, "Comments on the Conflict between Chinese Christians and Western Missionaries in the Church of Western Guangdong" (闻粤西教会中西冲突感言), *The True Light*, Vol. 25, Nos. 4–6 (July 1926), 65–66.
58. Cheng Jingyi, "The Relations between the Nationalist Revolution and the Christian Church" (国民革命与教会关系), *Annals of the Chinese Christian Church*, No. 10 (1928), Part One, 2.
59. Wang Zhaoxiang 汪兆翔, "The Christians' Attitudes towards the Present Situation and Their Countermeasures" (基督教对于最近时局当有的态度和措施), *The Chinese Christian Literature Society Monthly*, Vol. 2, No. 8 (June 1927), 3.
60. Cheng Jingyi, "The Relations between the Nationalist ReVolution and the Christian Church," op. cit., Part One, 7.
61. Wang Zhaoxiang, "The Christians' Attitudes towards the Present Situation and Their Countermeasures,," op. cit., 3.
62. Ibid., 6.
63. Ibid., 3.
64. Cheng Jingyi, "The Relations between the Nationalist Revolution and the Christian Church," op. cit., Part One, 7.
65. Zhang Junjun 张君俊, "Christian Churches in Hunan after the Mighty Storm" (暴风疾雨以后的湖南教会), *Annals of the Chinese Christian Church*, No. 10 (1928), Part Two, 3.

66 Cheng Jingyi, "The Relations between the Nationalist Revolution and the Christian Church," op. cit., Part One, 3.
67 Yang Tianhong, *Christianity and Modern China*, 393–394.
68 See: Zhang Junjun, "Christian Churches in Hunan after the Mighty Storm," op. cit., Part Two, 4.
69 Ibid., 389–391.
70 Cheng Jingyi, "The Relations between the Nationalist Revolution and the Christian Church," op. cit., Part One, 5.
71 Zhao Guanhai, "Christianity and the Nationalist Government" (国民政府下之基督教), *The Chinese Christian Literature Society Monthly*, Vol. 2, No. 7 (May 1927), 27.
72 Wang Zhixin, "We Christians' Perception of Revolution" (我们的革命观), *The Chinese Christian Literature Society Monthly*, Vol. 2, No. 7 (May 1927), 28–36.
73 Ye Yunlong 叶运隆, "Hangzhou Chinese Christian Church: A Fruit of the Hangzhou Christian Independence Movement" (杭州基督徒独立运动结果成立杭州市中华基督教会), *Annals of the Chinese Christian Church*, No. 10 (1928), Part Three, 22.
74 Huang Jiting 黄吉亭 and Yang Duo 杨铎, "Causes and Effects of Christian Reform in Wuhan" (武汉基督徒革新运动之前因后果), *Annals of the Chinese Christian Church*, No. 10 (1928), Part Three, 25.
75 Ibid., 25–26.
76 Shen Sizhuang 沈嗣庄, "Chinese Christians' Manifesto Issued on Christmas Day of 1927" (1927年圣诞节中国基督徒对于时局的宣言), *The Chinese Christian Literature Society Monthly*, Vol. 3, No. 1 (November 1927), 3.
77 Huang Jiting and Yang Duo, "Causes and Effects of Christian Reform in Wuhan," op. cit., Part Three, 26–27.
78 Anon, "Changsha Chinese Christians' Manifesto of Reform" (长沙基督徒革新运动宣言), *Annals of the Chinese Christian Church*, No. 10 (1928), Part Three, 42.
79 Anon, "Chengdu Chinese Christians' Manifesto of Reform" (成都基督徒革新运动宣言), *Annals of the Chinese Christian Church*, No. 10 (1928), Part Three, 43.
80 Anon, "Key Resolutions of the Fourth Annual Conference of the NCCC" (协进会第四届年会之要案), *Chinese Christian Education Quarterly*, Vol. 2, No. 3 (October 1926), 94.
81 Ibid., 99.
82 Sun Juewu 孙觉悟, "An Open Letter Urging Chinese Christians to Found an Independent Chinese Church as Soon as Possible" (告华信徒速筹备自立教会), *Holy News*, Vol. 16, No. 6 (July 1926), 11.
83 Ye Yunlong, "Hangzhou Chinese Christian Church: A Fruit of the Hangzhou Christian Independence Movement," op. cit., Part Three, 23.
84 Anon, "Xiangtan Chinese Christians' Manifesto of Independence of Christian Church" (湘潭基督徒教会自办运动大会宣言), *Annals of the Chinese Christian Church*, No. 10 (1928), Part Three, 63.
85 Anon, "Shanghai Chinese Christian Conference: A Manifesto" (上海中华基督徒大会宣言), *Annals of the Chinese Christian Church*, No. 10 (1928), Part Three, 57.
86 *Guangdong Chinese Christian Church Monthly* (广东协会月刊), Vol. 1, No. 2, 1. See: Zhao Zichen, "The Chinese Christian Church Is Rising in Unrest" (风潮中奋起的中国教会). Quoted in Zhang Xiping and Zhuo Xinping eds., *The Experiment of Indigenizing Christianity in China*, 316.

87 *Rehabilitation* (改进), Vol. 1, No. 12. See: Zhao Zichen, "The Chinese Christian Church Is Rising in Unrest." Quoted in Zhang Xiping and Zhuo Xinping eds., *The Experiment of Indigenizing Christianity in China*, 316.
88 Ibid., 317.
89 Cheng Jingyi, "The Relations between the Nationalist Revolution and the Christian Church," op. cit., Part One, 4–5.
90 Zhao Zichen, "The Chinese Christian Church is Rising in Unrest." op. cit., 317.
91 Sun Juewu, "An Open Letter Urging Chinese Christians to Found an Independent Chinese Church as Soon as Possible," op. cit., 11.
92 Wang Yuting 王雨亭, "Chinese Christians Should Strive for Independence" (勉华信徒努力自立), *Holy News*, Vol. 16, No. 7 (July 1926), 9.
93 See: Anon, "Why the Chinese Church Must be Independent and How to Achieve It" (全国教会必须自立的原因和自立的方法), *Holy News*, Vol. 16, No. 7 (September 1926), 3–4.
94 Zhu Jingyi 朱敬一, "Open Discussions on the Self-Support of the Rural Christian Church" (乡村教会自养之商榷), Vol. 2, No. 4 (February 1927), 73–77. Publisher unknown.

Bibliography

Anon, "Feng Yuxiang's Open Letter to All Oppressed Christians Worldwide" (冯玉祥告世界被压迫之基督徒书). *The Life Monthly* (生命月刊). Vol. 5, No. 9 (June 1925).

Anon, "Nanjing Chinese Christians' Response to the Shanghai Massacre: An Angry Manifesto" (南京中华基督徒对沪案之愤恨宣言). *The Life Monthly* (生命月刊). Vol. 5, No. 9 (June 1925).

Anon, "Shanghai Council of Chinese Christians' Open Telegram Regarding the Shanghai Massacre" (上海中华基督徒联合会为沪案通电). *The Life Monthly* (生命月刊). Vol. 5, No. 9 (June 1925).

Anon, "The Manifesto of the Kaifeng Chinese Christian Church Founded by the Kaifeng Members of the China Inland Mission Who Choose to Break with the British CIM Due to the Shanghai Massacre" (开封内地会全体教友因沪案与英人完全绝交新组成开封中华基督教会之宣言). *The Life Monthly* (生命月刊). Vol. 5, No. 9 (June 1925).

Anon, "To British Missionaries: An Open Letter Penned by the Supporting Corps of Chinese Christians in Fenzhou of Shanxi" (山西汾州基督徒沪案后援会特告英传教士的忠言). *The Life Monthly* (生命月刊). Vol. 5, No. 9 (June 1925).

Anon, "Wenzhou Chinese Christians' Annunciation Against Foreign Brutality" (温州基督徒反对强暴宣言). *The Life Monthly* (生命月刊). Vol. 5, No. 9 (June 1925).

Anon, "Wenzhou Chinese Christians' Response to the Shanghai Massacre: An Announcement of Independence" (温州圣道会自理宣言). *The Life Monthly* (生命月刊). Vol. 5, No. 9 (June 1925).

Anon, "The National Christian Council of China's Open Letter to All Chinese Christians" (中华全国基督教协进会致全国基督徒书). *The Christian Occupation of China*. No. 54 (10 July 1925).

Anon, "The Executive Office's Letter to the Shanghai Municipal Council on June 8, 1925" (本会致工部局函（6月8日）. *The Christian Occupation of China* (中华归主). No. 54 (10 July 1925).

Anon, "A Manifesto Announcing Independence from the United Methodist Church Mission" (脱离圣道会宣言). *Holy News* (圣报). Vol. 15, No. 7 (July 1925).

Anon, "A Manifesto of the Christians of the Baptist Church in Guangdong and Guangxi" (两广浸会基督徒救国联合会宣言). *The True Light* (真光). Vol. 24, No. 7 (July 1925).

Anon, "Announcement of the Shanghai Chinese Christian Church" (上海中华基督教会通启). *The True Light* (真光). Vol. 24, No. 7 (July 1925).

Anon, "A Recent Investigation of Campaigns Criticizing Christianity" (最近非基督教运动种种活动调查记). *The Christian Occupation of China* (中华归主). No. 58 (10 January 1926).

Anon, "The Chinese Christian Church's Opinion about the Relationship between Missionary Work and Treaties with China" (中国教会对于传教条约问题之意见). *The Christian Occupation of China* (中华归主). Vols. 63–64 [a combined issue] (10 September 1926), 9.

Anon, "Western Missionary Societies' Opinion about the Relationship between Missionary Work and Treaties with China" (西国宣教会对于传教条约问题之意见). *The Christian Occupation of China* (中华归主). Vols. 63–64 [a combined issue] (10 September 1926).

Anon, "Why the Chinese Church Must Be Independent and How to Achiever It" (全国教会必须自立的原因和自立的方法). *Holy News* (圣报). Vol. 16, No. 7 (September 1926).

Anon, "Key Resolutions of the Fourth Annual Conference of the NCCC" (协进会第四届年会之要案). *Chinese Christian Education Quarterly* (中华基督教教育季刊). Vol. 2, No. 3 (October 1926).

Anon, "Changsha Chinese Christians' Manifesto of Reform" (长沙基督徒革新运动宣言). *Annals of the Chinese Christian Church* (中华基督教会年鉴). No. 10 (1928), Part Three.

Anon, "Chengdu Chinese Christians' Manifesto of Reform" (成都基督徒革新运动宣言). *Annals of the Chinese Christian Church* (中华基督教会年鉴). No. 10 (1928), Part Three.

Anon, "Shanghai Chinese Christian Conference: A Manifesto" (上海中华基督徒大会宣言). *Annals of the Chinese Christian Church* (中华基督教会年鉴). No. 10 (1928), Part Three.

Anon, "Xiangtan Chinese Christians' Manifesto of Independence of the Christian Church" (湘潭基督徒教会自办运动大会宣言). *Annals of the Chinese Christian Church* (中华基督教会年鉴). No. 10 (1928), Part Three.

Biaofeng 表峰. "Comments on the Conflict between Chinese Christians and Western Missionaries in the Church of Western Guangdong" (闻粤西教会中西冲突感言). *The True Light* (真光). Vol. 25, Nos. 4–6 (July 1926).

Cheng, Jingyi 诚静怡. "The Relations between the Nationalist Revolution and the Christian Church" (国民革命与教会关系). *Annals of the Chinese Christian Church* (中华基督教会年鉴). No. 10 (1928), Part One.

Cheng, Xiangfan 程湘帆. "Notes to *Manifesto of Chinese Christian Educational Circles*" (中华基督教教育界宣言). *The True Light* (真光). Vol. 24, Nos. 7, 8–10 (1925).

Cheng, Xiangfan 程湘帆. "Christians' Statements Against Imperialism and Unequal Treaties" (基督教人士之反对帝国主义及不平等条约宣言). *The Life Monthly* (生命月刊). Vol. 5, No. 9 (June 1925).

Huang, Jiting 黄吉亭 and Yang Duo 杨铎. "Causes and Effects of Christian Reform in Wuhan" (武汉基督徒革新运动之前因后果). *Annals of the Chinese Christian Church* (中华基督教会年鉴). No. 10 (1928), Part Three.

Li, Rongfang 李荣芳. "The Awareness that Foreign Missionaries Should Have at Present" (现时西教士在中国应有的觉悟). *The Life Monthly* (生命月刊). Vol. 5, No. 9 (June 1925).

Lin, Buji 林步基. "Christian Education and Nationalism" (基督教教育与国家主义). *Chinese Christian Education Quarterly* (中华基督教教育季刊). Vol. 1, No. 4 (December 1925).

Lin, Buji 林步基. "The Basic Goal of Christian Education" (基督教之教育宗旨), *The Episcopal Church News* (圣公会报). Vol. 19, No. 10 (May 1926).

Liu, Ganzhi 刘淦芝. "Christian Schools in China Should Be Awakened at Present" (现在中国教会学校应有的觉悟). *The Life Monthly* (生命月刊). Vol. 6, No. 1 (October 1925).

Liu, Tingfang 刘廷芳. "Christianity and the Chinese National Character" (基督教与中国国民性). *The Life Monthly* (生命月刊). Vol. 5, No. 9 (June 1925).

Liu, Tingfang 刘廷芳. "How Does Christianity Stop Slandering by Self-Rectification?" (基督教在中国今日当如何自修以止谤). *The Life Monthly* (生命月刊). Vol. 6, No. 2 (November 1925).

Liu, Tingfang 刘廷芳. "What Do You Think I Am?" (你们说我是谁). *The Life Monthly* (生命月刊). Vol. 6, no. 3 (December 1925).

Liu, Weihan 刘维汉. "Christians Should Pay Attention to Three Matters of Great Urgency in the Condemning Christian Movement" (非基督教声中基督教人应当注意的三个问题). *The True Light* (真光). Vol. 25, No. 1 (January 1926).

Liu, Weihan 刘维汉. "Unexpectedly Some Say Christianity Is a Talisman Defending Imperialism and Capitalism!" (竟还有人说基督教是帝国主义及资本主义的护符). *The True Light* (真光). Vol. 25, Nos. 7–8 (September 1926).

Liu, Zhan'en 刘湛恩. "The Shanghai Massacre and Christian Schools" (五卅惨案与教会学校). *Chinese Christian Education Quarterly* (中华基督教教育季刊). Vol. 1, No. 3 (October 1925).

Lutz, Jessie G. 鲁珍晞. *China and the Christian Colleges, 1850–1950* (中国教会大学史). Trans. Zeng Jusheng 曾钜生 (Hangzhou: Zhejiang Education Press, 1988).

Miao, Qiusheng 缪秋笙. "New Experiments in the Reform of Religious Education" (宗教教育的几个新实验). *Chinese Christian Education Quarterly* (中华基督教教育季刊). Vol. 2, No. 1 (March 1926).

Nianwu 稔五. "The State of Condemning Christianity Movement in Guangzhou" (广州市反基督教运动的近况及批评). *The True Light* (真光). Vol. 25, No. 1 (February 1926).

Shen, Sizhuang 沈嗣庄. "Chinese Christians' Manifesto Issued on Christmas Day of 1927" (1927年圣诞节中国基督徒对于时局的宣言). *The Chinese Christian Literature Society Monthly* (文社月刊). Vol. 3, No. 1 (November 1927).

Shi, Yufang 施煜方. "My Opinions Regarding Improvement of Religious Subject in Church-Run Secondary Schools" (改进教会中学宗教教育科的我见). *Theological Review* (神学志). Vol. 12, No. 1 (Spring, 1926).

Sun, Juewu 孙觉悟. "An Open Letter Urging Chinese Christians to Found an Independent Chinese Church as Soon as Possible" (告华信徒速筹备自立教会). *Holy News* (圣报). Vol. 16, No. 6 (July 1926).

Tan, Jiansun 谭健荪. "Reaction to the 1st and 2nd Volumes of *Semiweekly Criticizing Christianity*" (反基督教半周刊第一第二期). *The True Light* (真光). Vol. 25, Nos. 7–8 (September 1926).

Wang, Yuting 王雨亭. "Chinese Christians Should Strive for Independence" (勉华信徒努力自立). *Holy News* (圣报). Vol. 16, No. 7 (July, 1926).

Wang, Zhaoxiang 汪兆翔. "The Christians' Attitudes towards the Present Situation and Their Countermeasures" (基督教对于最近时局当有的态度和措施). *The Chinese Christian Literature Society Monthly* (文社月刊). Vol. 2, No. 8 (June 1927).

Wang, Zhixin 王治心. "We Christians' Perception of Revolution"(我们的革命观), *The Chinese Christian Literature Society Monthly* (文社月刊). Vol. 2, No. 7 (May 1927).

Wang, Zhongxin 王忠欣. *Modern Chinese Education and Christianity* [中国近代教育与基督教] (Wuhan: Hubei Education Press, 2000).

Wei, Fulan 魏馥兰 (Francis John White). "How to Carry through the Sinicization of Christian Universities and Colleges" (怎样贯彻基督教大学之中国化). *Chinese Christian Education Quarterly* (中华基督教教育季刊). Vol. 2, No. 2 (June 1926).

Wu, Leichuan 吴雷川. "The Shanghai Massacre and the Future of Chinese Christianity" (沪案与中国基督教的前途). *The Life Monthly* (生命月刊). Vol. 5, No. 9 (June 1925).

Wu, Leichuan 吴雷川. "Results of the Official Registration of Christian Schools in China" (教会学校立案以后). *The Life Monthly* (生命月刊). Vol. 6, No. 2 (November 1925).

Xu, Baoqian 徐宝谦. "The Condemning Christian Movement and How We Christians Should Respond to It" (反基督教运动与吾人今后应采之方针). *The Life Monthly* (生命月刊). Vol. 6, No. 5 (February 1926).

Xu, Songshi 徐松石. "Whether or Not Christian Schools Should Make Reading the Bible Compulsory?" (教会学校是否应以读经为必修课). *The True Light* (真光). Vol. 25, Nos. 4–6 (July 1926).

Yang, Tianhong 杨天宏. *Christianity and Modern China* [基督教与近代中国] (Chengdu: The People's Press of Sichuan, 1994).

Ye, Yunlong 叶运隆. "Hangzhou Chinese Christian Church: A Fruit of the Hangzhou Christian Independence Movement" (杭州基督徒独立运动结果成立杭州市中华基督教会). *Annals of the Chinese Christian Church* (中华基督教会年鉴). No. 10 (1928), Part Three.

Ying, Yuandao 应元道. "The Background and Main Content of Chinese Christian Thoughts in the Recent Five Years" (近五年来中国基督教思想之时代背景及其内容之大概). *The Chinese Christian Literature Society Monthly* (文社月刊). Vol. 1, Nos. 9–10 (1926).

Zhan, Wei 詹渭. "The Nationalist Christian Education" (国家主义的教会教育). *Progress of the Youth* (青年进步). No. 90 (February 1926).

Zhang, Junjun 张君俊. "Christian Churches in Hunan after the Mighty Storm" (暴风疾雨以后的湖南教会). *Annals of the Chinese Christian Church* (中华基督教会年鉴). No. 10 (1928), Part Two.

Zhang, Qinshi 张钦士. *Trend of Religions in China in the Last Decade* [国内近十年来之宗教思潮] (Beijing: Jinghua yinshuju, 1927).

Zhang, Shizhang 张仕章. "A Study of the Campaign for Taking Back the Right of Education" (收回教育权运动的研究). *Progress of the Youth* (青年进步). No. 92 (April 1926).

Zhang, Xiping 张西平 and Zhuo Xinping 卓新平 eds. *The Experiment of Indigenizing Christianity in China* [本色之探] (Beijing: China Radio and Television Press, 1999).

Zhao, Guanhai 招观海. "The Church Should Reexamine Itself in the Condemning Christianity Movement" (反教风潮中教会应有的自省). *The Chinese Christian Literature Society Monthly* (文社月刊). Vol. 1, Nos. 9–10 (1926).

Zhao, Guanhai 招观海. "Christianity and the Nationalist Government" (国民政府下之基督教). *The Chinese Christian Literature Society Monthly* (文社月刊). Vol. 2, No. 7 (May 1927).

Zhao, Zichen 赵紫宸. "Religious Thoughts and Life in Present-Day China" (今日中国的宗教思想和生活). *Progress of the Youth* (青年进步). No. 91 (March 1926).

Zhong, Ketuo 钟可托 and Li Zeling 李则灵. "Part One of Lecture on the Shanghai Massacre" (演讲（五卅惨案）之一). *Holy News* (圣报). Vol. 15, No. 7 (July 1925).

Zhu, Jingyi 朱敬一. "Open Discussions on the Self-Support of Rural Christian Church" (乡村教会自养之商榷). Vol. 2, No. 4 (February 1927). Publisher unknown.

Index

April 12 Anti-Communist Massacre, the 193

baojiaoquan (the West's alleged right to protect missionary work in China) 112
Beida (Peking University) 5, 7
Bible-reading class/course/session, the 169, 172–4
Bolshevism 13, 118; Bolsheviks 13
Boxer, 8, 9, 81, 112, 113, 120, 157, 159, 193
Buddhism and Christianity in China 53, 114, 179, 188; assimilation into Confucianism 73; Christian branch of Buddhism, the 117; Christian Church should learn from Buddhism 32, 75; mutual action 75, 76, 77, 114; similarity in the historical perspective 57, 143, 146
Bu Fangji (Francis Pott) 157; crackdown on patriotic students, the 157–8

Cai Yuanpei 7, 8, 12, 97, 100, 111, 175
Campaign for Taking Back the Right of Education, the 96, 101, 118–20, 121, 166, 175, 177; education sovereignty 102, 104, 125, 130, 176
Chen Duxiu 8, 11, 12, 14, 32, 96, 111
Cheng Jingyi 24, 47, 63, 116, 192, 194, 203; discussion of indigenization of Chinese Christian Church 24–5, 27–8, 35, 54
Cheng Xiangfan 115, 122, 124, 156
Chen Qitian 103, 176
chijiao (bad persons' dependence on Christian Church) 36, 204
China Association for Improving Education, the (CAIE) 97, 101;
Resolution on Banning Propagation of Religion in All Schools (*Ban*) 101–3
China Continuation Committee (CCC) 1, 22, 23, 97
China's Ministry of Education (MOE) 170; six-article law regarding Christian education in China, 170–1
Chinese Christian Education Quarterly (*Education Quarterly*) 124, 125
Chinese Education Mission, the (CEM) 97–9
Chinese Manifesto (regarding indigenization of Chinese Church) 40, 42, 43, 46, 53, 56
Chinese Marxists, the 11, 96
The Chinese Recorder 85, 122
Christian Education Society, the 84
Christianity and Confucianism 73–5, 135
Christian Occupation of China, The (a religious movement) 1, 2, 27, 42; *The Christian Occupation of China* (a church-run journal) 26, 85, 184, 186; *The Christian Occupation of China* (a report) 1, 23, 47, 60, 97
Christianity in China: apologists 12, 117, 178; Christianity and capitalism 3, 4, 17; Christianization (of Chinese nation, society, education, family and Confucianism) 2, 98, 99, 123, 124, 126, 139, 141, 179, 200; crimes committed by Christianity 3, 7; criticism of Jesus Christ, the 182; criticism of the Church, the 64, 147, 180–2; Gospel and imperialism 4, 198; indigenization of Chinese Church, the 25, 28, 40, 42, 49, 51, 53–6, 64, 145, 166, 180, 182, 196
Committee of the Indigenized Chinese Church (CICC) 49, 50; discourses on

the indigenization of Chinese Church 49–50
Communist Party of China, the (CPC) 95, 96, 100, 110, 111
Condemning Christianity Movement (CCM) 1, 8, 21, 70, 86; Beijing 8; Chinese Christian Church's response 12, 13: Condemning Religion Alliance (CRA) 5, 11, 108: *Beida* conference 7; criticism against Christianity, the 5–7; *The Manifesto* 6–7; second open telegram, the 8–10: Condemning Christianity Students Association (CCSA) 2, 4, 11, 13, 14; criticisms against the movement 10; effects on the Chinese Christianity 15, 16; favorable comments 12; relation to indigenization of Chinese Christianity 17: second round, the (the 2nd CCM) 95: CPC's support of the 2nd CCM, the 111; Church's response 115, 177; interaction with the Northern Expedition 191; Second Condemning Religion Alliance, The (SCRA) 108, 110, 111, 112; *1924 Manifesto* 109–10; Society for Young China's (SYC) role, 11, 95, 99, 131, 176; taking back the right of education 96, 100, 101, 104–6, 111, 118, 119, 121, 130, 168, 169, 175, 177
Confucianism 53, 57, 73–6, 114, 135, 136, 140–2, 179, 188; *de* (the Virtue) 140; *ren* (benevolence) 73, 140; *junzi* 139; *zhong* and *shu* (Confucian virtues) 140, 141
Confucius 29, 135, 136, 140, 145; Confucius and Jesus 74
Constitution of the National Christian Council of China, The 40, 43; discourses on the indigenization of Chinese Church 40–1

Daoism 53, 57, 75, 142
The Doctrine of the Mean 73, 75, 136
Duan Guanglu 137

Fan Bihai 51, 80, 139
Feng Yuxiang 156, 203
foreign missionaries 14–16, 21, 24, 27, 29, 30, 34–6, 56, 61, 64, 65, 80, 81, 98, 107, 143, 146, 160–2, 167, 181, 182, 193, 201; apologists for imperialism 157, 159, 183, 186, 188, 191, 195, 199; *jiaoan* (conflicts with Chinese residents) 85; their attitude towards massacres 157, 158, 163; their manipulation of education 170–1

Guomindang 95, 96, 100, 110–12, 194, 198
Gu Ziren 32

Holy Spirit 73, 74, 202
Hu Shi 14, 97, 100, 101, 106

Jesus Christ 8, 15, 41, 54, 56, 58, 59, 70, 75, 112, 114, 116, 159, 162, 167; Dao, Jesus and Confucius 74, 135–7; Jesus as patriot 129, 166; Jesus as worker 80; Jesus's close relation to the Chinese culture 144–5; mean trumpeter of capitalists, a 4; Mozi and Jesus 76; personality of Jesus, the 129, 130, 134, 179, 183; spirit of Jesus, the 60, 136, 196; sympathy for the poor and original spirit 17
Jia'nan (Cannan) Hall 61
Jian Youwen 16, 28, 51, 61, 62
Jiang Jieshi (Chiang Kai-shek) 111, 193
jiao (religions) 74, 135, 136
jiaomin (Chinese Christian converts) 187
Jia Yuming (Xingwu) 29, 30, 35
Jinling (Nanking) University 171; 1927 Incident, The 193
Jinling Seminary 82, 83

Kaifeng 100, 106, 169, 190; 1924 NAE conference, the 101; Kaifeng Christians renouncing their relations with British empire 161

Liang Qichao 10
Liang Shuming 137, 138
Li Dazhao 7, 8, 96
Li Denghui 118
Li Shizeng 7
The Life Monthly 2, 12–14, 26, 50, 66
Liu Tingfang 13, 15, 17, 26, 35, 38, 51, 52, 54, 62, 64, 66, 77, 120, 122, 123, 146, 164, 166, 180, 182
Luo Bingsheng 123

Manifesto of Chinese Christian Educational Circles (*Education Manifesto*) 126–8

Index 217

May Fourth Movement (MFM) 23, 52, 86, 118
Mude (John R. Mott) 1, 35, 188

Nanjing praxis (Christian institutions taking inspirations from Buddhism) 82–3
Nanjing Road 21, 153
National Association for Education, the (NAE) 101
National Christian Council of China, The (NCCC) 24, 40, 43, 45, 46, 48, 83, 84, 115, 163, 188–90; aim, organization and responsibilities 43–5; indigenization programme 45–6; conference on the abrogation of unequal treaties 198–200
National Congress of Christianity (NCC) 21, 47, 48: *Chinese Manifesto* 40: indigenization of Chinese Christian Church, the 40–1, 53–4; *The Constitution*, 40, 43; women Christians' presence 23, 24
National Student Union (NSU) 167, 168, 177, 178
nationalism: Chinese nationalism, the 22, 39, 52, 97, 101, 106, 107, 110, 118, 147, 191; nationalism and Christianity 129, 131–3, 143, 165, 183; nationalism and internationalism 118, 132; nationalism and patriotism 97, 131; nationalism and the national education, the 99, 121, 125, 126, 167, 169, 175, 176; parochial British nationalism, the 162
Nationalist Revolution, The 171, 174, 191; Chinese Christians' attitude towards the Revolution 193–5, 197–9; effects on Christians and Church 192, 193, 196, 200
New Culture Movement (NCM) 22, 24, 25, 28, 32, 33, 37, 39, 48, 52, 57, 64, 86, 96, 97, 115
Northern Expedition, the 95, 177, 195; effects on Chinese Christianity and Christians 191, 193, 194; Guangzhou Government 191; Nationalist Revolutionary Army 197, 198; Northern Expedition Army (NEA) 191, 192; slogans condemning Christianity 192

Other World 37, 134; This World 58, 74, 134, 141

Paris Peace Conference 96
patriotism: Christian education and patriotism 118, 126–8; critical attitude towards Christianity, the 42, 117, 181, 182; foreign missionaries' dislike of patriotism 162; patriotic activities after Shanghai Massacre 96, 153, 165; patriotic feeling of Chinese Christians, the 43, 52, 54–5, 81, 130, 131, 154, 160, 161, 166, 171, 185, 190; patriotism and Christianity 77–80, 163, 164; patriotism and internationalism 52; patriotism and the abrogation of unequal treaties 183; young people/students 4, 28, 102, 126, 155, 166, 167, 184: missionary schools' oppression of patriotic students 157, 158, 167, 169, 178
Peng Jinzhang 50, 51, 62, 131; Christianity and imperialism 132
Progress of the Youth 2, 12, 13, 26

Qinghua (Tsinghua University) 1, 4; Tsinghua school 3, 4
qi (vital breath) 73

rural Christian church, the 36, 84; indigenization endeavor, the 84–6, 204, 205; problems 57; rural churches in the Northern Expedition 192

self-governing 32, 41, 44, 56, 60, 62, 64, 161, 162, 183, 201, 202, 204, 205; self-propagating 41, 44, 56, 60, 64, 161, 166, 183, 201, 202; self-supporting 26, 32, 41, 44, 45, 56, 60–3, 83, 85, 132, 161, 166, 182, 183, 201, 202, 204, 205
Shaji (Shakee) Massacre 155, 157
Shanghai Council of Chinese Christians (SCCC) 154, 159, 161
Shanghai Massacre 95, 108, 131, 133, 147, 153, 166, 178, 185; atrocity perpetrated by imperialists 153, 154; Chinese Christians' response 156, 158, 159, 162, 164, 165; foreign missionaries' response to the atrocity 157–60, 163, 167, 169: Bai Shide (Alexander Baxter) 158: effects on the effort to take back the right of education 166, 171, 176–7; effects on the indigenization of Chinese Christian Church 160; effects on the second Condemning Christianity

Movement 96; killings perpetrated by British imperialists 155, 168; misleading reports by *North China Daily News* 157
Shanghai Municipal Council (SMC) 154, 155, 157, 163, 168
Shen Shizhuang 30
Sinicization of Christianity 14, 15, 28, 30–2, 47, 48, 50, 58, 68–70, 77, 78, 139, 143, 146; Sinicization of Christian education 98, 124–6, 170, 172, 174, 175; Sinicization of the Bible 30, 31, 42
Situ Leideng (John L. Stuart) 34, 122
Society for Chinese Christian Education (SCCC) 121–4
Sun Yat-sen 96, 111, 132

Theological Review 26, 50, 51, 58
theology 7, 31, 34, 51, 53, 55, 58, 59, 67, 71, 145, 183
Tri-Benefit Society (TBS) 51, 61, 62
The True Light 12, 13
Truth Weekly 50, 51

unequal treaties: abrogation of unequal treaties, the 81, 95, 96, 111, 130, 131, 155–7, 161, 163, 173, 182–7, 190, 191, 198–200; *Boxer Protocol* 113; Christianity and unequal treaties 113, 128, 130, 158, 162, 164, 165, 176, 181, 183, 186, 188, 195; foreign missionaries and extraterritoriality 52, 53, 80, 86, 98, 106, 165, 182, 185, 199; NCCC's 14 questions regarding the abrogation of unequal treaties 188–9

Wang Jingwei 7, 12, 13, 101, 111
Wang Zhixin 47, 50, 52, 53, 72, 76, 142, 185, 187, 194
Wei Pengdan (Wei Que) 123

Wei Zhuomin 123
Wenzhou: local Christians' anti-imperialist endeavor 162, 190; self-government and self-support 203, 205
World Student Christian Federation (WSCF) 1–3, 9, 10: rejection of WSCF Conference, the 1, 2, 4, 5, 10, 13: WSCF's response to criticisms 13–14, 16
Wu Leichuan (Wu Zhenchun) 50–3, 72, 73, 76, 117, 129, 130, 160, 165
Wuhan Christian Reform Manifesto 197
Wu Yaozong 50–2, 57, 79

Xie Fuya 133
Xu Baoqian 130, 179, 183
Xu Zuhuan 51, 55, 142

yangjiao (foreign religion) 37, 49, 54, 77
Yanjing (Yenching) University 13, 122, 157, 164, 172
Yi Wensi (Robert K. Evans) 35, 39
YMCA 1, 6, 7, 14, 16, 57, 80, 103, 115, 122, 164; YMCA (an organization of Chinese young Christians) 2; YWCA 2, 115, 164, 168
Yu Jiaju 11, 99, 101
Yu Rizhang 35, 47, 115, 122

Zhang Chunyi 75, 114, 117, 203
Zhang Qingshi (C. S. Chang) 12, 50, 51, 60
Zhang Shizhang 17, 175
Zhang Yijing 12, 184
Zhang Zhidong 131; *Exhortation to Chinese Learning* 131
Zhao Guanhai 128, 131, 132, 182, 194
Zhao Zichen 16, 35, 36, 51, 52, 54, 63, 69, 79, 179, 203
Zhenru 31, 32
Zhu Zhixin 8, 12

For Product Safety Concerns and Information please contact our EU
representative GPSR@taylorandfrancis.com
Taylor & Francis Verlag GmbH, Kaufingerstraße 24, 80331 München, Germany

www.ingramcontent.com/pod-product-compliance
Lightning Source LLC
Chambersburg PA
CBHW050534300426
44113CB00012B/2092